DATE DUE	

OVERDUE FINE
$0.10 PER DAY

DEADLY
MEDICINE

DEADLY
MEDICINE

**CREATING
THE
MASTER
RACE**

United States
Holocaust Memorial
Museum

Washington, D.C.

United States
Holocaust Memorial Museum
100 Raoul Wallenberg Place, SW
Washington, DC 20024-2126

Museum Shop
800.259.9998

Project Director: Susan Bachrach
Editor: Dieter Kuntz
Exhibitions Director: Stephen Goodell

Publications Director: Mel Hecker
Art Director: Lea Caruso
Production Manager: Dwight Bennett
Copy Editor: Gerald Zeigerman
Production Editor: Laura Glassman

Project Coordinator: Kathleen Mulvaney
Project Assistance: Clare Cronin, Neal Guthrie,
Gregory Naranjo, Edward Phillips, Paul Rose,
Laura Surwit
Photography: Max Reid

Book Design: Studio A, Alexandria, Va.
Typeset in DIN and TheSerif

Printed by: Proost NV
Printed in Belgium

Cover and page iii: Calipers.
Deutsches Historisches Museum, Berlin

Distributed by
The University of North Carolina Press
P.O. Box 2288
Chapel Hill, NC 27515-2288

Additional copies of this publication may be
ordered by calling 800.848.6224 or from the
Press's Web site, www.uncpress.unc.edu.

ISBN 0-8078-2916-1

The publication of this volume was made possible in part by the major sponsorship of The David Berg Foundation, with additional support from Lorraine and Jack N. Friedman, The Blanche and Irving Laurie Foundation, and The Viterbi Family Foundation. Published in association with the exhibition Deadly Medicine: Creating the Master Race, *held at the United States Holocaust Memorial Museum, Washington, D.C., April 22, 2004. to October 16, 2005.*

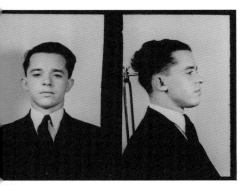

Contents

ACKNOWLEDGMENTS

During its first ten years, the United States Holocaust Memorial Museum has confronted a host of difficult and deep-rooted moral questions in its exhibitions and programs. The study of Holocaust history invariably raises fundamental issues about human nature, social responsibility, and the obligation of individuals and institutions to act with conscience in the face of unspeakable crimes.

In this landmark exhibition, *Deadly Medicine: Creating the Master Race,* the Museum focuses on the physicians, psychiatrists, anthropologists, public health officials, and others who supported and, ultimately, implemented the Nazi racial eugenics program that culminated in genocide: the Holocaust. The topic is especially timely as our society debates such issues as cloning and the legal definitions of life and death. The exhibition sounds useful warnings against the unchecked subordination of individual rights to the welfare of the larger community, as well as abuses of scientific knowledge in the name of progress or the "greater good."

As the nationally mandated steward of Holocaust history and memory, the Museum has a unique obligation. Even as there are fewer and fewer eyewitnesses to tell the story, the Museum must sustain its imperative to teach this history. Why teach about the Holocaust? Surely, it is to memorialize the victims and educate the public about this cataclysmic human event. But there is more to the obligation. The United States Holocaust Memorial Museum is about *responsibility*—our *responsibility* to the past and to the memory of the victims and survivors, our *responsibility* to our fellow human beings in the present, and, perhaps most important, our *responsibility* to future generations.

During the Holocaust, every institution established to uphold civilized values failed—the academy, the media, the judiciary, law enforcement, the churches, the government, and, yes, the medical and scientific disciplines as well. In the name of utopian ideals, many traditionally charged with the protection of the public good subscribed to the grossest violations of human rights—even mass murder. And they succeeded because so few resisted. As has often been said, indifference is always evil's great accomplice. This points precisely to the mission of our Museum: to teach not just the history of the Holocaust but its lessons as well; to teach that nations require of their institutions and citizens an attentive commitment to individual rights, social justice, and respect for humane values.

Exhibitions are the core teaching tools of any museum. They use objects and documents—the evidence, the "real stuff" of history—to tell stories. Our exhibitions present history in such a way that visitors can examine themselves, their decisions, and their actions in both personal and professional contexts.

What makes our exhibitions so powerful—and *Deadly Medicine* is surely a case in point—is that the history of the Holocaust is fundamentally about human nature and the entire spectrum of human behavior, from unimaginable evil to extraordinary goodness. It is about us and what it means to be a human being.

This exhibition speaks directly to issues that matter now, in our own time. What responsibility do medical professionals have to their patients? What are the implications of the ways we acquire and apply scientific information? Is it always possible to balance the needs of the society as a whole with the rights of the individual?

In presenting *Deadly Medicine*, the Museum furthers its commitment to education, remembrance, and conscience. It is our hope that the questions it raises will challenge our visitors to make connections between the past and the present, and, as a result, be more responsible and responsive human beings.

On behalf of the United States Holocaust Memorial Museum, I wish to acknowledge all who have helped to realize this important exhibition. From curators, researchers, and translators to designers, filmmakers, webmasters, and preparators; from conservators and editors to registrars, educators, and photographers, exhibitions are quintessentially team efforts. But the team is far broader than the dedicated staff and volunteers directly involved in the creation of the exhibition. Exhibitions require the support and endorsement of museum leadership, the encouragement of governance, the willing participation of lenders and donors, the expertise of scholars and advisors, and the generosity of benefactors. On behalf of Fred S. Zeidman and Ruth B. Mandel, Chair and Vice-Chair of the United States Holocaust Memorial Council, I commend everyone listed on the following pages for their contribution to this project. And to all who have enabled the realization of this exhibition, we not only express heartfelt appreciation but also acknowledge, with a profound sense of privilege, your essential partnership in our mission.

Sara J. Bloomfield
Director
United States Holocaust Memorial Museum

CREDITS

EXHIBITION SPONSORS

The David Berg Foundation
Lorraine and Jack N. Friedman
The Blanche and Irving Laurie Foundation
The Viterbi Family Foundation

ARTIFACT DONORS
Bruno Lambert
Zentrum für Soziale Psychiatrie Rheinblick, Eltville

ARTIFACT AND PHOTOGRAPH LENDERS
Austria
Dokumentationsarchiv des österreichischen
     Widerstandes (DÖW), Vienna
Naturhistorisches Museum, Vienna
Oberösterreichisches (OOE) Landesarchiv, Linz
Wiener Stadt- und Landesarchiv

Belarus
Belorusskiy gosudarstvennyy arkhiv
     kinofotofonodokumentov, Dzerzhinsk
Belorusskiy gosudarstvennyy muzey Istorii Velikoy
     Otechestvennoy Voyny, Minsk

France
Musée de l'Armée, Paris

Germany
Archiv der Klinik Wiesengrund,
     Humboldt Krankenhaus, Berlin
Archiv der Rheinischen Landesklinik,
     Bonn, Courtesy of Linda Orth
Archiv des Diakonischen Werkes der EKD, Berlin
Archiv des Landeswohlfahrtsverbandes Hessen,
     Fotosammlung, Kassel
Archiv zur Geschichte der Max-Planck-
     Gesellschaft, Berlin
Berliner Medizinhistorisches Museum
Bildarchiv Preussischer Kulturbesitz, Berlin
Bundesarchiv Berlin
Bundesarchiv Koblenz
Deutsches Blinden-Museum, Berlin
Deutsches Historisches Museum, Berlin
Deutsches Hygiene-Museum, Dresden
Diakonie-Kork Epilepsiezentrum, Kehl-Kork
Diakonie Neuendettelsau
Diakonie Stetten

Dokumentations- und Kulturzentrum Deutscher
  Sinti und Roma, Heidelberg
Evangelische Stiftung Alsterdorf, Hamburg
Gedenkstätte Pirna-Sonnenstein
Hessisches Hauptstaatsarchiv, Wiesbaden
Institut für Zeitgeschichte, Munich
Institut für Zeitungsforschung, Dortmund
Jüdisches Museum Berlin
Jüdisches Museum der Stadt Frankfurt
Karl-Bonhoeffer-Nervenklinik, Berlin
Katholische Nachrichtenagentur, Bonn
KZ-Gedenkstätte Dachau
Landesarchiv Berlin
Max-Planck-Institut für Psychiatrie (Deutsche
  Forschungsanstalt für Psychiatrie), Historisches
  Archiv, Bildersammlung GDA, Munich
Museum für Kunst und Gewerbe Hamburg
Rott Collection from the University Archives,
  Freie Universität, Berlin
Sächsisches Hauptstaatsarchiv, Dresden
Sammlung Prinzhorn, Heidelberg
Schulgeschichtliche Sammlung, Bremen
Staatliche Naturwissenschaftliche Sammlungen
  Bayerns, Munich
Staatsarchiv Bamberg
Staatsarchiv Freiburg
Staatsbibliothek zu Berlin
Stadtarchiv Chemnitz
Stadtarchiv Offenburg
Stadtarchiv und Landesgeschichtliche Bibliothek,
  Bielefeld
Stiftung Liebenau, Meckenbeuren
SV-Bilderdienst, Munich
Ullstein Bild, Berlin
Universitätsbibliothek, Regensburg
Unternehmensgeschichte/Archiv der Bayer AG,
  Leverkusen
Zentrum Soziale für Psychiatrie Rheinblick, Eltville

Israel
Ghetto Fighters' House, Kibbutz Lohamei HaGetaot
Yad Vashem, Jerusalem

Lithuania
Lietuvos Centrinis Valstybes Archyvas, Vilnius

Poland
Archiwum Akt Nowych, Warsaw
Archiwum Panstwowe w Lublinie
Instytut Pamieci Narodowej—Komisja Scigania
  Zbrodni przeciwko Narodowi Polskiemu,
  Warsaw
Muzeum Historyczne Miasta, Cracow
Panstwowe Muzeum Auschwitz-Birkenau w
  Oswiecimiu
Zydowski Instytut Historyczny, Warsaw

Russia
Gosudarstvennyy arkhiv Rossiyskoy Federatsii,
  Moscow
Tsentral'nyi Muzei Vooruzhennykh Sil, Moscow

United Kingdom
AKG, London
Galton Collection, University College London
Imperial War Museum, London
Popperfoto.com
U C London Library, Special Collections

United States
American Eugenics Society (AES) Records,
  American Philosophical Society, Philadelphia
American Geographical Society Library, University
  of Wisconsin (UW)-Milwaukee Libraries
American Jewish Joint Distribution Committee,
  New York
AP/Wide World, New York
Buffalo Museum of Science
California Institute of Technology,
  Institute Archives, Pasadena
California State Archives, Dept. of Mental Health,
  Sacramento
Corbis Corporation, New York
Dittrick Medical History Center, Case Western
  Reserve University, Cleveland
Getty Images, New York
Hrdlicka Historical Reprint Collection, Department
  of Anthropology, Smithsonian Institution,
  Washington, D.C.
Leopold Page Photographic Collection,
  Beverly Hills, Calif.
Library of Congress, Washington, D.C.
Mara Vishniac Cohn, Courtesy International Center
  of Photography, New York
National Anthropological Archives, Smithsonian
  Institution, Washington, D.C.
National Archives and Records Administration
  (NARA), College Park, Md.
National Library of Medicine, National Institutes
  of Health (NIH), Bethesda, Md.
The New Yorker Collection, cartoonbank.com
The New York Times Co., New York
Proquest Information and Learning, Ann Arbor, Mich.
SUNY Albany, Special Collections and Archives
Truman State University, Kirksville, Mo.

Individuals
Henry Aron
Hans-Jochen Asemissen
Irene Eckler
Gershon Evan
Eduardo M. Fraifeld
Fritz Gluckstein
Eric Goldfarb
Wolfgang Haney, Berlin
Hans Hauk
Ingeborg Hecht
Paul A. Lombardo, University of Virginia
Ovitz Family, Haifa, Courtesy of Yehuda Koren
  and Eilat Negev
Friedrich Rösing
Wolfgang Schuhmann
Kriemhild Synder
Jerzy Tomaszewski
Esther Weisel

SCHOLARLY ADVISORS
Garland Allen
Peter Black
Gisela Bock
Michael Burleigh
Henry Friedlander
Willard Gaylin
Stephen J. Gould
Patricia Heberer
Daniel J. Kevles
Benoit Massin
Benno Müller-Hill
Steven Selden
Sheila Faith Weiss

EXHIBITION RESEARCH AND DEVELOPMENT
Curator
Susan Bachrach

Lead researcher
Jonathan Friedman

Development and coordination
Nancy Gillette
Gregory Naranjo

Registrar
Susan Blecher

Editor
Edward Phillips

Project oversight
Stephen Goodell
Alice Greenwald

Core research and coordination
Clare Cronin
Neal Guthrie
Satu Haase-Webb
Dieter Kuntz
Kathleen Mulvaney
Alexa Potter
Paul Rose
Laura Surwit

Special assistance
Vadim Altskan
Margaret Frankston
Elyse Gussow
Steven Luckert
Jürgen Matthäus
Jacek Nowakowski
Nava Schreiber
Alina Skibinska
Anatole Steck
Lisa Topelmann

Translators
Fritz Gluckstein
Kimberly Jaeger
Inge and Werner Katzenstein
Inger Crickenberger Montecinos
Gary Saltsman

EXHIBITION DESIGN AND PRODUCTION
Design
LaymanDesign, Glenview, Ill.
Archegraph, Crete, Ill.

Fabrication
Display Dynamics Inc., Clayton, Ohio
MCA Construction, Inc., Alexandria, Va.

Production manager
Richard Ernst

Lighting
David Bobeck

Artifact research, conservation,
mounts, and installation
Charles Bills
Eileen Blankenbaker
Lizou Fenyvesi
Lisa Holt
Emily Jacobson
Jane Klinger
Anne Marigza
Genya Markon
Diane Saltzman
Kyra Schuster
Gail Singer
Susan Goldstein Snyder
Joan Suttin
William Trossen

Archival Art Services, Inc., Washington, D.C.
Bessant Studio, Washington, D.C.

Artifact photography
Max Reid

Photograph research and assistance
Judith Cohen
Nancy Hartman
Curtis Millay
Sharon Muller

AUDIOVISUAL

Production
Joshua Blinder
Peter Bonta
Duane Brant
Raye Farr
Izhar Harpaz
Lindsay Harris
Sandra Kaiser
Bruce Levy
Regina Longo
Adele O'Dowd
David Stolte
Lawrence Swiader
Leslie Swift

Firstlight Pictures, Montclair, N.J.
Larry Asbell Editing, Takoma Park, Md.

Film sources
Bundesarchiv Berlin
CineMedia Film, AG
Friedrich Wilhelm Murnau Stiftung
National Archives and Records Administration
    (NARA), College Park, Md.
Rossiyskiy gosudarstvennyy arkhiv
    kinofotodokumentov, Krasnogorsk, Russia

Oral histories
Dorothea Buck
Paul Eggert
Helga Gross
Helmut Heinze
Irene Hizme
Antje Kosemund
Elvira Manthey
Benno Müller-Hill
Rita Prigmore
Simon Rozenkier
Theresia Seible
René Slotkin

*In addition, the Museum thanks the following
individuals for their research assistance and advice:*

Burkhard Asmuss, Thomas Beddies, Rosmarie
Beier-de Haan, Gunnar Berg, Margit Berner,
Linda Bixby, Bettina Brand, Olaf Breidbach,
Andrew Campana, Tina Campt, Helen
Chatterjee, Michael von Cranach, Carl Diercke,
Allysa Dowden, Michael Engel, Gerda
Engelbracht, Johann Gross, Lilo Gruner, Horst
Gundlach, Margret Hamm, Christina Härtel,
Johann Hauck, Michael Häusler, Marga Hess,
Ute Hofman, Uwe Hossfeld, Alois Kaufmann,
Brigitte Kepplinger, Verena Kleinschmidt,
Wolfgang Lamsa, Dana Ledger, Hans Oskar Baron
Löwenstein de Witt, Petra Lutz, Thomas Matzek,
Andreas Michaelis, Jennifer Nieves, Asmus
Nitschke, Klara Nowak, Linda Orth, Martin
Pernick, Marla Petal, Aubrey Pomerance,
Darlene Prickett, Hartmut Reese, Byrony Reid,
Frank Reuter, Anke Ricklefs, Jovanka Ristic,
Thomas Roeske, Susanne Rössiger, Carola
Sachse, Paula Sarach, Ulf Schmidt, Thomas
Schnalke, Marion Schneider, Jeannie Sklar,
Paolo Tappero, Maria Teschler-Nicola, Achim
Tischer, Anna-Maria Treutel-Gennrich, Christina
Vanja, Elissa Vinnik, Dieter Vorsteher, Anke
Wachter, Matthias M. Weber, Esther Weisel,
Jürgen Wetzel, Ilse Wolfsdorff, Michael Wunder,
Friedrich Zawrel

ES BEWUNDERN DIE MENSCHEN

DAS RAUSCHENDE MEER

DIE FLIESSENDEN GEWÄSS.

DEN ANBLICK DES HIMMELS

UND VERGESSEN

ÜBER ALLEM BEWUNDERN DER DINGE

DAS WUNDER

DAS SIE SELBER SIND

INTRODUCTION

BY SUSAN BACHRACH

From 1933 to 1945, Germany's National Socialist (Nazi) government, under Adolf Hitler, attempted to rid Germany and German-controlled territory of people who did not fit its vision of a healthy and ethnically homogeneous community. Driven by a racist ideology, the Nazis promoted a nationalism that combined territorial expansion with claims of biological superiority—an "Aryan master race"—and virulent antisemitism. In the name of "applied biology," the term used by Hitler deputy Rudolf Hess, the Nazis eventually murdered six million Jews. Many others also became victims of persecution and murder through Nazi "racial hygiene" programs designed to cleanse German society of individuals believed to be biological threats to the "health" of the nation: "foreign-blooded Gypsies," persons diagnosed as "hereditarily ill," homosexuals, and, in German-occupied eastern territories during World War II, Poles and others belonging to ethnicities deemed innately inferior. *Deadly Medicine: Creating the Master Race* examines the intersection of scientific racism and the Holocaust and documents how Nazi racial and antisemitic policies, which were explicitly expressed in biological and medical terms and developed as public health measures, culminated in mass murder and the genocide of European Jewry.

Nazi officials at a 1935 exhibition. In both the Weimar and Nazi eras, the transparent "glass man" drew large crowds to German Hygiene Museum shows promoting health and eugenics. *NARA, College Park, Md.*

Portrait of British scientist Francis Galton, published in a German eugenics journal edited by an official in the Prussian Ministry of Welfare, February 1931. *USHMM Collection*

Biomedical language pervaded the crude, pseudoscientific Nazi propaganda that depicted Jews as "microbes" infecting the German "national body" *(Volkskörper)* and slandered Jewish doctors as sexual predators. More dangerous were the subtler, scientifically framed versions of racism and antisemitism presented by medically trained experts who helped develop and promote Nazi policies and gave them legitimacy in the eyes of the German public. Many were psychiatrists, geneticists, and anthropologists who, in most instances, continued their careers after the demise of the Third Reich. Often assuming multiple roles as professors, researchers, public speakers, and policy makers, these professionals participated during the Nazi years in the total reorientation of medical ethics from a focus on individual care to the hereditary health of the larger community—the Germanic people *(Volk)*. In this context, the term *Volk* had clear biological connotations, embracing Germanic peoples within and beyond Germany's political borders and effectively excluding Jews and other ethnic minorities living within those borders as racially alien "foreigners." Well before Adolf Hitler took power in 1933, many German scientists in the biomedical fields had supported proposals for *racial* (as opposed to *individual*) health care; such ideas for "improving the race" were known in Germany as racial hygiene *(Rassenhygiene)* or eugenics *(Eugenik).*

A long path led from racial hygiene before the Third Reich to Nazi racial hygiene and the Holocaust, and the first travelers on that route could not have imagined its horrific ending. Eugenics in Germany had a far-reaching history and was part of a larger, international movement, animated by reformist impulses and galvanized by revolutionary advances in medicine and the new science of human genetics. In

EUGENIK

ERBLEHRE ∗ ERBPFLEGE

August Forel †

BAND 1   AUGUST 1931   HEFT 11

VERLAG ALFRED METZNER · BERLIN SW61 · GITSCHINER STRASSE 109

Swiss psychiatrist August Forel (1848–1931), an early proponent of eugenics. *USHMM Collection*

the late nineteenth and early twentieth centuries, utopian dreams of perfecting humanity by manipulating heredity seduced many scientists and scientific-minded reformers. In 1865, the British scientist Francis Galton (1822–1911), inspired by his cousin Charles Darwin's theory of evolution by natural selection, optimistically wrote: "If the twentieth part of the cost and pains were spent in measures for the improvement of the human race that is spent on the improvement of the breed of horses and cattle, what a galaxy of genius might we not create!"[1] It was Galton who coined the term *eugenics*, in 1883, from the Greek meaning "good birth." The hereditarian beliefs of Galton and like-minded thinkers in Germany, Sweden, the United States, Canada, and elsewhere were greatly buttressed by the dissemination, after 1892, of the German biologist August Weismann's theory of immutable "germ plasm," his term for hereditary matter, and the rediscovery of the Austrian botanist Gregor Mendel's laws of heredity, in 1900, by the German biologist Carl Correns and others. (The term *gene* was first used, in 1909, by Wilhelm Johannsen, a Dane, who distinguished between the "phenotype," the observable physical appearance of an organism, and its counterpart, the invisible "genotype.")[2]

The biography of Alfred Ploetz (1860–1940), founder of the German Society for Racial Hygiene, in 1905, perfectly reflects the development of German eugenic thinking. The son of a factory manager, Ploetz was a native of Breslau (now Wroclaw, Poland), a manufacturing center whose population, like that of all large German cities, expanded rapidly, from 200,000 to 500,000, between the 1870s and 1900. On a mission to help his nation use science to solve the problems created by rapid urbanization and industrialization, Ploetz studied economics, imbibed the teachings of the renowned

4

A door, ca. 1850, from an isolation cell used into the twentieth century at the Eichberg Psychiatric Clinic, in Eltville, Germany. *USHMM Collection, Gift of Zentrum für Soziale Psychiatrie Rheinblick, Eltville*

Wittenau Psychiatric Clinic, Berlin, 1930. *Landesarchiv Berlin (A Rep. 003-04-04 Nr. 3)*

German zoologist and social Darwinian Ernst Haeckel, and lived briefly in a utopian socialist community in Iowa.[3] Ploetz later studied medicine under the eminent Swiss psychiatrist August Forel. Forel inspired his followers with such declarations as, "The law of heredity winds like a red thread through the family history of every criminal, of every epileptic, eccentric, and insane person. Should we sit still and witness our civilization go into decay and fall to pieces without raising the cry of warning and applying the remedy?"[4] Ploetz and his contemporaries also adopted the theories of the Italian psychiatrist Cesare Lombroso, whose concept of the "born criminal" was widely disseminated in Europe in the late nineteenth century. Lombroso articulated that era's middle-class fears of social disorder and of the poor, urban masses crowded into unhealthy tenements. He also provided methods of research for anatomists, who dissected the brains of executed murderers to identify pathologies, and for physical anthropologists, who studied faces for measurable signs of criminality, applying Lombroso's anthropometry theory that associated physical appearance with social behavior.[5]

Girl being measured in 1932 as part of a large anthropological research study, on the hereditary composition of the German population, conducted at dozens of sites. *Ullstein Bild, Berlin*

World War I (1914–18) was an important turning point in the development of German racial hygiene. The nation's humiliating defeat in the war, two million dead on the battlefield, and ensuing political and economic crises that threatened the survival of the young, democratic Weimar Republic (1919–1933) provided fertile new ground for German support of eugenics. As before the war, but with increased urgency, eugenic reformers, inspired by Darwinian principles of "the survival of the fittest," argued that modern medicine, charity, and welfare programs interfered with the process of natural selection by artificially sustaining the weak and "unfit." At the same time, racial hygiene proponents warned of the dangers of Germany's falling birthrate and pointed to a new trend among the "productive" middle class, of persons marrying later and limiting family size to an average of two children. During the 1920s, the quest for race improvement found wider support beyond the elite circles of such proponents as Ploetz and reinforced the highly nationalistic drive to restore the country to world preeminence. Advocates of eugenic solutions to Germany's problems spanned the political spectrum, and included government officials and academics in the biomedical fields. Two newly established, government-supported scientific institutes embodied the growing state interest in eugenics: the Kaiser Wilhelm Institute for Psychiatry, in Munich, opened in 1924, and the Kaiser Wilhelm Institute for Anthropology, Human Heredity, and Eugenics, in Berlin-Dahlem, in 1927.[6]

To arrest what they decried as the biological decline or degeneration of the population, racial hygiene advocates classified and ranked individuals as "superior" or "inferior," using such scientific techniques as observation, family genealogies,

Calipers used to measure skull size at the Kaiser Wilhelm Institute for Psychiatry, in Munich, ca. 1930. The institute's director, Dr. Ernst Rüdin, was a leader of the German eugenics movement. *Staatliche Naturwissenschaftliche Sammlungen Bayerns, Munich*

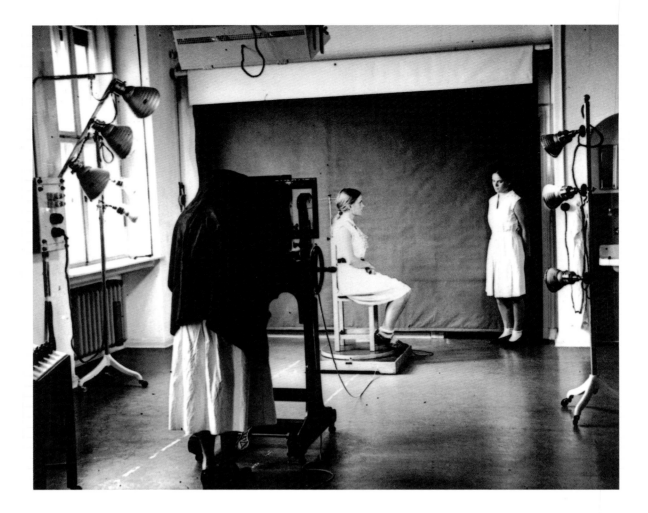

Geneticist Otmar von Verschuer's laboratory for twin research at the Kaiser Wilhelm Institute for Anthropology, 1928.
Archiv zur Geschichte der Max-Planck-Gesellschaft, Berlin

physical measurement, and intelligence testing. They proposed, on the one hand, that the state implement policies to encourage the growth of "valuable" families, while, on the other hand, advocating drastically slashing public funding for mental hospitals, prisons, and care homes. To achieve this goal, occupational therapy engaged those able to work in the fields, laundries, and kitchens of institutions. To curb reproduction of persons deemed "less valuable," popular educational materials and premarital counseling advised couples to look for hereditary taints in their family trees.

Although few citizens supported the idea of "euthanasia" or physically eliminating persons considered unproductive and incurably ill, the concept had long been debated in Germany. A treatise entitled *Authorization of the Destruction of Life Unworthy of Life*, cowritten by a psychiatrist and a legal scholar, was widely discussed in professional circles after its publication in 1920. Growing numbers of Germans subscribed to the concept that individuals must justify their existence to the larger society. New medical procedures then introduced a less draconian measure to eliminate the reproduction of inferiors—surgical sterilization, a far more acceptable alternative than "euthanasia." The first reported vasectomies on men were performed at St. Mary's Hospital, in Chicago, in 1897, on two patients with prostate problems. Between 1910 and 1920, a German surgeon perfected a method for sterilizing women, by cutting the fallopian tubes.[7]

In the Weimar Republic, however, political and religious opposition prevented the enactment of racial hygiene measures, including a proposed sterilization law. The push for such a law greatly accelerated after the onset of an economic

crisis in 1929, when funds to provide care for persons in institutions dropped sharply. In other countries where eugenics organizations lobbied for their passage, political opposition similarly inhibited the enactment or enforcement of sterilization laws. In the 1920s, only Denmark introduced a national statute legalizing voluntary sterilization, although the law was actually little used. Eugenicists had more political success in promoting sterilization laws in countries where such laws were the prerogative of state and provincial governments—the United States, Canada, and Switzerland. The largest number of eugenic sterilizations occurred in the United States: A recorded total of 16,000 procedures were performed on men and women in the 26 years between 1907 and 1933.[8] Half of these sterilizations occurred in California. Marshalling their arguments on behalf of sterilization, German racial hygienists buttressed their case by citing American and other practices abroad.[9]

Before 1933 and the radical political change of Hitler's dictatorship, German proponents of racial hygiene saw themselves in the vanguard of promoting change. Yet, they also felt stymied at every turn by what they viewed as the entrenched status quo, including traditional beliefs that emphasized the role of education, rather than heredity, in shaping individuals.[10] It is not surprising, therefore, that Hitler's regime found many willing collaborators eager to realize long-held dreams of improving the race and, more practically, funding for their research on genetics and related subjects. In the 1920s, eugenic thinking had been absorbed into the ideology and platform of the nascent Nazi Party. Hitler stated in *Mein Kampf*, published in 1925:

By the late 1920s, the use of the more scientific-sounding word *eugenics* instead of *racial hygiene* had become a political choice in Germany. The pamphlet *(left)*, *Foundations of Racial Hygiene*, was published in 1924. The second edition *(right)*, published in 1929, bore the title *Foundations of Eugenics. USHMM Collection, Gift of Deutsches Hygiene-Museum, Dresden*

Anthropologist Eugen Fischer, ca. 1933–38, reading a journal published by the American Genetic Association. *Archiv zur Geschichte der Max-Planck-Gesellschaft, Berlin*

The national state...must set race in the center of all life. It must take care to keep it pure. It must declare the child to be the most precious treasure of the people. It must see to it that only the healthy beget children.... The state must act as the guardian of a millennial future in the face of which the wishes and the selfishness of the individual must appear as nothing.... It must put the most modern medical means in the service of this knowledge.[11]

In a similar vein, Hitler's minister of propaganda, Joseph Goebbels, proclaimed to a Nazi Party rally in 1938:

Our starting point is not the individual, and we do not subscribe to the view that one should feed the hungry, give drink to the thirsty, or clothe the naked.... Our objectives are entirely different: We must have a healthy people in order to prevail in the world.[12]

Ultimately, revolutionary political change and the establishment of a ruthless dictatorship backed by full police powers were necessary for the implementation of eugenic ideas in the form and scale carried out by Hitler's regime. The Nazis transformed racial hygiene ideas, practices, and institutions to fit their political agenda and to mesh with their racial ideology. They silenced opponents of eugenics and democratic defenders of individual and minority rights that had inhibited the enactment of eugenic measures in Germany before 1933. Through public health measures, including a sterilization law and a marital health law to strengthen the "national body," the Nazis intended to eliminate all sources of "hereditary illness" from the

Psychiatrist Paul Nitsche *(center, back to camera)* director of the Sonnenstein State Mental Institution, with members of his staff, ca. 1935. A founding member of the German Society for Racial Hygiene, Nitsche supported "mercy death" for "incurables," and later headed the medical office of the Nazis' "euthanasia" program, Operation T-4. *Gedenkstätte Pirna-Sonnenstein*

German gene pool. The Nazi regime also promoted the Blood Protection Law as a public health and racial hygiene measure. Targeting what they regarded as racially alien elements, by aiming to prevent future births of "racially mixed" children *(Mischlinge)*, this law prohibited marriage and sexual relations between Jews and persons of "German or related blood." Through further implementing of decrees, the law was also applied to Sinti and Roma peoples (Gypsies) living within the Reich. Brutally implemented, Nazi racial hygiene measures sought not to perfect mankind, as Galton originally envisioned, but aimed solely to create a "superior, Germanic (Aryan) race."

Many German physicians and scientists embraced the new regime's emphasis on biology and heredity. Yet, German racial hygiene before 1933 had not been characteristically antisemitic, and no one advocated "purifying the race" of Jewish genes. Although eugenic ideas had supporters on both the political left and right, the emphasis and tone of ideas varied. Most German Jewish adherents preferred the term *eugenics* to *racial hygiene,* because of the ambiguous connotations of "race" and their desire that eugenics not become entwined in discussions of racial differences. Other proponents of eugenics favored racial hygiene and welcomed the "exaltation of the Nordic race" as "eugenically advantageous."[13] Members of this group, such as geneticist Fritz Lenz, anthropologist Eugen Fischer, and geneticist Otmar von Verschuer, prospered under the Third Reich.

Many academics, who had privately harbored antisemitic views before the Nazi takeover, collaborated with the Nazi regime after 1933 in removing Jewish colleagues from academic positions, integrating antisemitic material into revised racial hygiene textbooks and lectures, and offering expert opinions on individuals' "racial" background

René and Renate Guttmann, March 31, 1940. On December 15, 1943, the twins were deported with their mother from the Theresienstadt ghetto to Auschwitz, where they became subjects of Dr. Josef Mengele's research on heredity.
Irene Hizme

in disputed cases. Eugen Fischer, who served as the director of the Kaiser Wilhelm Institute for Anthropology, Human Heredity, and Eugenics from 1927 to 1942, minced no words when he stated in a 1939 lecture:

I do not characterize every Jew as inferior, as Negroes certainly are, and I do not underestimate the greatest enemy with whom we have to fight. But I reject Jewry with every means in my power, and without reserve, in order to preserve the hereditary endowment of my people.[14]

World War II (1939–1945) provided the Nazis a unique environment within Germany and in the occupied eastern territories for murderous programs of racial hygiene or "cleansing"—a progressive radicalization of policies characterized by ever greater depths of moral transgression. Using arguments advanced in the 1920s, the Nazis murdered in the name of euthanasia—"mercy death"—and enlisted hundreds of asylum directors, pediatricians, psychiatrists, family doctors, and nurses. Many proponents of eugenics who had earlier rejected killing came to support murder, in wartime, "for the good of the Fatherland." The first victims were the most vulnerable— newborns and young children with severe birth defects. The adult euthanasia program targeted adults judged unproductive, or "life unworthy of life." In 1940 and 1941, 70,000 male and female patients in private, state, and church-run institutions became the first victims of gas chambers at six facilities established in Germany and Austria. Later, adults were killed by starvation and drug overdoses in a more decentralized program. An estimated total of 200,000 adults were victims of Nazi euthanasia.

Gabriel and Theresia Reinhard, a German Gypsy couple, with their newborn twins, Rolanda and Rita, in Würzburg, Germany, March 1943. The twins became subjects of genetic study at the Würzburg University clinic, where Rolanda died during the course of the research. *Rita Prigmore*

Ultimately, Nazi racial hygiene policies would culminate in the near annihilation of European Jewry. The "Final Solution to the Jewish Question" began as special squads of SS and police, the *Einsatzgruppen,* followed German forces into the Soviet Union in the summer of 1941, and by the end of the year killed nearly one million Jews in open-air shootings. Seeking a "cleaner" and "more efficient" method of killing, SS chief Heinrich Himmler turned to the example of the euthanasia murder program and introduced gassing, but on a vastly larger scale. Nearly two million people, mostly Polish Jews, were deported for murder to four killing centers in occupied and annexed Poland. At Sobibor, Treblinka, and Belzec, staff redeployed from the German euthanasia centers manned the gassing installations and crematoria. More than one million Jews, deported from German-controlled countries from France to Greece, perished at Auschwitz-Birkenau. Auschwitz also became a site where Nazi doctors conducted sterilization experiments and genetic research, using Jews and Gypsies as human guinea pigs. The notorious SS physician Josef Mengele has come to embody deadly Nazi medicine and the perversion of medical ethics under the Third Reich. His studies and experimentation using twins were undertaken in full partnership with researchers at Berlin's Kaiser Wilhelm Institute for Anthropology, who analyzed the information and "human material" sent from Auschwitz.

In reconstructing the origins and development of the Nazi regime's murderous racial science policies, *Deadly Medicine* draws on extensive scholarship. Two works published in Germany 20 years ago were groundbreaking: geneticist Benno Müller-Hill's book, translated into English as *Murderous Science: The Elimination by Scientific Selection of Jews, Gypsies, and Others in Germany, 1933–1945,* and journalist Ernst

Files from the Wittenau Psychiatric Clinic, Berlin, of patients at the institution during the Nazi years. *Landesarchiv Berlin (A Rep. 03-04-04)*

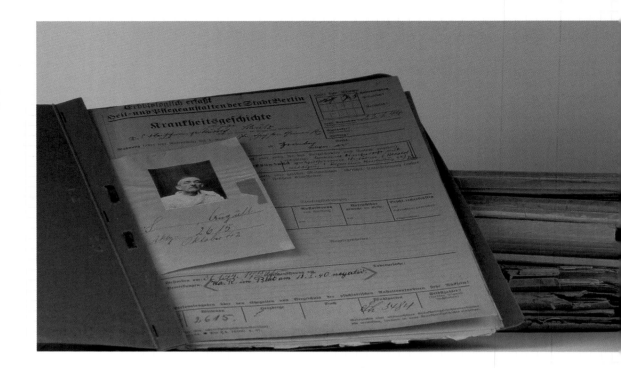

Klee's work *Euthanasia in the National Socialist State*, which brought the little-known history of the Nazi murder program to a larger German audience.[15] Some of the most recent research has been done by psychiatrists, psychologists, nurses, and others who have delved into the history of their own institutions, salvaging patient files and other institutional documents from old basements being cleared for renovation. Such individuals as Dr. Michael Wunder, a psychologist at the Alsterdorf institution for mentally retarded persons, in Hamburg, Christina Härtel, a psychologist at the Bonhoeffer Psychiatric Clinic, in Berlin, Ilse Wolfsdorf, the director of the nursing staff at the Kork institution for epileptics, and many others in this book's acknowledgments contributed their expertise to this exhibition project.

The exhibition also benefited greatly from many research projects and exhibitions developed by other Germans and Austrians. A major endeavor directed by Dr. Hartmut Reese, with Dr. Brigitte Kepplinger, has involved the renovation and conversion of the Hartheim euthanasia center to a memorial and education center.[16] In Vienna, anthropologists, including those at the Natural History Museum led by Dr. Maria Teschler-Nicola, have been conducting historical research on the activities of Viennese anthropologists under the Third Reich. A systematic inventory of the museum's massive holdings found in long-forgotten storage crates uncovered a unique collection of anthropological masks made of Jewish subjects, as well as photographs, measurement sheets, and other materials that document museum anthropologists' complicity with the Nazi regime.[17] In Berlin, an important project has brought together scholars, under the direction of Dr. Carola Sachse, to document the history of the Kaiser Wilhelm Society in the National Socialist era.[18]

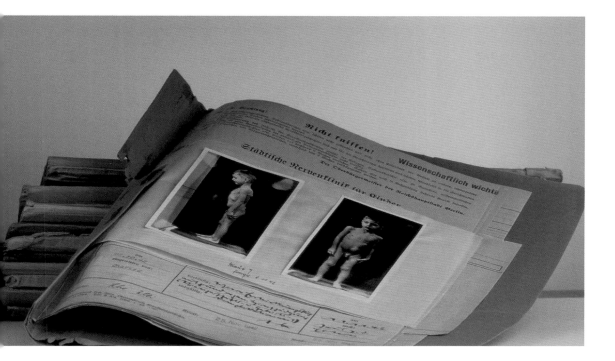

Several exhibitions in Austria and Germany have also explored diverse aspects of this subject. The first exhibitions on eugenics and Nazi euthanasia included one created at the Hadamar memorial, one of the former gassing sites; *The Value of the Human Being,* sponsored by Berlin's Chamber of Physicians; and an exhibition on the history of the Karl Bonhoeffer (formerly the Wittenau) Psychiatric Clinic during the National Socialist years.[19] More recent endeavors include the history of the victims of the pediatric euthanasia ward, Spiegelgrund, at Vienna's Steinhof Psychiatric Hospital; an exhibition on the artwork of psychiatric patients killed in the Nazi euthanasia program, at Heidelberg University's Prinzhorn Collection; and the exhibition *The [Im]Perfect Human,* created by the German Hygiene Museum, in Dresden.[20]

Each of the authors of the essays in this publication has made important contributions to our knowledge of the history of eugenics, the Nazi euthanasia program, and links to the Holocaust. By documenting the relationship between biological or scientific racism and the Holocaust, the essays help illuminate events often characterized as incomprehensible. They also provide opportunities to reflect upon issues of contemporary relevance. As Benno Müller-Hill states in his contribution, in light of both history and recent advances in the field of human genetics, "It must be made absolutely clear that science should never become the reason to justify injustices to a genetically defined group of persons."

GERMAN EUGENICS, 1890–1933

BY SHEILA FAITH WEISS

Racial hygiene, or eugenics—the strategy aimed at improving the genetic qualities of a population through control of reproduction—is commonly linked to the racial purity policies of the Third Reich, and is often portrayed as leading directly to the Holocaust. Simply to view the German eugenics movement as a direct and inevitable precursor to Nazism would be a distortion. German racial hygiene, unlike Nazi racial ideology, was rooted not in antisemitic concepts but in reform movements concerned with public health and social welfare. Still—and very important—both eugenics and Nazi racial theory shared common beliefs in the central role of heredity in determining physical and mental traits and in the innate inequality of individuals and groups. The roots of Nazi eugenics that culminated in the Holocaust were laid in the preceding decades, particularly in the 15 years following World War I, the period of the Weimar Republic.

From its beginnings, Anglo-American eugenics and its German counterpart, racial hygiene, presupposed a belief in the innate inequality of individuals and "races." Proponents of eugenics viewed individuals and groups in terms of their genetic "value," ranking them from "superior" to "inferior." In the name of a higher good—the health of humanity as a whole, or of a nation (in Germany, of the *Volk*), and of the

Health Is Life's Fortune was published by the National Committee for Hygienic Education, for National Health Week, in 1926. Weimar eugenics was largely "positive," focusing on public health campaigns, sex education, and combating such diseases as syphilis, tuberculosis, and alcoholism that increased the rate of female infertility, infant mortality, and birth defects. *Rott Collection, Freie Universität, Berlin*

16

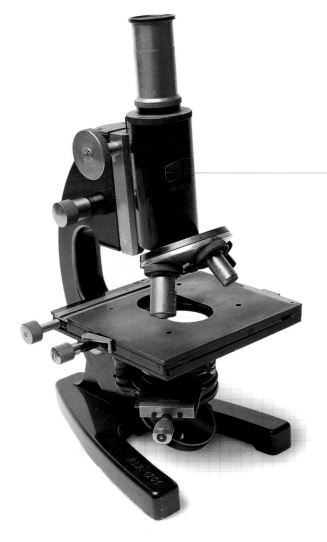

Berlin's Charité Hospital was one of
the best teaching hospitals in the world
in the 1920s. This microscope was
used at Charité for pathology studies
by a student of the renowned microbiologist
Rudolf Virchow. Ca. 1930. *Berliner
Medizinhistorisches Museum*

need to decrease the burden of care for mentally and physically disabled persons, viewed as "defects" or "inferior"—eugenicists everywhere argued that populations should be scientifically managed. Part of the program, referred to as "negative" eugenics, was the control of individual reproduction by means of physically segregating and surgically sterilizing the "unfit," who, it was believed, were multiplying at faster rates than the "fit."

Nazism also presupposed innate or biological differences between individuals and races, and, like eugenics, privileged heredity's role in determining physical and mental traits. During the 1920s, the turbulent political and economic years of the Weimar Republic, eugenics became well established in government circles, and within the German medical and scientific community. It also reached a wider audience, including the nascent Nazi Party. Eugenic ideas were absorbed into the ideological platform of the party. Even before Hitler took power in 1933, anti-Nazi writers were beginning to express fears of the form that medicine and public health might take under a Nazi regime. Hitler and other Nazis had publicly expressed contempt for traditional religious and charitable care that permitted the unfit to continue to procreate and multiply. In the Nazi view, they were but "human ballast" that should be jettisoned.[1]

In view of the institutional development and increasing popularity of eugenics during the 1920s and the early years of the Great Depression, it is not surprising that many racial hygienists welcomed the Nazi takeover as an opportunity to see eugenic measures implemented, such as a compulsory mass sterilization law, that, owing to democratic opposition, had been politically unfeasible before. At the same time, Hitler's regime, embracing a radical and racialized interpretation of eugenic

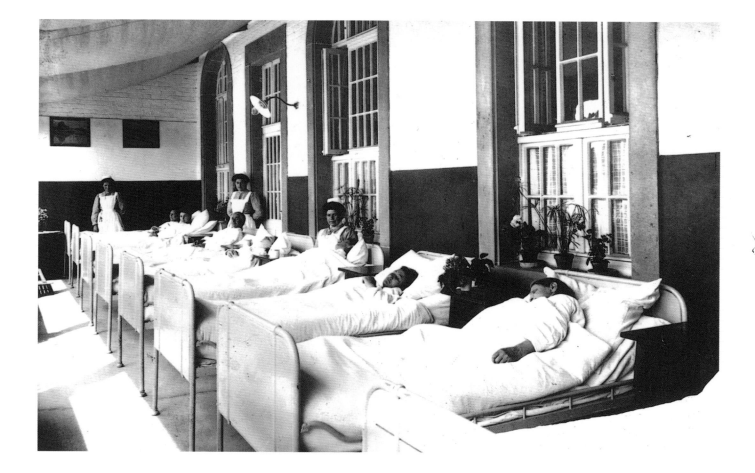

ideas, would welcome the collaboration of academic experts, proponents of eugenics, as they would lend legitimacy to and help implement Nazi racial hygiene policies. The relationship would be a symbiotic, mutually beneficial one.

A ward for psychiatric patients in the Baden State Hospital, Wiesloch, Germany, ca. 1924–25. Racial hygienists labeled persons diagnosed with mental illness as "inferior" or "less valuable" (minderwertig), and feared the steady increase of these and other institutionalized "degenerate" populations. *Deutsches Hygiene-Museum, Dresden*

ORIGINS OF GERMAN RACIAL HYGIENE, 1890–1918

Eugenics in Germany originated in the late nineteenth century as a reform movement looking for a scientific solution to social problems created by the nation's rapid industrialization and urbanization—poverty, crime, alcoholism, and such chronic afflictions as tuberculosis and venereal diseases.[2] Advocates of eugenics comprised a small group of educated, middle-class intellectuals with medical backgrounds. German eugenics developed independently of its British counterpart, although both were heavily influenced by Charles Darwin's principles of evolution.

In Germany, the zoologist Ernst Haeckel popularized social Darwinism—the extension of Darwin's theory of survival of the fittest (natural selection) to competition in human society. Haeckel's writings substantiated the fears of a falling birthrate among the "better" (or "productive") elements of society and pointed ominously to an increasing hereditary "degeneration"—the transmission of physically and mentally unhealthy traits—of the human species. The work of German biologist August Weismann lent additional scientific support to the concern that natural selection no longer operated effectively in contemporary society, because modern medicine and social welfare enabled the unfit to survive and reproduce their own "genetically defective" kind.[3]

A care facility for epileptic children, Kork, Germany, 1930. Racial hygienists also stigmatized epileptics as innately "inferior." Today, experts do not regard most cases of epilepsy as the result of hereditary disease but, rather, the combination of a genetic disposition and an outside "trigger," such as an accident or infection. *Deutsches Historisches Museum, Berlin*

Attempting to counteract this process, a small but growing group of medical experts began to promote eugenics as the best way to restore Germany's long-term health. Physicians enjoyed extraordinary prestige in Germany because of the medical breakthroughs of the nineteenth century, reinforcing their view of themselves as the one professional group possessing the expertise to safeguard the health and welfare of the German people. The medically trained cofounders of the German eugenics movement, Wilhelm Schallmayer and Alfred Ploetz, both wrote their first eugenics treatises during the last decade of the nineteenth century.

A prize competition in 1900, funded by the Krupp munitions family, brought the ideas of what, in Germany, would be known as "racial hygiene" to a limited public audience. Schallmayer's work, *Heredity and Selection in the Life Process of Nations*, won first prize for answering, "What can we learn from the theory of evolution about internal political development and state legislation?" He argued that long-term national power depended upon the biological vitality of its citizens, and neglect of the genetic fitness of its population led to the downfall of the state. Adopting a eugenics program was urgent, as the future of the nation depended on the "good management" of its human resources.[4] Schallmayer's treatise outlined early racial hygiene goals: a heavy emphasis on "positive" eugenic measures designed to increase the number of the so-called fit—or socially productive individuals—who seemed headed for extinction because of late marriages and birth control; caution in the area of "negative" measures to limit the reproduction, through such means as surgical sterilization, of those in the population deemed unfit—or unproductive; and a special preoccupation with education and propaganda to promote eugenic goals. For

EUGENIK

E R B L E H R E ∗ E R B P F L E G E

Dr. Alfred Ploetz

BAND 1   SEPTEMBER 1931   HEFT 12

VERLAG ALFRED METZNER · BERLIN SW61 · GITSCHINER STRASSE 109

In 1905, Alfred Ploetz, a physician and economist by training, founded the German racial hygiene movement, the world's first eugenics organization. *USHMM Collection*

Schallmayer, the rational administration of Germany's human resources was the most effective way to redress the perceived imbalance between genetically inferior and superior human material. His plan of population management focused attention on the least productive (yet, to him, the seemingly fastest multiplying) individuals within German society, the "hereditary degenerates"—especially criminals, alcoholics, the insane, and the feebleminded.

Ploetz, however, was the far more influential of the two cofounders of German eugenics. In his 1895 book *The Fitness of Our Race and the Protection of the Weak,* he originated the word *"Rassenhygiene"* (racial hygiene) as a German synonym for "eugenics," a term coined in 1883 by Francis Galton, the founder of British eugenics. Ploetz viewed a *Rasse* (race) as any interbreeding human population that, over the course of generations, could demonstrate similar physical and mental traits.[5] In 1904, he established the first journal in the world dedicated to eugenics, the *Journal of Racial and Social Biology (Archiv für Rassen- und Gesellschafts-Biologie),* and in 1905, the German Society for Racial Hygiene, the world's first eugenics organization.[6] He intended the society to be international—to include members from all "civilized" nations—but, ultimately, his international society fell victim to World War I.[7]

German racial hygiene during the first two decades of the twentieth century consisted of a narrow, elite, social network composed primarily of Ploetz's literary and scientific acquaintances—among them, the psychiatrist Ernst Rüdin, the anthropologist Eugen Fischer, the human geneticist Fritz Lenz, and the biologist Agnes Bluhm.[8] All had medical degrees and all remained active during the Third Reich. Attended by 5.5 million, the 1911 International Hygiene Exhibition, in Dresden,

displayed tables and charts of racial hygienists who sought to spread the new "applied science" in Germany. But the early racial hygiene movement failed to attract official support before the war or have any impact on public policy.[9]

Most of Ploetz's personal group of converts were (at least, privately) sympathetic to political doctrines of Aryan supremacy. But early German racial hygiene was diverse in its politics and its aims. Some, including the social hygienist Alfred Grotjahn, were on the political left. And both Catholics and Jews also had agendas that varied from those of Ploetz and his circle. But even those in his circle with a political weakness for "Aryanism" were not calling for the total elimination of the Jews from Germany—rather, most shared the "respectable" form of antisemitism common among Germany's non-Jewish, educated middle classes and academic elite. It would be misleading to view racial hygiene in Germany at this time as a mere prelude to "Nazi eugenics." The early German racial hygiene movement was preoccupied with eugenic issues common in most other countries with similar movements.[10] There were no public pronouncements seeking to advance exclusively the "Aryan," or ethnic German, segments of the German Empire. The primary objective was rational management of the population—to make the nation more efficient through control of the birthrates of various groups and classes of German society.

By applying eugenics using modern managerial methods and biological principles, eugenicists hoped to secure the long-term vitality of the state. Among the proposed plans to stimulate reproduction were financial incentives for eugenically desirable couples to marry early and have large families, ranging from tax benefits and inheritance law reform to the creation of homesteads and colonies on Germany's

Visitors to the International Hygiene Exhibition, Dresden, 1911. *Deutsches Hygiene-Museum, Dresden*

Opposite: A 1911 exhibition at the German Hygiene Museum, in Dresden, included a display on human heredity and measures to improve it. This poster, designed by Munich artist Franz von Stuck, features the Enlightenment's all-seeing eye of God, adapted from the ancient Egyptian "eye of Ra," which symbolized "fitness" or "health." *Deutsches Hygiene-Museum, Dresden*

War casualties at Plötzensee, near Berlin, summer 1916.
Library of Congress, General Collections, Washington, D.C.

Cemetery for German soldiers, Meissemy, France,
undated. Eugenicists pointed to the loss of population
and future generations as catastrophies of World War I.
Bundesarchiv Koblenz

German dead after the third battle at
Ypres, Belgium, 1917. *Imperial War
Museum, London (Q3117)*

eastern borders. Eugenicists also devised strategies to fight venereal disease and lower infant mortality. To evaluate the biological vitality of individuals, racial hygienists proposed medical genealogies and health passports. They envisioned these as accompanying marriage applications, to enable the state to prevent the marriage of unsuitable couples.[11]

POSTWAR EUGENICS, 1919–1933

World War I and its aftermath affected no country more than Germany. It toppled the monarchy, led to the birth of the largely unloved Weimar Republic—Germany's first attempt at democracy—and was, in no small measure, responsible for Hitler and his Nazi Party's rise to power. Worldwide, most eugenicists viewed the war as a necessary, if dysgenic, upheaval. The German racial hygiene movement, too, was profoundly altered by the aftershocks of the war. Tensions that simmered beneath the surface during the relatively untroubled prewar years ultimately erupted in the face of Germany's defeat and the harsh treaty concluding the war. Exacerbating the situation were attempts from the political right and left to overthrow the government, the occupation by the French of Germany's resource-rich Ruhr region, catastrophic inflation, devastating depression, and, finally, the appointment of Hitler as chancellor on January 30, 1933. Racial hygiene became an integral part of the Republic's health, welfare, and social policy, and inaugurated an active role for medical experts and eugenicists in managing that policy. Weimar racial hygiene also laid some of the necessary foundations for later developments under National Socialism.[12]

Wittenau Psychiatric Clinic, Berlin, 1930. *Landesarchiv Berlin (A Rep. 003-04-04 Nr. 3)*

Medical examination in Alsterdorf, an institution for mentally retarded persons in Hamburg, Germany, 1931. *Evangelische Stiftung Alsterdorf, Hamburg*

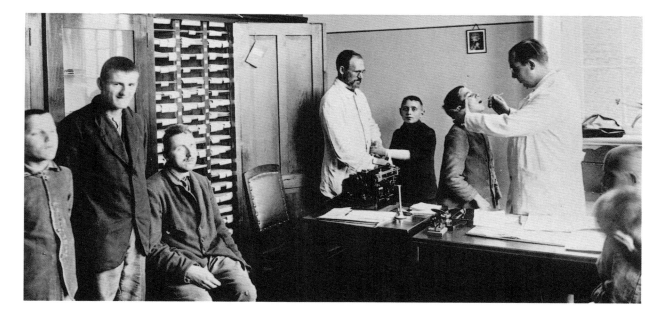

NATIONALISM AND NORDICISM

The major concerns of racial hygiene before the war—the degeneration of the national hereditary stock, population policy, and the alleged financial drain of maintaining the unfit in mental institutions, hospitals, and care homes—continued to preoccupy the postwar movement. Following military defeat and the loss of two million men, Weimar racial hygiene centered increasingly on restoring the health of the German nation, as biomedical professionals saw themselves as healers of the nation. Racial hygienists, aligning themselves with the fields of public welfare and social hygiene, aimed to save Germans from the scourges of crime, venereal disease, tuberculosis, alcoholism, the falling birthrate, and other social ills. Racial hygiene was also tied to the notion, prevalent during the 1920s, of reducing social tensions and social costs by rational state planning.[13]

A state training home for mentally retarded children, Rosenharz, Germany, 1926. *Stiftung Liebenau, Meckenbeuren*

German racial hygienists never entirely lost their international orientation. Many continued to correspond with their counterparts worldwide and, after the early 1920s, participated in international eugenics conferences. Yet, most harbored resentment toward Allied policies, particularly toward the German "war-guilt" clause of the detested Versailles Treaty. They were especially angered at France for using colonial soldiers (including Arab and black African troops) to police the occupied and demilitarized Rhineland region. These events helped push some members of the Ploetz circle more and more toward the political right. Both Fischer and Lenz, for instance, joined the extreme right-wing, nationalist, anti-Republic German National People's Party (DNVP) during the Weimar period.[14] Viewing their fatherland as engaged in a life-or-death geopolitical and economic struggle, and forced to suffer foreign

Brochure for the 1932 German Hygiene Museum exhibition *Healthy Woman, Healthy Nation*. Eugenicists regarded maternal health as an important means of lowering infant mortality and birth defects and, therefore, of improving both the quantity and quality of the German population. *Deutsches Hygiene-Museum, Dresden*

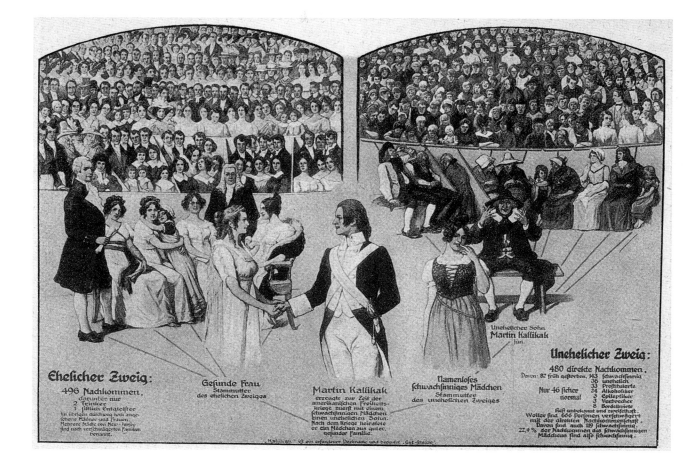

domination by people "culturally beneath them," as the renowned German geneticist and racial hygienist Erwin Baur put it, those in the vanguard of the first generation of the movement, as well as the growing number of new converts in the burgeoning Weimar health and welfare bureaucracy, became increasingly attracted to eugenic solutions.[15]

The larger group of welfare eugenics experts, centered in Berlin, served as an important political counterweight to the conservative, nationalist circle based in Munich. This older group of nationalist racial hygienists was committed to promoting the "Nordic race" as the most biologically desirable of the so-called European races within the German population. They postulated the idea that Germany was populated by several so-called "European races" as well as "non-European races," such as the Jews—normally viewed as a mixture of non-European races. Almost all assumed that the Nordic race stood at the pinnacle of the European races and humanity as a whole. Racial mixing between European and non-European races was viewed as problematic, even dysgenic.

This illustration, from the 1924 educational booklet *Foundations of Racial Hygiene*, typified eugenic fears of population decline. "Kallikak," the pseudonym given to an American Revolutionary War hero who fathered children out of wedlock with a "feebleminded" woman, was the subject of a study by the American psychologist Henry H. Goddard in 1912. The graphic is also an example of the Germans' frequent referral to international eugenics research. *USHMM Collection*

THE POPULARIZATION OF EUGENICS

Owing to the veritable army of medical experts within the left-leaning Prussian government's health and welfare bureaucracy, who found racial hygiene appealing as a means of dealing with a host of health-related issues, eugenics became increasingly more popular in the Weimar years. Race hygienists now reached a wider audience in a variety of ways, including traveling exhibitions, brochures, pamphlets, newsletters, and other teaching materials, as well as through the innovative use of public health

The Wittenau Psychiatric Clinic, in Berlin, was internationally known for its alcohol treatment programs. Many psychiatrists and proponents of eugenics viewed alcoholics as biologically "degenerate," like individuals afflicted with venereal disease or tuberculosis, and likely to pass on their physical defects to any offspring. Ca. 1930. *Landesarchiv Berlin (A Rep. 003-04-04 Nr. 3)*

and eugenics propaganda films that dealt with such topics as infant care, tuberculosis and alcoholism prevention, and the risks of sexually transmitted diseases.

Seeking a wider audience for the eugenics message, in 1925 racial hygienists in Berlin formed the German League for National Regeneration and Heredity *(Deutscher Bund für Volksaufartung und Erbkunde)*, a eugenics education organization. The league dedicated itself to spreading eugenic ideas to all Germans, particularly the working class, a target of eugenicists as a source of social problems and illnesses. Its name, "national regeneration" *(Volksaufartung)*, reflected the spirit of optimism and hope of national reconstruction of the mid-1920s, while its slogan, "Protect German Heredity and Thus the German Type," appealed to nationalism. The league was not antisemitic, yet its chairman, the physician, eugenicist, and high-ranking government official Karl von Behr-Pinnow, accepted the notion of racial hierarchy and regarded the Nordic race as spiritually and physically superior. It also endorsed both negative and positive eugenic measures, including sterilization of physical and mental degenerates. During the Weimar years, the league published three popular journals. Edited, in the late Weimar period, by the influential public health official with Social Democratic sympathies in the Prussian Ministry of Welfare, Arthur Ostermann, the journals and their contents had a strong influence in government circles.[16] Many of the 1,500 members who belonged to the league also found their way to the German Society for Racial Hygiene.

The league's journals were politically distasteful to some supporters of the Nordic idea, and to many on the political right—the extreme nationalist publisher Julius Lehmann, for one. Lehmann, a supporter of Adolf Hitler, became an important

Foundations of Human Genetics and Racial Hygiene—also known as Baur-Fischer-Lenz—was one of the definitive works on human heredity and eugenics in its time. Ideas from this work, published in 1921 and reissued in 1923, were incorporated into the ideology of the fledgling Nazi movement. *USHMM Collection*

Dr. Fritz Lenz, a geneticist and one of Germany's leading proponents of racial hygiene. *Archiv zur Geschichte der Max-Planck-Gesellschaft, Berlin*

propagandist for the Nordic wing of racial hygiene. Although specializing in medical books and journals, Lehmann's firm also published many antisemitic and radically nationalist tracts, such as amateur anthropologist Hans F. K. Günther's popular *Racial Study of the German People (Rassenkunde des deutschen Volkes)*.[17]

During the Weimar years, proponents in cultural and political arenas further popularized eugenics. In the Catholic sphere, eugenics centered on Hermann Mucker-mann, a Jesuit biologist and steadfast eugenics advocate, whose ties to the Catholic Center Party gave him influence in some government circles. His tireless lecturing on eugenics won him a reputation as a leading propagandist for the cause. The Social Democratic Party was also attracted to eugenic ideas, which is not surprising considering the wide interest in scientific methodology shared by both socialists and eugenicists—a scientific approach that both embodied the utopian vision of transforming humankind and lent itself to various social engineering projects under way in Weimar Germany's health and welfare sectors.[18] By the late Weimar years, eugenics also made its way into the German secondary-school biology curriculum, further encouraging the spread of the eugenics gospel beyond the confines of a narrow, intellectual band of advocates.[19]

INSTITUTIONALIZING WEIMAR RACIAL HYGIENE

Along with its popularization, German racial hygiene experienced a high degree of professionalization and institutionalization in the Weimar period. One of the people who did most to help professionalize racial hygiene during the Republic, as well as

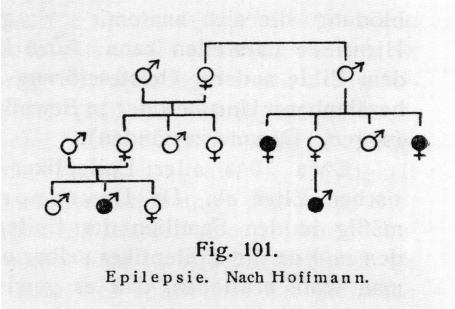

Family trees showing the manifestation of epilepsy across two generations, from *Foundations of Human Genetics and Racial Hygiene*. USHMM Collection

Fig. 101.

Epilepsie. Nach Hoffmann.

lend an air of international respectability to eugenics in Germany, was Fritz Lenz. He wrote more than six hundred articles and book reviews in his lifetime. Lenz, who was active in the Munich chapter of the society before the war, came to the attention of the international eugenics community, in 1921, as coauthor of what became the discipline's standard work, *Foundations of Human Genetics and Racial Hygiene*. The treatise comprised two volumes and went through four editions in German; its third edition (the last to be published prior to the Third Reich) was translated into English in 1931.[20] It was the racial hygiene text Hitler was said to have read during his stay in prison following his failed 1923 beer-hall *putsch*, in Munich. The Baur-Fischer-Lenz, as the *Foundations* was dubbed (for its authors, Erwin Baur, Eugen Fischer, and Fritz Lenz), was reviewed in more than 300 professional journals, including 27 in non-German-speaking countries.[21]

Like many anthropologists and geneticists of his day, Lenz believed that psychological and physical traits were racially determined. Along with many of his colleagues worldwide, he accepted a hierarchy that classified and ranked groups into races based on cultural achievement and physical appearance. His support of ideologies of Nordic racial supremacy and his scientific variety of antisemitism were both clearly evident in the *Foundations*. According to Lenz (and many Jewish anthropologists), Jews were a composite of two main races, the Near Eastern and the Oriental. He considered them a "mental race," a people preoccupied with making money or making revolution. But he also praised Jews as a highly intelligent people whose presence in the "world of knowledge," particularly in the sciences, was far greater "than might be expected from their numbers." "To deny that the Jewish race has produced persons of outstanding genius," Lenz asserted, "would be absurd."[22]

Most Western anthropologists classified people into "races" based on such physical traits as head size and eye, hair, and skin color. This classification scheme by Eugen Fischer, published in the 1921 and 1923 editions of *Foundations of Human Genetics and Racial Hygiene*, identifies eight racial types.

Tafel 4.

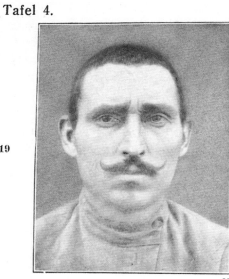 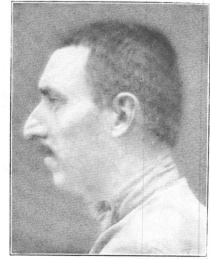

Vorderasiatische Rasse.
Aus Bessarabien. Aufn. F. Lenz.

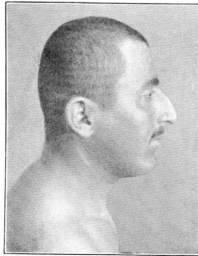 

Vorderasiatische Rasse. Aus Armenien.
Aufn. J. Weninger. (Mitt. Geogr. Ges. Wien 1920).

Dinarische Rasse, wenig nordischer Einschlag. Aus
Tirol. Aufn. des Anthropol. Instituts der Univ. Wien.

Dinarische Rasse.
Aus Südbaden. Aufn. Mattern.

Orientalische Rasse mit vorderasiatischem Einschlag.
Jüdin aus Belgien. Aufn. C. Ruf.

A Belgian-Jewish woman (right bottom) is classified as a mixed type, with Oriental and Near Eastern traits. *USHMM Collection, Gift of Friedrich Rösing*

25

26

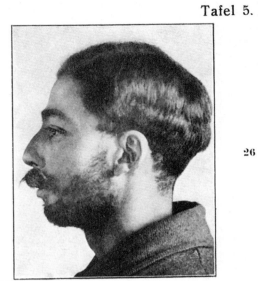

Orientalische Rasse.
Aus Algerien. Aufn. F. Lenz.

27

28

Mongolide Rasse.
Jakutin aus Jakutsk nach Jochelson-Brodsky.

Mongolide Rasse.
Vornehmer Japaner. Aufn. C. Ruf.

29

30

Mongolid-nordischer Mischtypus.
Aus Lettland. Aufn. F. Lenz.

Mongolid-nordischer Mischtypus.
Aus Zentralrußland (Gegend von Kursk). Aufn. F. Lenz.

The Kaiser Wilhelm Institute for Psychiatry, in Munich, was led by Dr. Ernst Rüdin, an early advocate of the compulsory sterilization of the "unfit." At the institute, researchers created family trees of psychiatric patients to identify the hereditary roots of mental illness. *Max-Planck-Institut für Psychiatrie, Munich*

Lenz projected his obsession with cultural productivity as a standard for genetic fitness onto race. For him, the Nordic race was the pinnacle of cultural efficiency as well as physical beauty—the standard-bearer of his idealized version of Western culture.[23] Yet, the bulk of his work was more concerned with medical genetics, the inheritance of talent, the methodology of genetic research, and practical suggestions for the implementation of racial hygiene. Lenz, therefore, is the best representative of the two faces of German racial hygiene—at once a supporter of Nordic supremacy as well as an advocate of social productivity as the main criterion for ascertaining the "value" of an individual. His discussion of human genetics and his work on statistics gave the German movement worldwide scientific respectability. The international reputation of German racial hygienists would be an extremely valuable resource for the Nazi state in the implementation of its racial policies.

The professionalization of Weimar racial hygiene coincided with substantial institutional expansion. In 1923, the University of Munich established a chair for the new discipline (held by Lenz), and by 1932, many German universities offered eugenics lecture courses—mostly in faculties of medicine.[24] Perhaps most significant for the establishment of eugenics' scientific respectability, both at home and abroad, was the creation of the prestigious Kaiser Wilhelm Society (KWS)—an umbrella organization encompassing, during the Weimar years, more than 30 research institutes in the natural and applied physical sciences.

Racial hygiene found its first home in the Kaiser Wilhelm Society in 1924, when it took over the German Research Institute for Psychiatry, originally founded, in Munich, in 1918. Ernst Rüdin, a conservative nationalist (although of Swiss origin) renowned for

The Kaiser Wilhelm Institute for Anthropology, Human Heredity, and Eugenics opened, in Berlin, in 1927. Modeled after Sweden's State Institute for Race Biology, in Uppsala, the institute's work raised government officials' confidence in the science of eugenics and eugenic proposals for solving public health and social problems. *Archiv zur Geschichte der Max-Planck-Gesellschaft, Berlin*

his vanguard work in psychiatric genetics, headed the institute's Department of Genealogy and Demography. Rüdin's long-standing connection to Ploetz, and his marriage to Ploetz's sister, strengthened his commitment to racial hygiene. In his pioneering work on schizophrenia, published in 1916, Rüdin popularized his methodology of hereditary prognosis—the collection and study of patients' genealogical data—as a way to document the genetic transmission of schizophrenia and other psychiatric disorders. Many of his future coworkers at the institute adopted this methodology during the Weimar years.[25] The Kaiser Wilhelm Society's willingness to fund Rüdin's research was probably not unrelated to Weimar health policy concerns; its interest in data on genetic disorders in families and hereditary data banks, like the kind established by Rüdin and his institute, was a way to screen large-scale populations.[26] Before Rüdin became director of the German Research Institute for Psychiatry in 1931, he had earned a national, even international, reputation in his field.

In 1927, the German government established a second eugenics-related Kaiser Wilhelm Institute (KWI)—the KWI for Anthropology, Human Heredity, and Eugenics, directed by the internationally respected anthropologist Eugen Fischer. KWS president Adolf von Harnack convinced the Social Democratic–Center Party coalition government in Prussia, an important source of funding, of the "great national task" of establishing such an institute. He argued that the Kaiser Wilhelm Institute for Anthropology would serve as a counterweight to the "inadequate and dilettantish" manner in which the fields of anthropology (increasingly known as "racial science"), human heredity, and eugenics were frequently treated. Offering his solemn pledge that "the Kaiser Wilhelm Society [would take] full responsibility" in guaranteeing the objective

Eugen Fischer, director of the Kaiser Wilhelm Institute, achieved prominence with his 1913 study of mixed Dutch and Hottentot children *(Mischlinge)* in colonial German South-West Africa. *Archiv zur Geschichte der Max-Planck-Gesellschaft, Berlin*

nature of the science pursued within the walls of the proposed new institute, he won the necessary financial backing from the Prussian state and the Reich. "True racial science," the aging KWS president argued, "will bring segments of the nation closer together, not divide them."[27]

Fischer himself headed the Department of Anthropology as well as serving as institute director until 1942, and simultaneously held a chair of anthropology at the University of Berlin. Fischer had always sympathized with the Nordic point of view, but was astute enough to realize that emphasizing this side of German racial hygiene would not be welcomed in the political climate of Berlin of the middle Weimar years. The use of the term *eugenics* rather than *racial hygiene*, as part of the institute's official title, was deliberate. Fischer instituted a clearly thought-out research program that focused on the inheritance of racial and pathological traits and on an analysis of the genetic foundations of a population. The first two research foci, he believed, found their culmination in the third, eugenics. He appointed Hermann Muckermann head of the division of eugenics. During the Weimar years, Muckermann delivered some 600 talks on eugenics. (He would be forcibly removed from his post when the Nazis assumed power in 1933.)

Fischer selected his medically trained former student, an extreme nationalist and racial hygiene enthusiast, and, later, close personal friend and confidant, Otmar von Verschuer, to head the Department of Human Heredity. Verschuer established the Kaiser Wilhelm Institute for Anthropology as one of the world centers for twin research, at the time the most innovative approach in the study of human genetics. Adept at finding ways to locate subjects for his research at hospitals, schools, and

During the Weimar period, anthropologists turned their focus inward to the study of local populations in Germany. Academics from the Kaiser Wilhelm Institute for Anthropology, Human Heredity, and Eugenics, in Berlin, selected 63 sites and collected family data and thousands of physical measurements. The photographs, taken in 1932, document a study conducted in Schleswig-Holstein by two Kiel University professors. Anthropological tools included hair color kits. *Ullstein Bild, Berlin; Staatliche Naturwissenschaftliche Sammlungen Bayerns, Munich*

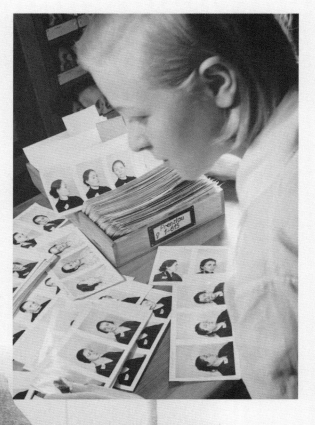

Kaiser-Wilhelm-Institut
für Genealogie und Demographie
München N 23   Kraepelinstr. 2
Direktor Prof. Dr. Rüdin
Telefon 36099

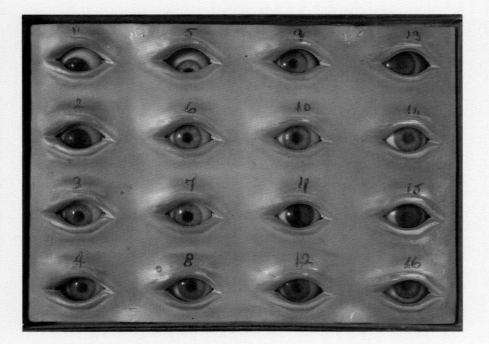

Eye chart. *Galton Collection, University College London*

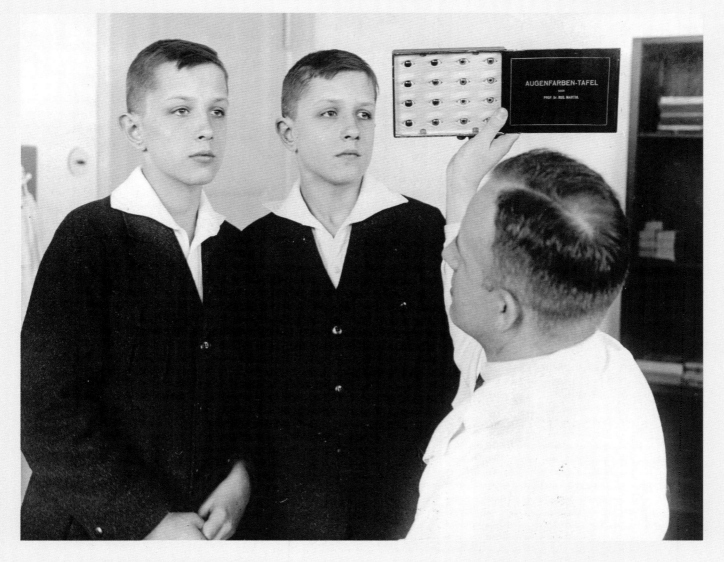

Verschuer, with identical twin subjects, at the Kaiser Wilhelm Institute, 1928. *Archiv zur Geschichte der Max-Planck-Gesellschaft, Berlin*

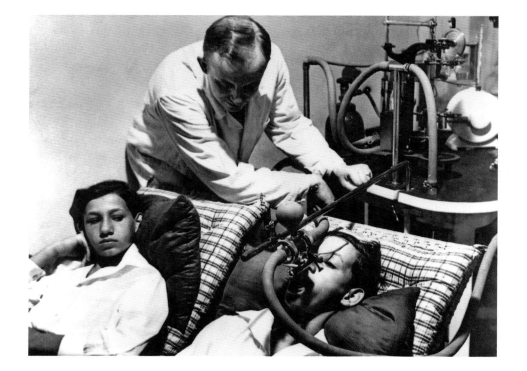

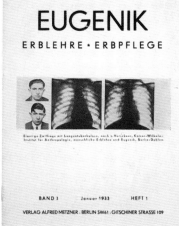

Eugenik, January 1933, which published Verschuer's investigation of the genetic links to tuberculosis. *USHMM Collection*

Dr. Otmar von Verschuer examines the lung capacities of twins, 1930. Ethical questions surfacing from the deaths of 75 children in an unrelated tuberculosis vaccine experiment in Lübeck led to the adoption, in 1931, of strict national guidelines for human medical experimentation. *Ullstein Bild, Berlin*

through newspapers, Verschuer quickly filled his files with data from hundreds, and, later, thousands, of twins. His research focused on the heritability of criminality, feeblemindedness, tuberculosis, and cancer, and in 1927, he recommended the forced sterilization of the "mentally and morally subnormal." Earlier, Verschuer had belonged to the ultranationalist organization of war veterans, the *Freikorps*, and typified those academics whose interest in Germany's "national regeneration" provided motivation for their research.[28]

Chairs like this forced subjects to sit straight for photographs and standard research conducted by anthropologists. After extensively measuring such physical traits as skull shape and eye and hair color, researchers produced statistical models that lent their findings an air of irrefutable authority. *Naturhistorisches Museum, Vienna*

THE RADICALIZATION OF EUGENICS

Two years after the festive opening of the KWI for Anthropology, the effects of the Great Depression began to alter both German politics and the attitudes of German racial hygienists. Not only did the Depression eventually leave more than six million people unemployed, it also forced a reexamination of the Weimar welfare state. Political leaders sought ways to trim Germany's welfare budget and to allocate Germany's dwindling financial resources in the most cost-efficient manner.[29] Racial hygienists and government officials looked for alternatives to pouring ever-increasing sums into asylums and prisons. They began formulating such ideas as "differential welfare," a concept supported by eugenicists like Hans Harmsen, a member of the Protestant Church's charitable organization, the Inner Mission. In determining who should receive health care and material assistance, Harmsen urged that distinctions had to be made between the chronically useless and those "from whom full productivity could reasonably be expected."[30]

Geh nicht blind
in die Ehe!

Abb. 36.

(Aus einer Flugschrift „Elternpflicht", herausgegeben von der Abteilung
zur Bekämpfung der Geschlechtskrankheiten des Staatsgesundheitsamtes
in Louisiana, Vereinigte Staaten.)

Educating the public about carefully selecting a spouse was a form of "positive" eugenics, the term used at the time. Captioned "Don't Go Blindly into Marriage!," this drawing illustrated a 1924 pamphlet that urged couples to be informed about the health, including genetic health, of prospective spouses. This image was first published by Louisiana's Department of Health. *USHMM Collection, Gift of Deutsche Hygiene-Museum, Dresden*

Although German racial hygienists—of all political persuasions—had previously been fairly reticent about mandating "negative eugenic measures," mainly sterilization, during the last troubled years of the Republic qualms about the legal and ethical problems associated with such measures began to fade. By 1930, many racial hygienists supported compulsory sterilization of the unfit, and, to almost all professional German racial hygienists, at least voluntary sterilization seemed reasonable. After prolonged debate, in 1932 the Prussian Health Council drafted a sterilization law that permitted the voluntary sterilization of certain classes of hereditarily "defective" individuals—including those with hereditary mental illness, feeblemindedness, and epilepsy. It required proof that these traits were, in fact, genetic, with evidence such as genealogical records evaluated by two physicians. There was no mention of sterilization on either racial or social grounds. Owing to the political chaos following the ouster of Prussia's center-left coalition government by the Reich in July 1932, the sterilization draft never became law during the Weimar Republic.[31]

It is important to note that the ever-increasing eugenics radicalism of German racial hygienists did not provoke any public criticism in the genetics community. Geneticists working in fields not related to human heredity were either sympathetic to racial hygiene—like the nationalist plant geneticist Erwin Baur, of the KWI for Breeding Research, and the Jewish geneticist Richard Goldschmidt, of the KWI for Biology—or were publicly silent on the topic.[32] In fact, virtually all members of the German human genetics community were advocates of racial hygiene, and most human genetics research was informed by racial hygiene concerns. Nor was there a strong anti-eugenics movement within either of Germany's two main churches

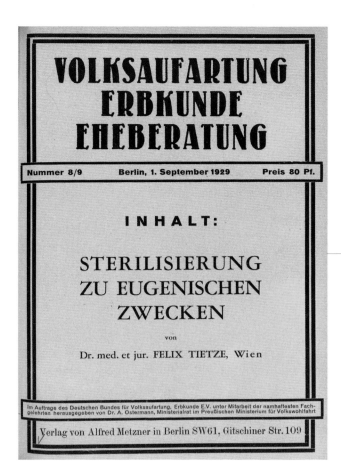

during the Weimar years. Muckermann used his ties to the Catholic Center Party to advance racial hygiene in Germany; he was even willing to negotiate with members of the Nazi Party, who sought his expert opinion on eugenic policy before 1933. Despite political differences, Muckermann saw eugenics and the Nazis "sharing the goal of overcoming national biological degeneration."[33]

With the coming of the Depression, many in the movement felt a sense of frustration that in bureaucratic, strife-ridden Weimar Germany relatively little in the way of practical eugenic policies could be implemented; some racial hygienists on the political right began to pin their hopes on Hitler and the Nazi Party. Lenz argued, as early as 1931, that the Nazi Party was the only party from which one might expect to see the type of racial hygiene measures commensurate with the genetic dangers facing Germany, although he regretted its one-sided antisemitism.[34] Even those, like Fischer, who did not publicly support Hitler prior to 1933, resented the deep budget cuts their institutes experienced during the last years of the Republic. They were not disinclined, therefore, to adopt a "wait and see" attitude toward the Nazis.[35]

Those racial hygienists willing to cooperate with the National Socialists believed that, as internationally respected scientific experts, they would be making the important decisions about future racial hygiene state policy. Once the Nazis were in power, many racial hygienists were ready to come to terms with Hitler's regime. In so doing, they not only showed few qualms in working to validate Nazi racial theories but, ultimately, many participated directly in the implementation of the Nazis' barbarous racial hygiene policies.

INTERNATIONAL EUGENICS

BY DANIEL J. KEVLES

Eugenics is rightly associated with the brutalities of the Nazis, but it was rooted in the pervasive social Darwinism of the late nineteenth century, with all its metaphors of fitness and competition and rationalizations of inequality. Indeed, the concept in its modern form originated with Francis Galton, a British scientist and a cousin of Charles Darwin. Galton coined the word *eugenics*, in 1883, and used it to promote the idea of improving the human race by, as he put it, getting rid of the "unde-sirables," multiplying the "desirables."[1] Eugenics began to flourish after the rediscovery, in 1900, of the Austrian monk and naturalist Gregor Mendel's theory that the biological makeup of organisms is determined by certain "factors," later identified with genes. After the turn of the century, eugenics movements blossomed in the United States, Canada, Great Britain, Scandinavia, and Russia, not to mention elsewhere in conti-nental Europe and parts of Latin America and Asia. Eugenics was, therefore, not unique to the Nazis. It could—and did—strike root almost everywhere.[2]

Eugenicists universally feared that their societies were beset by social degenera-tion. They were sure that "feebleminded" people—to use the broad-brush term then commonly applied to persons believed to be mentally retarded—were responsible for a wide range of social problems and were proliferating at a rate that threatened

In 1935, the Buffalo Museum of Science, in New York, acquired this model of the "glass man" produced by the German Hygiene Museum, in Dresden. In the late 1980s, officials at the Buffalo museum "donated" it back to the German museum, considering the object tainted by its Nazi associations. *Deutsches Hygiene-Museum, Dresden*

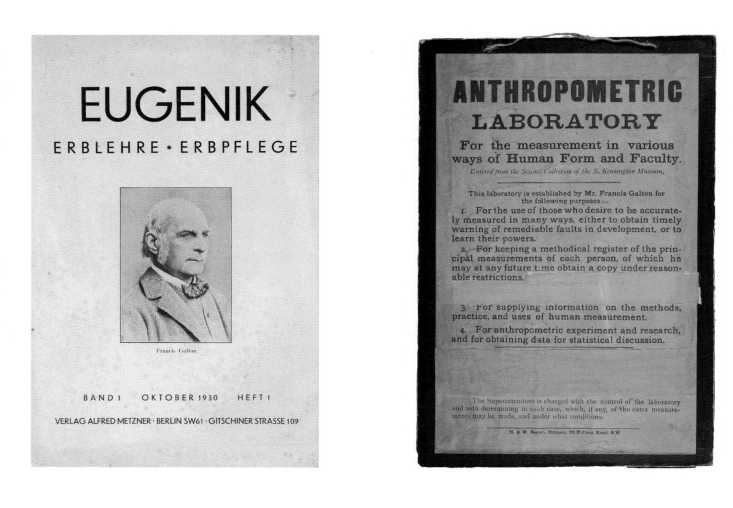

VERLAG ALFRED METZNER · BERLIN SW61 · GITSCHINER STRASSE 109

Above: The German journal *Eugenik*, of October 1930, honored Francis Galton. *USHMM Collection*

Above right: Laboratory regulations sign posted outside Francis Galton's Anthropometric Laboratory. Galton established the laboratory in order to obtain data on human heredity. He pioneered the use of gathering such statistics and interpreting inheritance factors. *Galton Collection, University College London*

social resources and stability. Anglo-American eugenicists fastened on the so-called "differential birthrate"—the theory, based on British data, that half of each succeeding generation was produced by no more than a quarter of its married predecessors and that the prolific quarter was disproportionately located among the dregs of society. Feebleminded women were held to be driven by a heedless sexuality, the product of biologically grounded flaws in their moral character that led them to prostitution and illegitimacy. Such biological analyses of social behavior found a receptive audience among middle-class men and women, many of whom were sexually prudish and apprehensive about the discordant trends of modern urban, industrial society, including the growing demands for women's rights and sexual tolerance.[3]

Eugenic doctrines were bolstered by the research that poured out of institutes for the study of eugenics, or "race biology," that were established in a number of countries, including Denmark, Sweden, Great Britain, Germany, and the United States. In the English-speaking world, one of the most prominent was the Galton Laboratory for National Eugenics, at University College London, under the directorship of the statistician and population biologist Karl Pearson. An adamant anti-Mendelian, Pearson probed the hereditary underpinnings of traits by calculating correlations among relatives or between generations for the frequencies of occurrence of different diseases, disorders, and behaviors.[4] The approach used in most eugenic laboratories, however, was Mendelian evaluation—the analysis of physical characteristics and family data to account for the inheritance of a variety of medical afflictions and social behaviors in genetic terms.

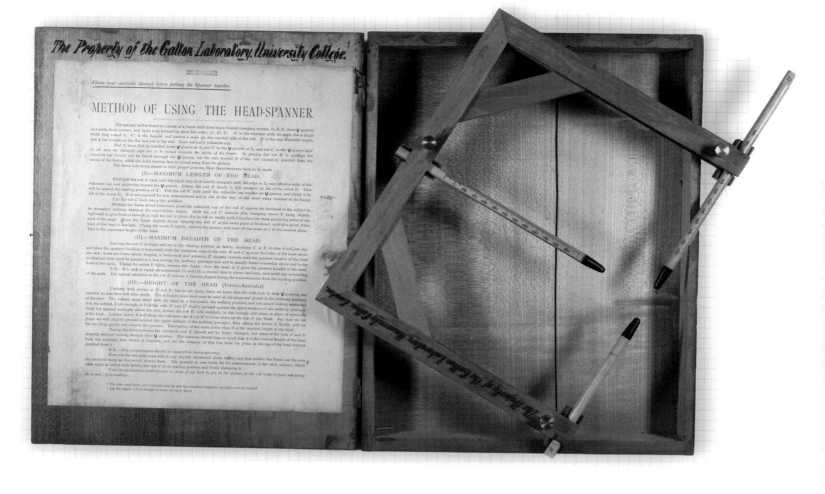

Calipers used by Galton to measure skull size. *Galton Collection, University College London*

Mendelism dominated the work of the Eugenics Record Office, which was affiliated with, and eventually became part of, the biological research facilities that the Carnegie Institution of Washington sponsored at Cold Spring Harbor, on Long Island, New York, under the directorship of the biologist Charles B. Davenport. Staff at, or affiliated with, the laboratory gathered information bearing on human heredity by examining medical records or conducting extended family studies, often relying upon field-workers—many of them recent alumnae from women's colleges—to construct trait pedigrees in selected populations (say, the residents of a rural community) on the basis of interviews and the examination of genealogical records.[5]

Wherever family pedigrees seemed to show a high incidence of a given character, Davenport concluded that the trait must be biologically inheritable, and he attempted to fit the pattern of inheritance into a Mendelian frame. Such findings were widely disseminated in popular articles, lectures, and books, including Davenport's own *Heredity in Relation to Eugenics*, published in 1911, and they made their way into the educated culture of the day.[6] It was a commonplace of the creed, to quote a chart displayed at the Kansas Free Fair in 1929, designed to illustrate the "laws" of Mendelian inheritance in human beings, that "unfit human traits such as feeblemindedness, epilepsy, criminality, insanity, alcoholism, pauperism, and many others run in families and are inherited in exactly the same way as color in guinea pigs."[7]

In most nations, eugenics' advocates included medical practitioners, especially those who worked with people suffering from mental diseases and disorders, and scientists, notably biologists, like Davenport, involved in the new discipline of genetics. In a number of countries, many women played a prominent role in the movement, having

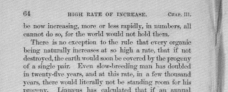

First edition of Charles Darwin's *On the Origin of Species*, given to Galton by his cousin, the book's author. Darwin's work sparked great interest in biological determinism and the application of the principle of natural selection to human society. Here, inspired by Darwin's assertion that various animals increased in number in a state of nature, Galton jotted down a logarithm of his own that projected population growth among humans. *U C London Library, Special Collections*

Illustration from a pamphlet published by the Eugenics Education Society, London, entitled *Those Who Come After*, ca. 1930, portraying the comparative educational cost, in pounds, shillings, and pence, for the normal child *(far left)*, and for children with various disabilities.

been drawn to it as club women or because of their involvement with issues of children, wayward girls, and the mentally retarded.

Eugenics drew significant support from social conservatives, concerned to prevent the proliferation of lower-income groups and save on the cost of caring for them. Eugenically minded women were often discomfited by the alleged wanton sexuality of feebleminded females; they saw the eugenic emphasis on limiting the reproduction of the unfit as a way of controlling sexual expression that deviated from middle-class norms.

But the movement also belonged, in no small part, to the wave of progressive social reform that swept through Western Europe and North America during the early decades of the century. For progressives, eugenics was a branch of the drive for social improvement that many reformers of the day thought might be achieved through the deployment of science to such good social ends as clean cities, greater temperance, child welfare, and public health. In the American Deep South, for instance, eugenics was introduced in the manner of the campaigns against hookworm, tuberculosis, and venereal disease by reformist missionaries from the North, particularly activists from national organizations for mental health and care of the feebleminded. They found a responsive audience among Southerners worried about Caucasian "degenerates," in the words of a white Louisiana physician, who threatened their own race with physical, mental, and moral "decay."[8]

The radical reformism of the Bolshevik Revolution encouraged eugenicists in Russia to think they might transform their creed into biosocial policy. Like many of

American eugenicists Charles B. Davenport *(right)*, director of the biological research facility at Cold Spring Harbor, New York, and Harry Laughlin, head of the associated Eugenics Record Office. *Truman State University, Kirksville, Mo.*

Visitors at the 1929 *Eugenic and Health Exhibit*, Kansas Free Fair. Exhibitions at state fairs became a popular medium for eugenicists to report their findings on hereditary research and advocate for eugenic measures. *AES Records, American Philosophical Society, Philadelphia*

Exhibit used at Fitter Families contests, sponsored at state fairs by the American Eugenics Society, ca. 1925–30. *AES Records, American Philosophical Society, Philadelphia*

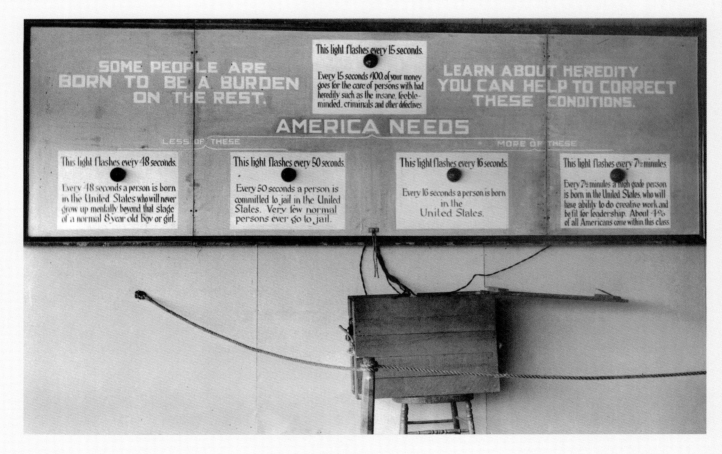

A 1923 Soviet poster, informed by eugenics, with babies *(from left to right)* demanding "Dry Clean Diapers," "Protection from Flies," "Mother's Breast," "Clean Air and Light," and "Healthy Parents & Midwives, and Not Old Women." *Gosudarstvennyy arkhiv Rossiyskoy Federatsii, Moscow*

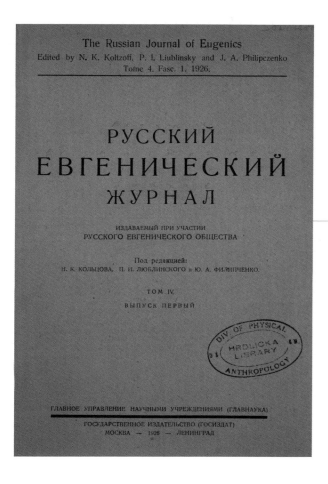

The Russian Journal of Eugenics
Edited by N. K. Koltzoff, P. I. Liublinsky and J. A. Philipczenko.
Tome 4. Fasc. 1. 1926.

РУССКИЙ
ЕВГЕНИЧЕСКИЙ
ЖУРНАЛ

ИЗДАВАЕМЫЙ ПРИ УЧАСТИИ
РУССКОГО ЕВГЕНИЧЕСКОГО ОБЩЕСТВА

Под редакцией:
Н. К. КОЛЬЦОВА, П. И. ЛЮБЛИНСКОГО и Ю. А. ФИЛИПЧЕНКО.

ТОМ IV
ВЫПУСК ПЕРВЫЙ

ГЛАВНОЕ УПРАВЛЕНИЕ НАУЧНЫМИ УЧРЕЖДЕНИЯМИ (ГЛАВНАУКА)
ГОСУДАРСТВЕННОЕ ИЗДАТЕЛЬСТВО (ГОСИЗДАТ)
МОСКВА — 1926 — ЛЕНИНГРАД

A 1926 issue of the *Russian Eugenics Journal*, featuring hereditary research using twins. Soviet eugenics, reflecting political ideology, rejected Mendelian heredity theory and such "negative" eugenic measures as sterilization in favor of "positive" approaches focused on parental care and other environmental conditions. *Hrdlicka Collection, Department of Anthropology, Smithsonian Institution, Washington, D.C.*

their counterparts elsewhere, they comprised biologists, physicians, social scientists, and public health officials, and were predominantly political liberals concerned with the dysgenic effects of World War I, through the killing of so many able-bodied men, and the postwar famine. They founded the Russian Eugenics Society, established a eugenics research program, and began publishing articles on human heredity. Aleksandr Serebrovskii, a Mendelian geneticist and one of the leaders in the movement, proposed that the first Five-Year Plan include population improvement by the artificial insemination of willing women with the sperm of able men, contending that "one talented and valuable producer could have up to 1,000 children," and that the program would enable human selection to make "gigantic leaps forward."[9]

But, by the early 1930s, Soviet authorities were turning against eugenics as "bourgeois"—a link between biology and society that qualified as one of the sins of "Menshevizing idealism"—something inadmissible in the new socialist order. The Russian Eugenics Society was disbanded in 1930 and the leading eugenics research program was abolished. In 1936, Stalin flatly rejected a plan for a socialist eugenics advanced by the American biologist Hermann J. Muller that, like Serebrovskii's, was grounded in artificial insemination. By then, Lysenkoists—who argued that environment played a role in determining hereditary characteristics—were successfully waging war against Mendelian genetics and eugenics, claiming that both were fascist in character.[10]

Racism helped energize eugenics, but the degree to which it did varied considerably from one nation to the next. In this era, racial differences were attributed to ethnic and even national distinctions. Swedish analysts feared that the racial purity of their country might eventually be undermined if only because so many Nordics

Norwegian eugenicist Jon Alfred Mjöen, a pharmacist by training, lecturing on Mendel's laws at the Vinderen Biological Laboratory, ca. 1925–30. Mjöen, an anti-alcohol campaigner, enthusiastically promoted Nordic racial purity. *AES Records, American Philosophical Society, Philadelphia*

were emigrating. Swedish speakers in Finland feared the proliferation of Finnish speakers, holding them to be fundamentally Mongols and, as such, a threat to national quality.[11] In England, the Fabian Sidney Webb enlarged upon the theory of the differential birthrate by pointing out that the poorer districts characterized by prolific breeding were heavily populated by Irish Catholics and Jews, who tended to be fruitful and multiply for religious reasons. "This can hardly result in anything but national deterioration," he warned, "or, as an alternative, in this country gradually falling to the Irish and the Jews."[12]

Race was a minor subtext in British and Scandinavian eugenics compared with the role it played in the versions of the movement that developed in Canada and the United States. North American eugenicists were particularly disturbed by the contributions to population growth of the immigrants from Eastern and Southern Europe who had been flooding into their countries since the late nineteenth century. The new arrivals were considered not only racially different from but also inferior to the Anglo-Saxon majority, partly because they were disproportionately represented among the criminals, prostitutes, slum dwellers, and feebleminded in North American cities. Davenport, for example, found the Poles "independent and self-reliant though

clannish," the Italians tending to "crimes of personal violence," and the Hebrews "intermediate between the slovenly Servians and the Greeks and the tidy Swedes, Germans, and Bohemians," and given to "thieving" though rarely to "personal violence." He expected that the "great influx of blood from Southeastern Europe" would rapidly make the American population "darker in pigmentation, smaller in stature, more mercurial...more given to crimes of larceny, kidnapping, assault, murder, rape, and sex-immorality."[13] In all, the eugenics community in the United States reasoned that if immigrant deficiencies were hereditary and Eastern European immigrants outreproduced natives of Anglo stock, inevitably the quality of the American population would decline.

The progressives, the conservatives, and the racists in both camps found common ground in attributing such phenomena as crime, slums, prostitution, and alcoholism primarily to biology. Their beliefs were reinforced by the knowledge that they were part of a worldwide movement. In 1912, some 750 people from Great Britain, Europe, and the United States attended the first International Eugenics Congress, in London, where the Right Honorable Arthur Balfour delivered the inaugural address, receiving hearty applause when he mentioned the "dignity of motherhood."[14] The congress's sponsoring vice presidents included the Lord Chief Justice of Britain, the Right Honorable Winston Churchill, Alexander Graham Bell, and Charles William Eliot, the former president of Harvard University. A second International Eugenics Congress was held in New York, in 1921. General international contact was maintained before and after the congresses, and it was especially strong— notably between Great Britain and the United States and between Germany and

Plates from *The Racial Character of the Swedish Nation* (1926), by Herman Lundborg, a psychiatrist and head of the Swedish Institute of Race Biology. In addition to photographs that attracted wide international attention, the volume included myriad statistical analyses based on physical measurements taken of 100,000 Swedes, largely military recruits, but also teacher trainees, patients in hospitals and sanatoriums, and prisoners. *USHMM Collection*

Photos from the scrapbook of the American Eugenics
Society of winners in Fitter Families contests, 1925.
AES Records, American Philosophical Society, Philadelphia

the Scandinavian countries and the United States. European eugenicists corresponded with their American counterparts and several visited the United States, some to work at the Eugenics Record Office.[15]

Eugenicists on both sides of the Atlantic argued for a two-pronged program that would increase the frequency of socially good genes in the population and decrease that of bad genes. One prong comprised "positive" eugenics, which meant manipulating human heredity and/or breeding to produce superior people. The other was "negative" eugenics, which meant improving the quality of the human race by eliminating or excluding biologically inferior people from the population.

In Great Britain between the wars, positive eugenics thinking led to proposals for artificial insemination, along Serebrovskii and Muller's lines, and for family allowances that would be proportional to income. Both were unsuccessful. In the United States, positive eugenics fostered so-called Fitter Family competitions, a standard feature at a number of state fairs that were held in their "human stock" sections. At the 1924 Kansas Free Fair, winning families in the three categories—small, average, and large—were awarded a Governor's Fitter Family Trophy. "Grade A Individuals" received a medal that portrayed two diaphanously garbed parents, their arms outstretched toward their (presumably) eugenically meritorious infant. It is hard to know what made these families and individuals stand out as fit, but some evidence is supplied by the fact that all entrants had to take an IQ test—and the Wassermann test for syphilis.[16]

Much more was urged for negative eugenics, notably in the United States, limiting immigration from Eastern and Southern Europe, and, in many countries, discouraging

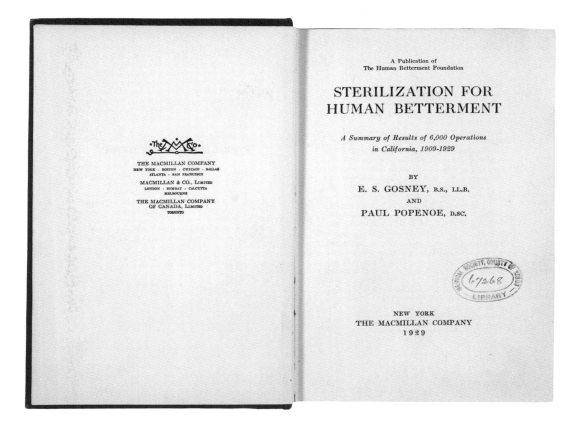

A Publication of
The Human Betterment Foundation

STERILIZATION FOR HUMAN BETTERMENT

A Summary of Results of 6,000 Operations in California, 1909-1929

BY

E. S. GOSNEY, B.S., LL.B.

AND

PAUL POPENOE, D.SC.

NEW YORK
THE MACMILLAN COMPANY
1929

THE MACMILLAN COMPANY
NEW YORK · BOSTON · CHICAGO · DALLAS
ATLANTA · SAN FRANCISCO
MACMILLAN & CO., LIMITED
LONDON · BOMBAY · CALCUTTA
MELBOURNE
THE MACMILLAN COMPANY
OF CANADA, LIMITED
TORONTO

A book, published in 1929, by Ezra Gosney, a Pasadena philanthropist, and Paul Popenoe, a journalist, on the history of eugenical sterilization in California. The authors portrayed the operations—vasectomies and tubal ligations—as low-risk, professional procedures that were actually welcomed by many grateful families. *USHMM Collection*

or preventing the reproduction of the allegedly unfit. Immigration restriction—a broad-based movement that included nativists as well as organized labor—would have succeeded in the United States without eugenics, but American eugenicists provided it with a scientific rationale. Using data from IQ tests administered to army draftees during World War I, they proclaimed that a large proportion of immigrants were almost, or actually, feebleminded, and that allowing them to continue to enter the United States freely menaced the country with "race deterioration." Harry Laughlin, superintendent of the Eugenics Record Office, at Cold Spring Harbor, advanced such arguments to the House Committee on Immigration and Naturalization in his capacity as the committee's "Expert Eugenical Agent." His claims bolstered Congress's drive to enact the Immigration Act of 1924, which severely restricted the number of newcomers from Eastern and Southern Europe.[17]

California's Mendocino State Hospital. Between 1909 and 1935, doctors performed 295 eugenic sterilizations at this mental hospital. Most patients were discharged after the operation, resulting in savings for the public institution that were tallied in written reports. *Dept. of Mental Health, California State Archives, Sacramento*

Emphasis in the drive to prevent the allegedly unfit—in the main, the so-called feebleminded—from reproducing resulted, initially, in segregating them in public institutions, but it was costly to maintain them. If they were sterilized, however, they could be released into society. A newspaper in Jackson, Mississippi, expressed a trope common among sterilizationists on both sides of the Atlantic: "This institutional care and training of the feebleminded (1) Purifies human stock, and (2) Reduces taxes."[18]

In the United States, by the late 1920s, eugenic sterilization laws had been enacted in about two dozen states, largely in the Middle Atlantic region, the Midwest, and in California, the champion. As of 1933, California had subjected more people to eugenic sterilization than all other states of the union combined. Most of these states' laws mandated compulsory sterilization of certain mentally defective persons

Carrie Buck and her mother, Addie
Emmitt ("Emma"). Carrie was forcibly
sterilized after the 1927 U.S. Supreme
Court decision upholding the constitutionality
of Virginia's sterilization law. *Special
Collections and Archives, SUNY Albany*

UPHOLDS OPERATING ON FEEBLE-MINDED

Supreme Court Majority Finds Virginia's Sterilization Law Valid.

RIGHT TO PROTECT SOCIETY

Justice Holmes Draws Analogy to Compulsory Vaccination in Woman's Case.

Special to The New York Times.
WASHINGTON, May 2—The au-
thority of the State of Virginia to order the sterilization of mental defec-
tives was upheld by the United States
Supreme Court in an opinion handed
down today by Associate Justice
Holmes for the majority of the court.

*New York Times, May 3, 1927.
Copyright © 1927 by The New York Times
Co. Reprinted with permission.*

or certain types of criminals. Almost everywhere they were passed, the laws
reached only to the inmates of state institutions for the mentally handicapped or
mentally ill. People in private care or in the care of their families eluded them. Thus,
the laws tended to work discriminatorily against lower-income and minority
groups. Similar measures were passed in Canada, in the provinces of British Columbia
and Alberta.[19]

Even so, Southern eugenicists were far more concerned with poor whites than
with African Americans, perhaps because they had plenty of means to keep blacks
under social control and felt little obligation to care for those who were, by any
measure, "unfit." After World War II, when African Americans were the beneficiaries
of federally mandated welfare programs, North Carolina began subjecting them
disproportionately to the knife under its eugenic sterilization law. Between the
wars, black writers did attack claims of Nordic superiority and black inferiority,
pointing, for instance, to how educational opportunity, which most African Americans
lacked, might affect performance on intelligence tests. Educated upper–middle
class blacks also, somewhat surprisingly, did not reject eugenics as such; rather,
they tried to turn hard-line doctrine back on itself, claiming that eugenic measures—
for example, enriched socioeconomic environments—could be used to improve any
race, including their own.[20]

The sterilization laws implicitly rode roughshod over private human rights,
holding them subordinate to the allegedly greater public good of the prevention of
degeneration. Such reasoning figured explicitly in the United States Supreme
Court's decision, in 1927, in the case of *Buck v. Bell*, which concerned the state of

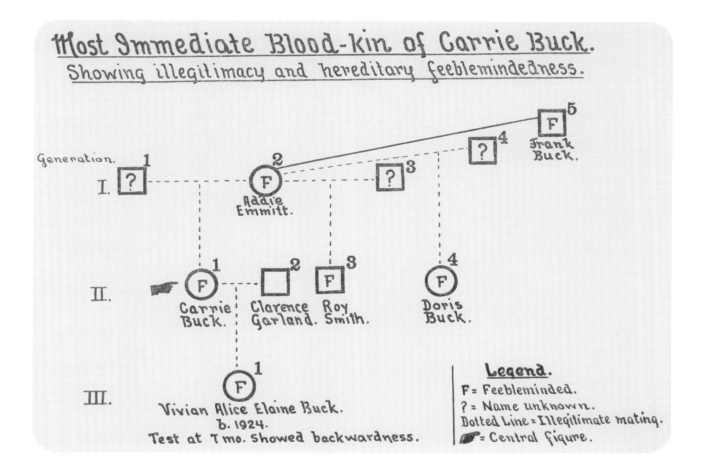

Virginia's desire to sterilize Carrie Buck under its eugenic sterilization law. Buck had given birth to a daughter, Vivian, out of wedlock. According to testimony, Carrie's mother, Carrie herself, and her infant daughter were all feebleminded. The court upheld the law by a majority of eight to one. Justice Oliver Wendell Holmes, Jr., writing for the majority, averred:

We have seen more than once that the public welfare may call upon the best citizens for their lives. It would be strange if it could not call upon those who already sap the strength of the State for these lesser sacrifices, often not felt to be such by those concerned, in order to prevent our being swamped with incompetence. It is better for all the world, if instead of waiting to execute degenerate offspring for crime, or to let them starve for their imbecility, society can prevent those who are manifestly unfit from continuing their kind. The principle that sustains compulsory vaccination is broad enough to cover cutting the Fallopian tubes.... Three generations of imbeciles are enough.[21]

In Alberta, Canada, the premier (provincial governor) called sterilization far more effective than segregation and, perhaps taking a leaf from Holmes's book, insisted that "the argument of freedom or right of the individual can no longer hold good where the welfare of the state and society is concerned."[22]

Sterilization rates climbed with the onset of the worldwide economic depression in 1929. In parts of Canada and the Deep South and throughout Scandinavia, sterilization acquired broad support, not primarily on eugenic grounds (although some hereditarian-minded mental-health professionals continued to urge it for that purpose)

The handwritten genetic chart of Carrie Buck showed the supposed inherited "feeblemindedness" of Carrie Buck and her daughter, based on intelligence testing. *Truman State University, Kirksville, Mo.*

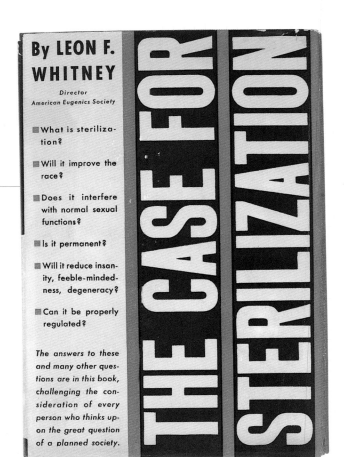

Leon Whitney, director of the American Eugenics Society, argued in favor of sterilization in his 1934 book. *Paul Lombardo, University of Virginia*

but on the economic ones of reducing the costs of institutional care and poor relief. Madge Thurlow Macklin, a geneticist at the University of Western Ontario, an organizer of the Eugenics Society of Canada, and an outspoken advocate of eugenic sterilization of the feebleminded, warned against the differential birthrate, declaring, "We care for the mentally deficient by means of taxes, which have to be paid for by the mentally efficient."[23] Even geneticists who disparaged sterilization as a panacea against degeneration believed that sterilization of the mentally disabled would yield a social benefit; it would prevent children being born to parents who could not care for them.

In Scandinavia, sterilization was broadly endorsed by Social Democrats as part of the scientifically oriented planning of the new welfare state. Alva Myrdal spoke for her husband, Swedish scientist Gunnar Myrdal, and for numerous liberals like themselves when, in 1941, she wrote:

In our day of highly accelerated social reforms the need for sterilization on social grounds gains new momentum. Generous social reforms may facilitate home-making and childbearing more than before among the groups of less desirable as well as more desirable parents.... [Such a trend] demands some corresponding corrective.

The legislation tended to authorize sterilization not only for eugenic reasons but also for what the Scandinavians called "social indications" (inability to care for children) and "medical indications" (preserving the health of the woman).[24]

In Germany, a sterilization law had been in the works before Hitler came to power in 1933. It had been advocated by the country's racial hygienists, as German eugenicists

Visitors to the German Hygiene Museum's traveling eugenics exhibition in Pasadena, California, in 1934, sponsored by the American Public Health Association. *Deutsches Hygiene-Museum, Dresden*

were known, who, like their counterparts elsewhere, had long contended that such socially deviant behavior as criminality and prostitution originated less in social conditions than in "the blood." They had regularly praised American policies, research, and writings and incorporated accounts of them into their works. In *Mein Kampf*, Hitler himself praised the U.S. sterilization laws and immigration restriction act.[25] Hitler's cabinet promulgated a eugenic sterilization law in 1933. It went far beyond American statutes: It was compulsory with respect to all people, institutionalized or not, who suffered from allegedly hereditary disabilities. The law went into effect on January 1, 1934. Within three years, German authorities had sterilized some 200,000 people, almost ten times the number treated in the previous 30 years in America.[26]

The Nazi sterilization program ran independently of the regime's antisemitic policies, although Jewish patients were certainly not exempt from the sterilization law, and zealots in Hitler's government did advocate mass sterilization of Jews. Antisemitism had not markedly characterized the German race-hygiene movement until the 1920s, when nationalist groups, for whom alleged racial differences counted a good deal, came to control most of its important institutional centers, such as leading journals, publishing houses, and professional societies. When Hitler seized power, German racial hygienists were ready with biological analyses of what ailed Aryan society—and with remedial enactments consistent with a slogan commonly found in Nazi literature: "National Socialism Is the Political Expression of Our Biological Knowledge." As Hitler turned ever more overtly against Germany's Jews, Nazi racial and eugenic policies merged, resulting in prohibitions against marriages betweens Jews and "Germans."

Display placards produced by the German Hygiene Museum for its traveling exhibition in the United States. *Buffalo Museum of Science; Dittrick Medical History Center, Case Western Reserve University, Cleveland*

In the early years of the Nazi regime, most eugenicists in the United States and Great Britain could not know—and likely did not want to know—that a direct line would lead from the sterilization law of 1933 to Auschwitz and Birkenau. Observers in both countries insisted that the Nazi sterilization program was without racially nefarious intent. German eugenicists said that they owed a great debt to American precedent, including the sterilization program in California. In 1936, the University of Heidelberg voted an honorary doctorate of medicine to Harry Laughlin, who was in charge of the Eugenics Record Office, at Cold Spring Harbor, Long Island, and was one of the United States' leading advocates of sterilization. Laughlin, who accepted the degree at the German consulate in downtown Manhattan, wrote to the Heidelberg authorities that he took the award not only as a personal honor but also as "evidence of a common understanding of German and American scientists of the nature of eugenics."[27]

Even as Laughlin wrote, the common understanding was eroding. During the interwar years, eugenics doctrines were increasingly criticized on scientific grounds

CENTRAL REGISTER OF HEREDITARILY DISEASED OR SUSPECT PEOPLE

10 hereditarily sound married couples have 17 children

10 hereditarily diseased married couples have

10 hereditarily diseased married couples have 35 children

We know that the hereditarily diseased are more prolific than the healthy ones.

In order to get a survey of all hereditarily diseased, the whole blood-relationship is examined, beginning with the suspect.

The result is recorded on the Central Register.

The latter thus becomes a sound basis for giving advice with regard to matrimony

and for their class and racial bias. Scientists pointed out that many mental disabilities have nothing to do with genes, and those that do are often complicated rather than simple products of them; most human behaviors, including the deviant variety, are shaped by environment at least as much as by biological heredity, if they are fashioned by genes at all. The biologist Julian Huxley and the anthropologist A. C. Haddon devastated claims that national groups or Jews constituted different races, pointing out that different populations differed from each other only in the relative proportions of genes for given characteristics that they possessed. "For existing populations," Huxley and Haddon maintained, "the word *race* should be banished, and the descriptive and noncommittal term *ethnic group* should be substituted."[28]

All along, many people on both sides of the Atlantic had ethical reservations about sterilization, and were squeamish about forcibly subjecting people to the knife. Attempts to authorize eugenic sterilization in Great Britain had failed, reaching their peak in the debates over the Mental Deficiency Act in 1913. More than a third of the states in this country declined to pass sterilization laws, as did the eastern provinces of Canada. Most American states that did pass such laws declined to enforce them, and British Columbia's law was rarely enforced.

The opposition to sterilization was energized partly by scientific dissent concerning eugenic theories, but even more so by objections from religious groups and civil libertarians insistent upon defending individual human rights. Some critics warned that compulsory sterilization constituted a Hitler-like suppression of private reproductive rights. In Alabama, for example, attempts to pass a sterilization law in the mid-1930s prompted a Methodist newspaper to warn that the "proposed

*"Tell me, Mrs. Creighton, has there ever been
any insanity in your family?"*

sterilization bill is a step" toward the "totalitarianism in Germany today." There, the "state is taking private matters—matters of individual conscience, and matters of family control—in hand, and sometimes it's a rough hand, and always it's a strong hand." In a letter to the governor, one opponent of the sterilization bill expressed a growing body of opinion: "The great rank and file of the country people of Alabama do not want this law; they do not want Alabama, as they term it, Hitlerized."[29]

Roman Catholics vigorously resisted sterilization, partly because it was contrary to Church doctrine, partly because a very high fraction of recent immigrants to the United States were Catholics and, thus, disproportionately placed in jeopardy of the knife. For many people before World War II, individual human rights mattered far more than those sanctioned by the era's science, law, and perception of social needs. The famed progressive lawyer Clarence Darrow spoke for them when he lambasted eugenics in the 1920s, declaring, "I, for one, am alarmed at the conceit and sureness of the advocates of this new dream. I shudder at their ruthlessness in meddling with life. I resent their egoistic and stern righteousness. I shrink from their judgment of their fellows."[30]

The revelations of the Holocaust discredited eugenics in many parts of continental Europe, Great Britain, and North America, but sterilization continued in the Scandinavian countries, in the western Canadian provinces, and in Virginia, North Carolina, and Georgia until the early 1970s. By then, molecular genetics, grounded in research into the features and operations of DNA, was raising the curtain on a new, potentially revolutionary era in the control of heredity, including the human variety. The working out of the genetic code inspired neo-Galtonian visions. As early

Nazi Decree Revives Sterilization Debate

Tho Legalized in Twenty-Seven States of the Union, and About to Be Used on Wholesale Scale in Germany, the Practise Evokes Disagreement Among Scientists

A HUNCHBACK won a throne by his wit. Another was called a wizard because he played with lightning in his laboratory. The maimed, the halt and the blind have scaled the heights of fame in spite of their handicaps. But, if the mass sterilization contemplated in Germany had been in force generations ago, the world might have been deprived of some of her greatest.

Some such reflections come to those who ponder this scheme to purify the Nordic strain. Nothing so extreme has been attempted before, no plan has opened so wide an avenue down which the outcast and despised could be driven; none has gone so far in discriminating among scientific theories and in assuming that human judgment can not err.

According to semiofficial reports emanating from Germany, 400,000 persons, about equally divided between the sexes, are to be sterilized. Nine diseases are designated by the law as

Idaho, Indiana, Iowa, Kansas, Maine, Michigan, Minnesota, Mississippi, Montana, Nebraska, New Hampshire, North Carolina, North Dakota, Oklahoma, Oregon, South Dakota, Utah, Vermont, Virginia, Washington, West Virginia and Wisconsin.

Of fifteen States reporting, 6,246 operations were performed on insane persons,

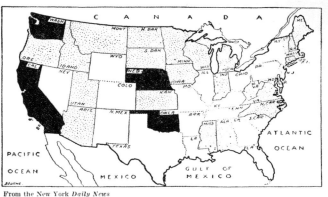

From the New York *Daily News*

Latest statistics available show twenty-seven States (black and stippled) have laws permitting sterilization. In black States crime is punishable by sterilization

flicted with hereditary feeble-mindedness or mental disease. If that be the situation, the individual should be sterilized because of his biologic heritage but not because of his commission of the crime. Criminality is an acquisition and, as such, is not transmissible to the offspring.

"So, too, the blind, the deaf, the deformed, the paupers, the inebriate, the lepers, the syphilitic, the drug fiends and others are the socially inadequate classes in our society that have primarily acquired their deficiencies. They do not transmit their shortcomings, as such, to their offspring. They ought not to be sterilized. They need vocational, mental or medicinal therapy. Where, however, in individual cases of these classes, the insufficiency was inherited and will be transmitted —then the potential progenitors of these weaknesses should be sterilized. The human sterilization program provides for the sterilization of individuals, not classes—whether they be social,

as 1969, Robert Sinsheimer, a prominent molecular biologist at the California Institute of Technology, declared that "for the first time in all time, a living creature understands its origin and can undertake to design its future"—and, in consequence, might eventually control its own evolution.[31] Yet, the international history of eugenics argues strongly that utopian genetic visions deserve to be treated with skepticism and caution. The record of eugenics everywhere powerfully suggests that the uses of genetic science and genetic information today warrant considerable attention in law and practice to civil liberties, individual rights, and social decency.

Literary Digest, January 13, 1934.
USHMM Collection

NAZI STERILIZATION AND REPRODUCTIVE POLICIES

BY GISELA BOCK

On June 28, 1933, five months after Hitler's rise to power, the Reich Minister of the Interior, Wilhelm Frick, outlined the Nazi program of "population and race policy" in a speech announcing an impending sterilization law.[1] Deploring the condition of the German people, he described a nation he saw mired in

Brochure for the 1939 German Hygiene Museum exhibition *Eternal People*, reflecting the Nazi adoption of the image of the "glass man" to promote its racial ideal. *USHMM Collection, Gift of Deutsches Hygiene-Museum, Dresden*

cultural and racial degeneration [created by] an exaggerated type of personal hygiene and welfare for the single individual without any regard for the insights of genetics, selection of life, and racial hygiene. This kind of modern "humanist value" and social welfare for the ill, weak and worthless individual has had enormously cruel effects on the people as a whole and has led to its ruin.

The result, Frick maintained, was the birth of more than one million genetically ill—both physically and mentally—whose "offspring were no longer desired." Estimating that as many as 20 percent of the population were undesirable as fathers or mothers, Frick underscored that it was precisely these "imbecilic and inferior" persons who were giving birth to disproportionately large numbers of children. He linked these antinatalist views with Nazi pronatalist population goals

Qualitativer Bevölkerungsabstieg
bei zu schwacher Fortpflanzung der höherwertigen

v.H.
100

75

50

25

am Anfang · nach 30 Jahren · nach 60 Jahren · nach 90 Jahren · nach 120 Jahren

So würde es kommen,
wenn Minderwertige 4 Kinder und höherwertige 2 Kinder haben.

"Qualitative Decline in the Population through Lower Reproduction Rates among Individuals of Higher Value: In the beginning, after 30 years, after 60 years, after 90 years, after 120 years. It could come to this, if individuals of lesser value have four children and those of higher value have two." Nazi propaganda poster, ca. 1938, used to promote public support for the mass sterilization program.
Staatsarchiv Bamberg

that aimed to raise the German birthrate, which, in 1932, was one of the lowest internationally. "Positive population measures" would encourage "German" and "hereditarily healthy" couples to have more children, he declared, concluding that "in order to raise the number of hereditarily healthy progeny we have, above all, the duty to diminish the expenses for the asocial, inferior and hopelessly hereditarily ill and to prevent the procreation of hereditarily tainted persons."

On July 14, 1933, almost four months after the Enabling Act had transferred the Reichstag's legislative powers to Hitler's cabinet, the latter approved a bill providing for compulsory and mass sterilization. The Law for the Prevention of Genetically Diseased Offspring took effect on January 1, 1934. Its purpose, as outlined in the official gazette, was to "eradicate biologically inferior hereditary taints," to "promote a gradual cleansing of the nation's ethnic body," and to aim at "the innumerable inferior and hereditarily tainted people" who "procreate without inhibition." The official commentary, published in 1934, claimed that this law demonstrated "the supremacy of the State in the field of life, marriage, and the family" and estimated that 1.2 million people should be sterilized.[2] Government officials discussed the number and reduced it to 400,000 for the short run. This was, in fact, the number of those sterilized under the law in the 12 years of the Nazi regime (about 300,000 up to 1939, plus another 60,000 after 1939 in Germany, and an additional 40,000 in annexed territories including Austria). It was a half percent of the German population at large and just over one percent of the population between 14 and about 50—the major age group targeted.[3] In a speech to his Nazi parliament, Hitler praised the law as "truly revolutionary" with respect to those "whose heredity placed them from

Medical experts, especially psychiatrists, increasingly defined and classified dozens of perceived mental, emotional, and physical defects. These images, captioned *(left to right)* "Woman displaying good-natured mania," "Alcohol-paranoia," and "Negativistic stupor in a woman," were among the dozens distributed as educational slides in the 1920s by the German Hygiene Museum. *Deutsches Hygiene-Museum, Dresden*

their birth on the negative side of *völkisch* (national) life." Many joined him, saying that this was "the first blood-and-soil law" and "the core piece of National Socialism—the idea of race."

PATHS TO NAZI STERILIZATION POLICY

The German discussions underlying the Nazi sterilization law—eugenics or racial hygiene—were, at this time, far from novel. They had been elaborated especially since World War I, although some of their elements had emerged earlier. In Germany, they had been discussed not only by Nazis but also by non-Nazis and not-yet-Nazis, and similar ideas emerged in various other countries. Eugenics was an international movement; its tenets, theoretical as well as practical and political, were built on five assumptions, most of which counted as "science" at the time.[4]

First, the cultural and political crises after World War I, reinforced by the economic crisis of the early 1930s and the perceived widespread "degeneration" *(Entartung)*, were attributed to a phenomenon called "counter-selection" *(Gegenauslese)*. This was the notion that modern medicine and social welfare violated the process of "natural selection," which otherwise would "eradicate the unfit." Second, the precise features of eugenic "inferiority"—most of all, emotional and mental defects—were increasingly defined and classified by psychiatrists, and psychiatry and medicine were to be transformed from a vehicle of degeneration and counter-selection into an agent to rectify counter-selection. Third, the undesirable features came to be considered as congenitally transmitted; therefore, psychiatry became a privileged field of human genetics. One

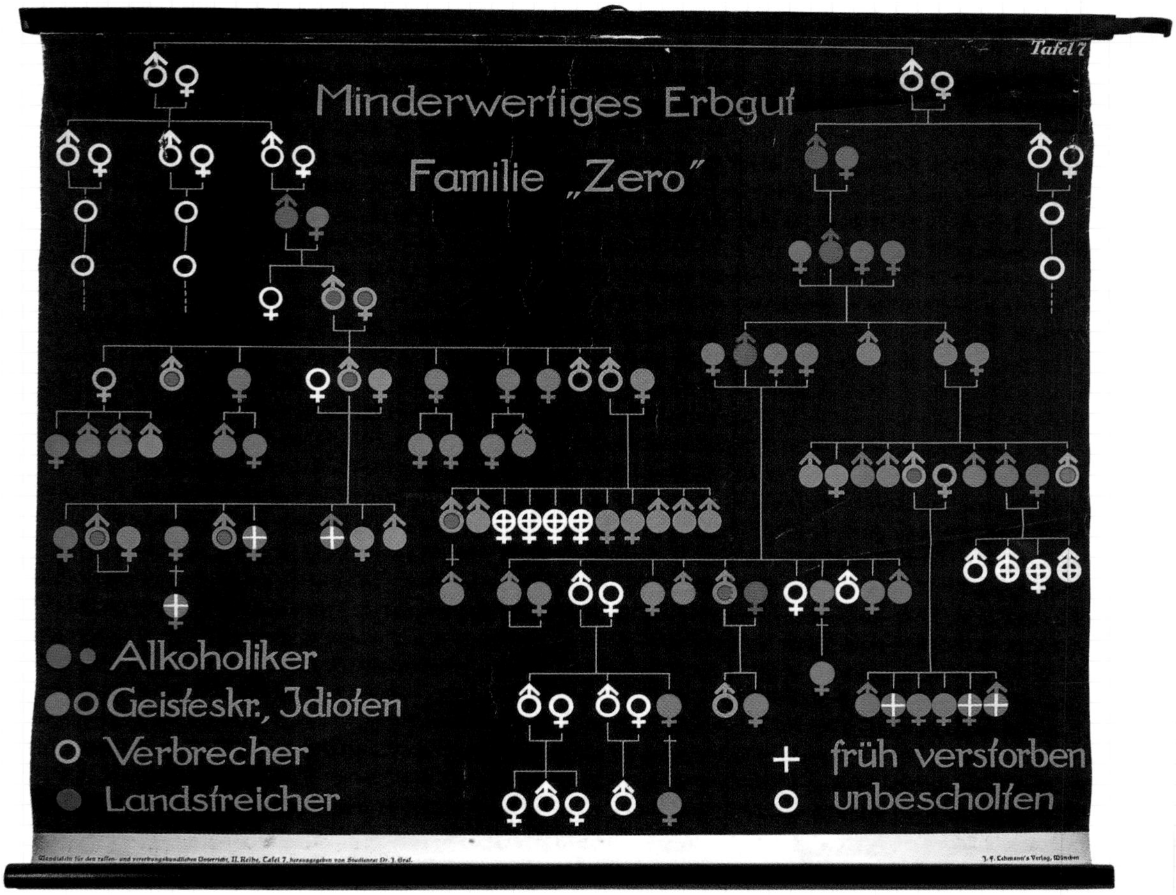

Racial hygienists in the 1920s used the genealogy of a Swiss family, known as the "Hereditarily Less-Valuable Family Zero," to demonstrate the hereditary transmission of inferior traits. The family tree was widely displayed in classrooms during the Nazi years. Legend *(left):* alcoholics; mentally ill, idiots; criminals; vagrants; *(right):* early death; without criminal record. *Schulgeschichtliche Sammlung, Bremen*

major scholar in this field was the psychiatrist and geneticist Ernst Rüdin. More popular was the two-volume book *Foundations of Human Genetics and Racial Hygiene*, by Erwin Baur, a plant geneticist, Eugen Fischer, an anthropologist, and Fritz Lenz, a human geneticist. Hitler probably drew on this book, while in prison in 1924, for the passages in *Mein Kampf* decrying the procreation of deficient people.[5] Discussions of heredity—both scientific and popular—turned into a veritable heredity hysteria and often served as a scheme to explain all of society's problems. Fourth, the individual human being as subject of suffering and object of healing was supplanted by a collectivity to be redeemed—the "German people" or "national body" *(Volkskörper).* Last, the heredity anxiety was supplemented by its apparent opposite—the vision of a world without illness, weakness, and misery that was proclaimed with revolutionary pathos. This vision included a powerful, even fanatical call to social and political action, in order to reach that vision, by "returning" to natural selection and "weeding out" *(ausmerzen)* the unfit and inferior through artificial social and political tools where "nature's" tools were no longer in force. One chosen tool—up to the late 1930s, the principal one—was the prevention of inferior offspring.

Surgical sterilization—known and studied since the turn of the century—was heatedly and publicly debated in Weimar Germany. Sterilizations on eugenic grounds were performed to some extent, but rather secretly (they were illegal under the penal-code clause against bodily injury), mostly on poor women, probably thousands of them. First, in 1923, and then again in 1925 and 1928, the medical doctor Gustav Boeters drew up, quite obsessively, various bills for the sterilization of many kinds of degenerates, which he recommended to the authorities of the state of Saxony

Ausmerzung des Kranken und Schwachen in der Natur

"Was nicht den Anforderungen des Seins genügt, das zerbricht"

This teaching chart's caption reads: "Eradication of the sick and weak in nature: Whatever does not meet the challenges of existence will be destroyed." From *Hereditary Teachings and Racial Science in Pictorial Representation*, by Alfred Vogel, 1938. *USHMM Collection*

and sent to doctors all over Germany.[6] In the final years of the Weimar Republic, which were marked by severe economic depression, virtually all strands of eugenic thought agreed on sterilization as the major method of eugenic intervention, and such "negative" eugenics took clear precedence over such "positive" measures as benefits for hereditarily healthy families. Now, many other groups—besides scientists, psychiatrists, and doctors—joined the lobby for eugenic mass sterilization. These included secular as well as religious welfare organizations, among them the Inner Mission of the Protestant Church, which maintained a charitable network of asylums throughout Germany. The Depression boosted the number of sterilization lobbyists to include such people on the left as the physicians Rainer Fetscher and Alfred Grotjahn, who both argued in favor of compulsory sterilization.

The reason why sterilization became so popular—and why the Nazi law of 1933 came about so easily and met with so little public criticism—was because it promised many things to many people. No children from "inferior" persons seemed to mean gains to communal and other public funds (with less demand for locally funded public assistance), reduced costs for institutional care, fewer illegitimate children, no more schools for backward children, and more financial assistance for the deserving unemployed and for the health care of the desirable part of the population. Nevertheless, doctors and psychiatrists were at the center of the campaign; for them, the major gain was not just a utilitarian but an idealistic one—the "regeneration" of the German people *(Volk)*.

In 1932, the Prussian Health Council promoted a sterilization bill (never enacted) for the state of Prussia; for this purpose, it convened a meeting of 78 experts from

Leaflet from the Nazi journal *New People*, ca. 1937, reads: "60,000 reichsmarks is what this hereditarily ill person will cost the national community over the course of his life. Citizen, this is also your money!" The Nazis built support for the implementation of the 1933 sterilization law with propaganda in party publications and films that tapped into popular resentment about the costs of care. *Deutsches Historisches Museum, Berlin*

many professions, particularly doctors. Rüdin presented a proposal for discussion that largely resembled the future Nazi sterilization law.[7] Held in July, the conference witnessed several National Socialists (among them, Leonardo Conti, at the time a member of the Prussian Parliament for the Nazi Party and, later, Reich Health Leader) pleading for outright compulsion "in the name of the NSDAP" (the Nazi Party).

Even though this bill included a clause of consent—in contrast to the Nazi law almost exactly one year later—its terms, and, even more, those of the debate, left no doubt that what was at stake was not the well-being of individuals but that of the national body and the requirements of population policy. One National Socialist in the assembly noted—and rightly so—that no one questioned "the generally recognized criterion of inferiority." Two dissenting voices deserve to be noted. A conservative, female medical doctor, who, in fact, favored sterilization on eugenic grounds, argued that it should not be a matter of "population policy" but of preventing actual individual misery, and that the individuals in question should have "fullest scope and legal protection." Only one doctor, a Catholic, spoke out "fully and entirely" against "brutal force" and the doctor's role of "hangman."[8] For "tactical reasons," most participants favored indirect forms of compulsion—for instance, placing a

Ernst Rüdin, one of the major figures in German psychiatry, genetics, and eugenics in the first half of the twentieth century, ca. 1931. Rüdin began his career in psychiatry in Munich. *Max-Planck-Institut für Psychiatrie, Munich*

person under the control of a trustee—since direct and state compulsion might have a negative impact on the popularity of such a law. At about the same time, Fritz Lenz thought that one-third of the population should have no children, and Rüdin joined him in this view.[9]

IMPLEMENTATION OF THE STERILIZATION LAW

Although the eugenics discussion in medicine and human genetics, as well as economic ideas about public expenses in a time of depression, formed a crucial background to the arrival of the sterilization law of 1933, even more so was the role of political, legal, and institutional power and, above all, Hitler's rise to power. In the words of a eugenicist in 1934, it was Nazism that "raised racial hygiene to the level of an explicit principle of government." That same year, Rüdin argued that "it was only through the political work of Hitler that the significance of racial hygiene has become publicly manifest in Germany, and it is only due to him that our thirty-year-old dream to put racial hygiene in practice has become a reality."[10] On May 26, 1933, the penal-code clause, which penalized bodily injury, was supplemented by a paragraph that permitted doctors to perform voluntary eugenic sterilizations. But this was not enough for the new regime, since it aimed not at permitting but at imposing sterilization and an overall racial hygiene ("population") policy. At this time, three men who would soon rise to important positions—the radical eugenicist and medical doctor Arthur Gütt, just hired by the Ministry of the Interior, the psychiatrist and geneticist Ernst Rüdin, and the lawyer Falk Ruttke—began to

68

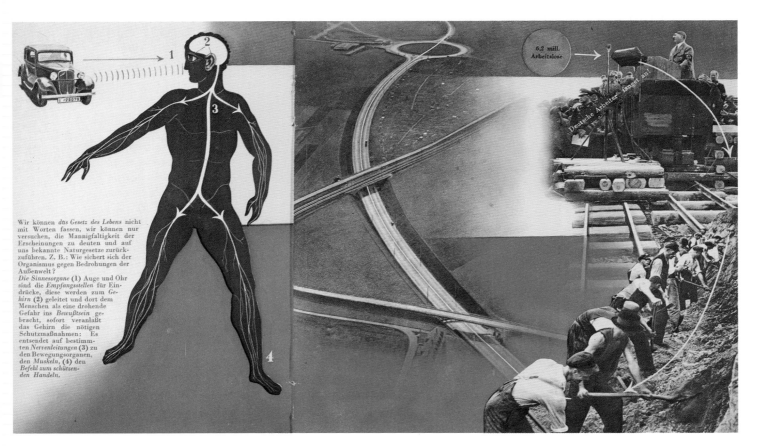

In this brochure for the 1935 exhibition *The Miracle of Life*, the new Nazi leadership of the German Hygiene Museum asserted that societies resemble organisms that follow the lead of their brains. Germany's leader, Adolf Hitler, is shown *(upper right)* guiding ordinary Germans in their biological "regeneration." *USHMM Collection*

elaborate the sterilization bill, the wording of its purpose, and, somewhat later, the extensive volume with the official commentary. In the cabinet session of July 14, the Catholic vice chancellor, von Papen, raised some objections as to the impending concordat with the Catholic Church (the Pope's 1930 encyclic, *Casti connubi*, had condemned sterilization). But Hitler insisted that the bill was "morally impeccable," "the hereditarily ill procreate to a high degree," and "all measures are legitimate which serve the preservation of the German people."[11]

The new law imposed sterilization on people "who suffer" from any of nine categories of disease, all assumed to be hereditary: feeblemindedness, schizophrenia, manic-depressive (now, bipolar) disorder, epilepsy, Huntington's chorea, blindness, deafness, malformation, and severe alcoholism (Article 1). Roughly 95 percent of the sterilizations were performed on the grounds of the first four of these categories. None of them was a precise disease, but they were umbrella categories for a number of different and lesser-known mental or emotional problems. Genetic transmission was not actually proven in any of them (Rüdin would often deplore this fact); therefore, it was not required to prove genetic transmission in each individual case.

One could apply for sterilization oneself (under Article 2)—although this provision came to be virtually irrelevant—or it could be done by a legal guardian; the latter clause led to placing many people under guardianship, often a collective one, precisely for the purpose of sterilizing.[12] Article 3 provided for applications by "state doctors" and the directors of hospitals, psychiatric asylums, and prisons. Soon, all doctors were required to report their patients to the sterilization authorities if they saw fit, and, in practice, anyone could denounce anyone else—and many did. Special

A storefront display of a measuring caliper and eugenic manuals. Berlin 1933. *The Roman Vishniac, © Mara Vishniac Cohn, Courtesy International Center of Photography, New York*

sterilization courts (Hereditary Health Courts) were established by Articles 5–10; in 1936, there were 205 first instance courts, plus another 18 appellate courts where a complaint could be filed.

    The actual sterilization was performed in specially selected hospitals (Article 11); by 1936, they numbered 108, and 144 surgeons had been specially nominated. Article 12 allowed the use of police force. Recalcitrant candidates were forcibly brought to the operating table, which happened in some regions to as many as 30 percent of those sterilized.[13] Police were also employed in three further situations. At the beginning of the procedure, a "state doctor" could ask to have a person brought in for examination as to the applicability of the law. In numerous cases, police searched for candidates who had fled or gone into hiding, and police could force a person into a psychiatric institution to be tested for disease or to prevent sexual intercourse or escape. A supplement to Article 12 was Article 14, which banned any sterilization outside this law—any voluntary one; therefore, in the last instance, all sterilizations under the law were nonvoluntary ones. This was, then, contrasting legislation for the "inferior" and the "superior." In the words of one German eugenicist, "Unequal value, unequal rights," and of another, "There is no equal right for all. Everyone's rights are determined by his value to the nation. The state has the right, even the duty, to distinguish between the superior and the inferior."[14]

    Racial hygiene was now legalized as well as institutionalized. The most remarkable innovation was the sterilization courts, an element that distinguished Nazi policy from other countries that also had eugenic sterilization laws. The courts included three judges, but only one was a judicial official, the other two being

Hereditary Health Court judges, from *Voice of the People,* March 24, 1934. Each court panel included a lawyer and two doctors, which lent an appearance of justice and due process. In fact, sterilization hearings lasted only a few minutes. Patients could appeal to a Superior Hereditary Health Court, but few lower-court decisions were reversed. *Institut für Zeitungsforschung, Dortmund*

The docket of the Hereditary Health Court in Hamburg, for February 21, 1934, shows that officials allotted only five minutes for each sterilization hearing. *Evangelische Stiftung Alsterdorf, Hamburg*

"doctors," usually psychiatrists, geneticists, population scientists, or anthropologists —for instance, Hans F. K. Günther, a major race theoretician of the time (in the court of Jena). The sentence was passed by majority vote. Scientists and doctors had become judges, "medical judges," with the full power of the law behind their judgment—an unheard-of event—and they exerted legal power over patients and procreation. Virtually all better-known eugenicists and psychiatrists, thousands in all, sat on such courts at one time or another; others were busy handing in expert advice.

Equally crucial was the institutionalization of decision making in the judiciary. On the one hand, the courts served to maintain the apparent legality of the procedure, and injustice appeared, therefore, as "justice." German racial hygienists were proud of this elaborate judicial system, contrasting it to the arbitrary way in which U.S. state governments enforced sterilization measures. On this, the American *Eugenic News* agreed: "From a legal point of view, nothing more could be desired."[15] This was the first instance when racial hygiene, and racism in general, infiltrated the judiciary (about 500 jurists sat on these courts until 1939). A leading judicial official, Erich Ristow, underscored this in 1935, exclaiming that "the activity of the Hereditary Health Courts entails the implementation of national socialist ideology, since National Socialism is applied racial science." The commentary to the law expressed the hope that "precisely the Hereditary Health Courts will inspire the entire German judiciary." The same view prevailed in SS chief Heinrich Himmler's staff.[16]

On the other hand, the judicial discussion revolved around the tribunal's decision making based upon the very vague psychiatric criteria for sterilization. The "gray zone," it was argued, had to be eliminated by separating "black from

Decision requiring August Alzen to submit to sterilization by reason of feeblemindedness, May 1937. *USHMM Collection*

Grounds.

The public health officer in Altenkirchen petitioned for the steriliza-tion of August Alzen, mentioned above. The outcome of the petition was also unbiased. According to the expert opinion submit-ted with the petition, the named person suffers from congenital feeblemindedness. August Alzen's intelligence examination has unobjectionably confirmed that he suffers from feeblemindedness. His school and general life knowledge is very limited. He cannot solve the simplest math problems. Memory and recollection are poor. Judgment and reasoning are strongly [diminished].

white" to allow judges to make "a clear-cut judgment." Judges discussed the issue in familiar Latin legal language: *in dubio pro patria* ("in case of doubt, decide for the Fatherland") now replaced *in dubio pro reo* ("in case of doubt, decide for the accused"). By 1936, the debate culminated in the official recommendation: "Racial hygiene must always follow the principle that it is better to sterilize too many rather than too few."[17] This was the outcome of the mid-1930s debate on whether someone with hereditary illness "may" be sterilized, as Article 1 of the law said, or "must" be sterilized. Ultimately, "must" prevailed.

Further institutional revolutions followed, especially the 1934 Law for the Unification of the Public Health System, which Gütt also devised. Its purpose was the centralization of public health, defined as *Erb- und Rassenpflege* ("heredity and racial care"—the official Nazi term encompassing both eugenic and ethnic racism). Public health was placed in the hands of newly created state doctors who operated the new State Health Offices, which included "Heredity and Racial Care" counseling centers. By 1943, there were more than one thousand such offices.

The task of this entire system was to implement what are regarded as the three core laws of National Socialist hereditary and racial policy: first, the Steriliza-tion Law; second, the infamous Blood Protection Law, of September 1935, which banned marriage and sexual intercourse between German Jews and non-Jewish Germans; and third, the Marital Health Law, of October 1935, which banned marriages between the "superior" (genetically fit) and the "inferior" (genetically ill) within the "German-blooded" population.[18] Originally, the two marriage bans were to be included in a single law, but they were separated for political reasons. Both aimed to prevent

"Ten Commandments for Choosing a Mate" *(excerpts)*, created by the Reich Committee for Public Health. From the treatise *May I Marry My Cousin?*, by Hermann Böhm, Berlin, 1935. *Staatsbibliothek zu Berlin*

1. Remember that you are a German.
Everything that you are is not of your own merit but, rather, through your nation.

2. If you are hereditarily healthy, you should not remain unmarried.
Everything that you are, all the characteristics of your body and mind, are transitory. They are an inheritance, a gift from your ancestors. They live on in you in an unbroken chain. Whoever remains unmarried without a compelling reason breaks this chain of the race. Your life is only a transient occurrence; family and nation will continue to exist. Mental and physical genetic makeup will celebrate its resurrection in your children.

3. Keep your body pure [of venereal disease]!
Maintain the health that has been given to you by pure parents in order to be able to serve your nation. Take care not to play with it needlessly and lightly. A moment's pleasure can permanently destroy your health and genetic makeup—a curse for you, your children, and grandchildren.

4. You should keep your mind and spirit pure!
Maintain the aptitudes that you have; become what you can be according to your aptitudes. Preserve your talents and use them to your best ability.... Prospects of money and property, prospects of getting ahead more quickly, prospects of pleasure, often tempt us to forget this.

5. As a German, choose only a spouse of the same or Nordic blood.
Where aptitude matches aptitude, harmony will reign. Where dissimilar races mix, there will be discord. The mixing of races that do not match each other (bastardization) frequently leads to degeneration and downfall in the life of people and nations, all the faster the less the races match each other. Beware of decline; keep away from those of foreign races of non-European origin. Happiness is only possible with those of your same kind.

6. In choosing your spouse, ask about his ancestors.
You are not marrying your spouse alone but, in a way, his ancestors, too. Worthy descendants can only be expected from worthy ancestors. Gifts of reason and mind are an inherited trait just like eye and hair color. Bad aptitudes are passed on just as good ones are. A good person can carry in himself germs (genetic makeup) that will turn into misfortune for his children. Therefore, never marry the one good person from a bad family.... If you are unsure, request a genetic-biological family chart, ask a trusted doctor familiar with questions of hereditary health, or contact the Reich Committee for Public Health, Berlin W 62, Einemstrasse 11.

There is nothing more valuable in the world than the seeds of noble blood. No medical art can change rotten genetic material.

7. Health is also a requirement for physical beauty.
Health offers the best protection for lasting happiness, for it is the prerequisite for beauty and mental stability. Ask your future partner to undergo a medical examination to deem worthiness for marriage, as you yourself should do.

8. Marry only for love.
Money is a transient possession and does not bring lasting happiness. Where the divine spark of love is missing, happiness cannot thrive.

9. Seek a companion in marriage and not a playmate.
Marriage is not a temporary game between two people but, rather, a lasting bond that is of great importance for the life of the individual as well as the entire nation. The purpose of marriage is having children and raising descendants.

Only among mentally, physically, and racially homogeneous people can this ultimate goal be achieved for the benefit of yourself and your nation, for every race has its own soul. Only similar souls will be compatible. An extreme age difference between spouses easily endangers the equilibrium in the marriage.

10. You should wish for as many children as possible.
Only with three or four children is the continuance of the nation ensured.... Many worthy children raise the value of the nation and are the best safeguard for its continuation. You will pass; what you give to your descendants will remain; in them, you will celebrate resurrection. Your Nation will live forever!

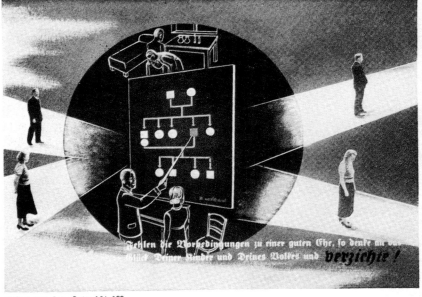

Abb. 4 und 5 zu Seite 154–188

"Crossroads of Marriage Choices," which illustrates the Nazi requirement to consider hereditary health when applying for a marriage license, appeared in the popular household manual *Love and Marriage* (1941), by Hanns Martin Elster. *USHMM Collection*

NAZI STERILIZATION AND REPRODUCTIVE POLICIES

undesired offspring. German officials applied the Blood Protection Law strictly, but they could not apply the Marital Health Law with the same rigor. Along with the State Health Offices, registrars of vital statistics (also thoroughly trained in racial hygiene) put marriage bans into practice.

The ideas of scientists had paved the way to the sterilization law; after 1933, though, their ideas were shaped by the sterilization law itself. The grand syntheses in the field of psychiatry that appeared under the Nazi regime were little more than further definitions and reflections on how to apply the law, expand its categories, and judge "who is inferior."[19] Much ink was spent—particularly in most journals of every profession involved in the complex issue—on single trials and on general principles of eugenics.

A researcher files family history cards that tracked information about disabilities and ethnic background. Undated. *Getty Images, New York*

Hitler's regime aimed to record the hereditary and racial history of the entire German population. By 1942, some ten million registry cards had been collected. The head of the Alsterdorf institution for the feebleminded, Dr. Gerhard Kreyenberg, began collecting patient family trees before 1933, and became an avid supporter of Nazi eugenics policies. Some of these cards were used as evidence in the sterilization courts, ca. 1936. *Evangelische Stiftung Alsterdorf, Hamburg*

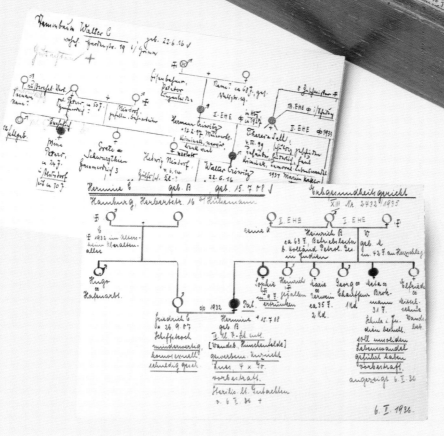

For Official Use Only*

Copy

Intelligence Examination Sheet

2. Knowledge acquired at school

(Hometown region?)	Silent
(Which state does it belong in?)	Don't know
(Capital of Germany?)	Berlin
(Capital of France?)	Don't know that either
(Who was Luther?)	Paulus
(Who was Bismarck?)	Don't know that either
(What form of government do we have?)	" " " "
(Who discovered America?)	" " " "
(When is Christmas?)	on Christmas Eve 24th
(What does Christmas signify?)	Because the savior was born then
(Other questions of similar nature)	
(How many days in a week?- forwards and backwards?)	7 Forwards +, backwards mixed up
(How many months?- forwards and backwards?)	Don't know January, February, March, April, May, June, August.

*Only to be given at health offices, hospitals, and similar institutions, etc., and by physicians.

Intelligence test administered to Ursula H. in the Wittenau Psychiatric Clinic, in Berlin, 1942. *Landesarchiv Berlin (A Rep. 003-04-04 Nr. 21)*

The major features of the law's implementation indicate similarities as well as differences compared to other countries that had sterilization laws. Everywhere, "degeneration" and "regeneration" were the catchwords and were often linked to visions of an ideal Nordic race. If inferiority was specified, "feeblemindedness" and insanity were the major targets everywhere. In Germany, almost two-thirds of the sterilizations were performed on persons judged to be mentally retarded and one-fifth on those deemed schizophrenic. Epilepsy accounted for 12 percent and manic depression for 3 percent.[20]

In Germany, more people were sterilized than in all other countries combined. From 1933 to 1945, up to 14 times as many people were sterilized than under the 30 sterilization laws in the United States (two-thirds of them included a compulsion clause), and if the greater U.S. population is taken into account, it was 30 times as many. Several reasons explain this difference. First, only Nazi Germany established a centralized and dense network of people and institutions to search for, examine, and judge sterilization candidates. Second, even though eugenic sterilization outside of Germany imposed much hardship on its victims, the juridical eugenicist Falk Ruttke correctly argued, in 1937, that the Scandinavian and North American sterilization laws existed "largely on paper only."[21] Third, Nazi racial hygiene was population policy in a strict sense—in principle, the entire population was on its records. The State Health Offices had the task of compiling a comprehensive genetic population census, starting with those judged to be inferior. No one in the United States had the "duty," as had so many in Germany, to denounce others to sterilization authorities. Over two-thirds of the U.S. laws were aimed exclusively at the

Ursula H. was forcibly sterilized by court order. The results of her intelligence test were used to support the action. *Landesarchiv Berlin (A Rep. 003-04-04 Nr. 21)*

This "Sterilization Book with Photos," from the Wittenau Psychiatric Clinic, in Berlin (1934–45), served as the registry of men in the clinic who were sterilized in outside hospitals. *Landesarchiv Berlin (A Rep. 003-04-04 Nr. 20)*

 73

 74

 75.

 76

 77

 78.

 79

 80

 81.

 82

 83

 84

Above: On December 20, 1934, a Hereditary Health Court ordered Else G., a patient at the Wittenau Psychiatric Clinic diagnosed with schizophrenia, to be sterilized. *Landesarchiv Berlin (A Rep. 003-04-04 Nr. 20)*

Left: Mathilde B. was forcibly sterilized by court order on the grounds of feeblemindedness. *Landesarchiv Berlin (A Rep. 003-04-04 Nr. 27)*

inmates of institutions, whereas the Nazi eugenicists went further—about two-thirds of the sterilization candidates lived outside of institutions, on their own, or in families. In other words, if the case of the United States demonstrated—as many Nazis argued—that eugenic sterilization was practiced "even" in a democracy, it also demonstrated that only under a dictatorship was it possible to implement the policies that German as well as American racial hygienists hoped for.

One major tenet of Nazi racial hygiene, the core of antinatalist population policy, followed from the logic of a discourse focusing on procreation and sexuality. Sterilization had to be performed especially on people with a "mild degree" of disease, since they were more likely to engage in sexual intercourse than those who were seriously ill. As a result, the mild cases, because of their "procreative danger," came to be a major object of racial hygiene argument and decision making. Rüdin—a medical judge in the Munich court—was just one among many who underlined how "infinitely greater" that "danger" was compared to the cases of people actually ill. No wonder then that many of the "inferior" opposed doctors' and judges' views, arguing that they were neither "diseased" nor "hereditarily diseased." Rüdin's answer was, "If we want to follow the spirit of the law, we need to sterilize the 'milder' cases."[22]

Although the notion of the mild cases applied to all sterilization trials, it did so, most of all, to those accused of feeblemindedness, who counted as being especially procreatively dangerous. It applied particularly to women; according to the racial hygienists, women must be expected to have sexual intercourse not only willingly but also against their will. Therefore, the rule was: "The same degree of feeblemindedness requires a different evaluation of the danger of procreation

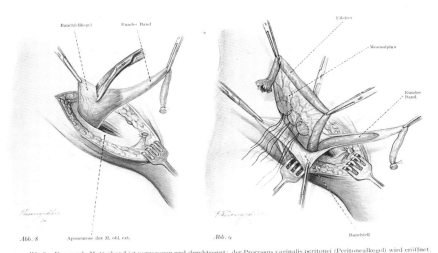

Arthur Gütt and Ernst Rüdin's *On the Prevention of Genetically Diseased Offspring* (1934) instructed physicians on procedures for a tubal ligation. Most men were sterilized through vasectomies as outpatients. In contrast, tubal ligations (tying the fallopian tubes) to sterilize women required full anesthesia and an abdominal incision, as shown in this drawing. *USHMM Collection*

Surgical retractor, ca. 1930, and scalpel, ca. 1930–40. *Deutsches Historisches Museum, Berlin*

in the case of women and men...female feeblemindedness is particularly procre-atively dangerous."[23]

By the mid-1930s, feeblemindedness was expanded into a veritable social diagnostic of its own. Its key concept was "conduct of life" or "social proof," largely directed against "moral feeblemindedness" and "antisocials" (such as prostitutes, beggars, vagrants, "work-shy," and "slovenly" or "unkempt" individuals). Between 1940 and 1944, a new law especially for the sterilization of antisocial individuals was elaborated, but did not come into effect. The category "social proof" differed considerably for men and women. Both men and women were assessed as to their work behavior, but women, in addition, as to their capacity and inclination for housework, child-rearing, and irregular heterosexuality. About 60 percent of those sterilized for feeblemindedness were women.

In 1933, the American journal *Eugenic News* underlined that the Nazi sterilization law was to be equally applied to all "hereditary degenerates...regardless of sex, race, or religion."[24] In fact, the available figures (although incomplete) suggest that the sex ratio among the sterilized was almost equal—52 percent men and 48 percent women. The difference is due to the 3 percent who were sterilized on the grounds of alcoholism, since they were usually only men (the figures for schizophrenia were gender-neutral, among epileptics men prevailed, and manic-depressives, for the most part, were women). Men were sterilized through vasectomy and as outpatients, but women underwent a major operation (salpingectomy), with full anesthesia, abdominal incision, and concomitant risk. The ensuing deaths led to a public outcry (according to the Nazis, such foreign articles as "Report from Hell" stemmed from

NAZI STERILIZATION AND REPRODUCTIVE POLICIES

Sterealifiert den Jud !
Dann vermifd)t fid) nid)t mehr
gefundes mit fdmierigem Blut!

This undated sticker for sealing envelopes reads, "Sterilize the Jew! Then, healthy and filthy blood will no longer mix!" Some Nazi zealots advocated sterilizing all German Jews. *Wolfgang Haney, Berlin*

Oktober 1937

Wittenauer-Heilstätten ,10.8.1937 Haus 9

The sterilization of Jews and "Gypsies" for reasons of "race" was not specified by the law, but individual members of these ethnic minorities were subject to the law and sterilized. Helene S. *(far left),* who was diagnosed as schizophrenic, was Jewish; she died of pneumonia before she could be sterilized as ordered. Else L., diagnosed as manic-depressive, and Kurt G., as schizophrenic, were both Jews forcibly sterilized. *Landesarchiv Berlin (A Rep. 003-04-04 Nrs. 10, 12, 13)*

the "Jewish press"). Hitler intervened in 1935, urging the use of X-rays instead, which were then introduced the next year for women over the age of 38. Yet, people continued to die from the sterilization operation; overall, the number of deaths may be estimated at 5,000, 90 percent of whom were women. Most of them died because physically they resisted right up to the operating table, and, afterward, rejected what had happened to them. In 1935, the sterilization law was amended by adding abortion, on eugenic grounds. It required the pregnant woman's "consent," but, in many cases, this rule was laid aside. Every eugenic abortion entailed a compulsory sterilization. Their number was about 30,000.

"Undesirable" religious and ethnic minorities were included in the law, even though Hitler argued (for a short time) that there was no reason to "improve alien races through sterilization."[25] The proportion among "alien races" was somewhat higher than among the "German-blooded" population—in any case, among African Germans, the 500 or so children of German mothers and black or Arabic fathers who had been among the French-occupation troops after World War I. As for other undesirables, the diseases outlined were flexible enough to identify many "Gypsies" as feebleminded. Some of the Jews from Eastern Europe were also judged feebleminded and some German Jews schizophrenic. Ample proof of the latter diagnosis was depression or a suicide attempt—although Jews had extremely good reasons for both.

On March 19, 1942, two months after the Wannsee Conference, where the "Final Solution" for the European Jews was announced to the minor levels of the Nazi hierarchy present and sterilization of Jewish–non-Jewish "hybrids" *(Mischlinge)* envisioned for the future, Jews were excluded from the implementation of the

A gynecological chair was used for medical experiments in Auschwitz's Block 10 barracks, which housed mostly Jewish women prisoners who were used as guinea pigs. *Panstwowe Muzeum Auschwitz-Birkenau w Oswiecimiu*

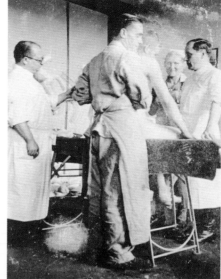

Early in his career as a research gynecologist, Carl Clauberg *(far left)* studied treatments to help infertile women conceive. In 1943 and 1944, on the authorization of SS chief Heinrich Himmler, Clauberg conducted experiments at Auschwitz intended to develop a method of mass sterilization. *Instytut Pamieci Narodowej, Warsaw*

sterilization law. It was not their future children but they themselves who were destined now for extinction. Yet, many Jewish women, along with Gypsy women, again confronted sterilization when SS physician Carl Clauberg used them, in Auschwitz, in experiments to sterilize women not only against their will but also without their knowledge. Clauberg, a research gynecologist, conducted experiments there in 1943 and 1944 to develop a method of mass sterilization. Using some 700 mostly Jewish women as expendable guinea pigs, he injected toxins into the uterus, causing severe pain and sometimes death. The purpose of his experiments, as he wrote in 1943, was for any doctor to be able to sterilize a woman "during the usual gynecological exam." This was the vision for the time after the "final victory," for a Europe under Nazi rule.

Prior to the beginning of the war, on August 31, 1939, the Ministry of the Interior had decreed that the implementation of the sterilization law should be drastically reduced to "urgent" cases—that is, those of a "particularly great danger of procreation" —and the decree pointed to the needs of the impending war. Two weeks earlier, on August 18, the ministry had decreed that doctors and midwives would have to report all children up to three years old who were "suspected" of certain diseases. Although the decree referred to the obligation to report the hereditarily ill under the sterilization law, what was at issue now was no longer sterilization but the impending murder of the disabled. It started with the killing of children, which ultimately claimed 5,000 lives, most of them having been born in the previous years, despite the sterilization law. Within barely six years, Nazi sterilization policy turned into a policy of mass murder.

A mother wearing an
Honor Cross of German
Motherhood, 1942.
SV-Bilderdienst, Munich

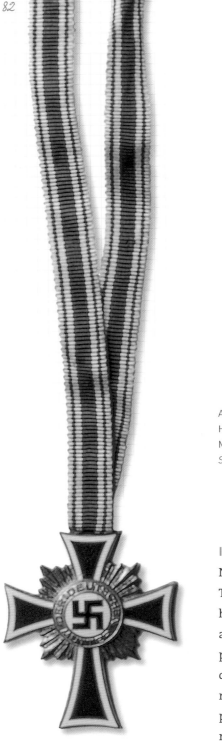

The Nazis awarded a bronze Honor Cross
of German Motherhood to women who
had four or five children, a silver for six or
seven, and a gold for eight or more. The
award, issued after 1938, sought to elevate
the status of racially and hereditarily "fit"
mothers. Jews and "Gypsies" were not
eligible, neither were women with backgrounds of prostitution or hereditary
illness nor women from large families
deemed "antisocial"—whose members
were habitual criminals or sex offenders.
USHMM Collection, Gift of Robert Jecklin

INTERACTIONS OF EUGENIC STERILIZATION WITH OTHER POLICIES

Nazi racial hygiene also promoted "positive eugenics," to encourage desirable births.
To this end, the regime introduced marriage loans in 1933, raised the tax rebates for
husbands and fathers with respect to wife and children in 1934, introduced child
allowances in 1936, supported the League of Large ("Child-Rich") Families, and cam-
paigned against voluntary abortion. Similar measures were also introduced in other
countries, but the Nazi version was unique; from the outset, it excluded encouragement of undesired births. Marriage loans were granted only after a public health
physician had examined the prospective couple for genetic diseases. This was the
major reason why only one-fourth of all couples applied. Jews, Gypsies, and antisocial persons were excluded from all the benefits. To genetically healthy superior
couples, child allowances were initially granted only from the fifth child onward,
but during the war this changed to the third child. The League of Large Families, in
existence since 1922, was transformed into a society for eugenic propaganda.

Anti-abortion policy was paramount for the Nazis, and many women were
convicted for voluntary abortion on the grounds of paragraph 218 of the penal code.
Nonetheless, in 1935, abortion on grounds of the pregnant woman's health was
legalized by the same amendment to the sterilization law that allowed for abortions
on racial hygienic grounds; in that same year, 11,800 health-motivated abortions
were performed. In late 1940, a decree of the Ministry of the Interior permitted
abortion on "racial" grounds (by 1941, it was applied 53 times), and in 1942, the same
ministry encouraged public health physicians to apply, outside the sterilization
law, for abortion and sterilization on antisocial German women—targeting

In *People in Danger* (1934), demographer Otto Helmut argued that Germany faced a crisis if it did not increase its birthrate. *USHMM Collection*

Flyer for a Nazi honor day for large "child-rich" families in Cologne, June 1936. *Archiv des Diakonischen Werkes der EKD, Berlin*

**Eine Schwangerschaft
darf nicht unterbrochen werden!**

**Hüte Dich vor
Ratschlägen und Eingriffen Unberufener!**

Placard from the traveling German Hygiene Museum exhibition *Healthy Woman, Healthy Nation*, ca. 1933–35, reads, "A pregnancy must not be terminated! Guard against advice and procedures by unqualified individuals!" *Deutsches Hygiene-Museum, Dresden*

prostitutes, especially. During the war, abortions were performed on an unknown number of forced laborers from Eastern Europe, probably in the hundreds of thousands.[26] In 1943, on the other hand, the death penalty was introduced for habitual abortionists (and five years of prison for the woman); some of the ensuing cases concerned Polish doctors who performed abortions on German women.[27]

Altogether, Nazi pronatalist policies, both through incentives ("positive eugenics") and suppression of voluntary abortion, were generally not successful. The birthrate rose until 1938, but only to the level of the late 1920s, when it was decried as "race suicide," and then declined. The actual convictions for abortion (about 40,000 women and men) did not exceed those of the Weimar years. Racial hygienists continued to complain that most families with many children were antisocial. The most "valuable," the families of SS members, had on average only 1.1 children in 1939, and 61 percent of the SS members were unmarried.[28]

In November 1933, a Law against Dangerous Habitual Criminals was enacted, providing castration for the largely male sexual offenders. Moreover, the first amendment (1935) to the sterilization law allowed for convicted male homosexuals to be castrated, with their consent and if a public health doctor judged castration to be useful for "liberating him from a degenerate sex drive." Up to 1943, 2,300 men were castrated according to these laws.[29] Homosexual men were a special target of Himmler, who created, in 1936, a Reich Central Office for Combating Homosexuality and Abortion, the assumption being that male homosexuals withhold their reproductive potential (no such fear arose in the case of lesbians). Himmler's argument fit into the eugenics discussion of cleansing the national

Paul Otto *(left)*, a homosexual man, with the woman he married to avoid persecution, and his long-term partner, Harry, in 1937. Eugenics proponents, such as psychiatrist Ernst Rüdin, regarded homosexuality as biologically "degenerate." Under the Nazi regime, the number of men arrested for homosexuality rose sharply, totaling some 100,000. *Private Collection, Berlin*

body of unwanted groups, but professional racial hygienists usually did not consider homosexuality as being genetically transmitted. Homosexuals were persecuted, like many other groups, outside eugenic laws and institutions; up to 50,000 men were convicted on the grounds of the penal code and some 5,000 to 15,000 were deported to concentration camps.[30]

In December 1935, Himmler created the organization Fount of Life *(Lebensborn)* as part of his struggle against abortion. The Lebensborn offered to (unmarried as well as married) women who were made pregnant by a very "valuable" man, usually an SS member, particularly good conditions in special confinement homes as an alternative to abortion. In the ten confinement homes in Germany, 1,371 such children were born before 1939. But most Lebensborn children (altogether 12,000) were born during the war and outside Germany, especially in Norway to women (about 6,000) who had relationships with German men of the occupying forces. From 1939, the Lebensborn homes in Germany were used mainly for "valuable" children who had been kidnapped in Eastern Europe and were now to be Germanized.[31]

Racial hygiene was part and parcel of Nazi racism. The core and common denominator of all forms of Nazi racism—in its discourse, "science," and practice—was the definition and treatment of certain social and cultural groups as being inferior. Eugenic racism targeted human beings considered inferior on eugenic grounds—their emotional, mental, social, and physical makeup—for the sake of "regeneration"; ethnic racism targeted those considered inferior on ethnic grounds—especially Jews, but also Gypsies, blacks, and Slavs. Eugenic racism based its scientific legitimacy on the discourse of heredity, ethnic racism on that of descent. Similar as well as

SS *Lebensborn* home in Germany, 1934.
Bundesarchiv Koblenz

different, they overlapped in many ways with regard to institutions, ideology, and actors. The major eugenicists were not necessarily among the major actors of anti-Jewish policies. Yet, different from the Weimar years, when many eugenicists, even such radical ones as Fritz Lenz, had harbored doubts about Hitler's anti-Jewish program and focused instead on the undesirable among the general population, none of the powerful old or new eugenicists of the 1930s and 1940s ever questioned the persecution of the Jews. The major reason why in Nazi Germany—and only in Nazi Germany—sterilization became a "population" policy in the strict sense, and why compulsory mass sterilization was one of the steps on the path to mass murder, was the fact that National Socialism conceptualized and practiced racial hygiene as an integral part of its overall racism.

Teddy bear used in SS *Lebensborn* home.
USHMM Collection

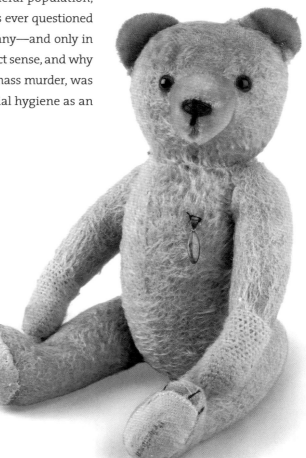

EUGENIK

ERBLEHRE ∗ ERBPFLEGE

Amenophis IV., schmalwüchsig, und ein breitwüchsiger Kopf, beide aus
El Amarna um 1370 v. Chr.

BAND 2   MÄRZ 1932   HEFT 6

VERLAG ALFRED METZNER · BERLIN SW61 · GITSCHINER STRASSE 109

THE "SCIENCE OF RACE"

BY BENOIT MASSIN

In 1934, Professor Otto Aichel, vice president of the German Society for Physical Anthropology, and Professor Otmar von Verschuer, one of the world's foremost specialists in twin research and medical genetics, introduced a collective volume in honor of Eugen Fischer, the director of the Kaiser Wilhelm Institute (KWI) for Anthropology, Human Heredity, and Eugenics, the largest research center in the field of "racial science" in Germany. The introduction to the volume underscored the important role of science in Nazi racial policy:

The Führer, Adolf Hitler, for the first time in the history of mankind, is taking measures to apply the knowledge of the biological foundations of nations—race, heredity, and selection. It is not by chance that this is occurring in Germany, for German science has given politicians the necessary tools.[1]

Ten years later, in 1944, Professor Eberhard Geyer, head of the Anthropological Institute at the University of Vienna, reiterated this point in his essay "Science at the Crossroads," confirming that "the study of race...has become the core of our new worldview."[2] Clearly, biomedical scientific disciplines—in particular, racial

Eugenik, March 1932. The cover juxtaposes narrow and wide-headed sculptures from ancient Egypt. The long head of the "Nordic race" was the eugenic ideal of Fritz Lenz, Eugen Fischer, and others of the Nordic school of German racial hygiene. *USHMM Collection*

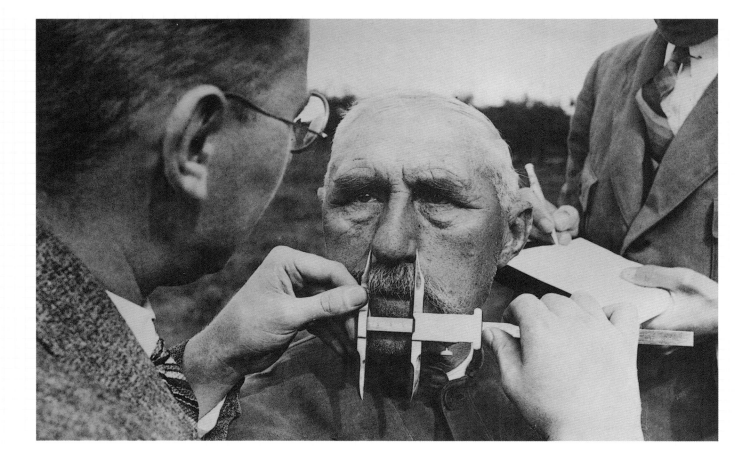

anthropology and medical genetics—occupied a central position in the Third Reich; they shaped Nazi policy and thereby influenced millions of lives.

Today, one views racism as an "irrational" prejudice that has little to do with science. But today's perspective should not obscure the role played by science and scientists in Nazi Germany. Along with psychiatrists, human geneticists, and the medical profession as a whole, racial anthropologists were deeply involved in Nazi medical and racial crimes. Scientists and medical experts advised Nazi government, party, and SS agencies. They gave scientific and medical expertise in the enactment and application of racial and eugenic laws; they provided scientific legitimization of these measures; they taught the medical personnel to implement racial hygiene on the home front; and they trained the SS racial experts who carried racial policy into occupied countries. In fact, on many occasions, the impulse for racial and eugenic policy came not from politicians but from scientists and the medical profession. Since the beginning of the twentieth century, German anthropologists and specialists in the "study of human heredity" (today, "human genetics") harbored a strong desire to influence governmental activity and advise policy makers. For its part, the Nazi government was willing to engage them, to achieve maximal efficiency in reaching its political objectives.

EUGENICS AND GERMAN PHYSICAL ANTHROPOLOGY

Physical anthropologists enthusiastically supported eugenics. During the Weimar Republic and the Third Reich, many anthropologists played key roles in the German eugenics movement. Eugen Fischer, the man who introduced a scientific revolution in

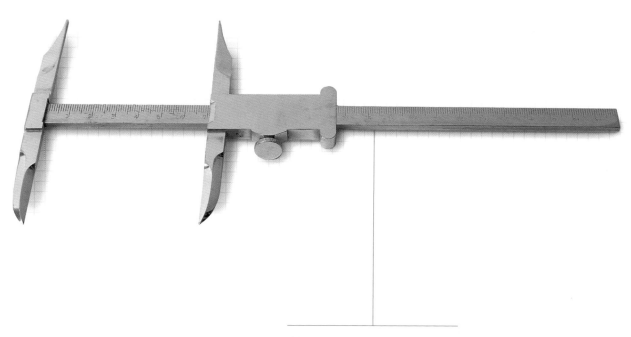

Calipers from the standard anthropological field kit. *Staatliche Naturwissenschaftliche Sammlungen Bayerns, Munich*

German physical anthropology by converting it to genetics, was particularly influential; at the end of the Weimar Republic, he presided over the German Society for Racial Hygiene. During the Third Reich, the editor of what was to become the official organ of the German Society for Racial Hygiene, the journal *People and Race (Volk und Rasse)*, was an anthropologist. From the 1920s on, eugenics and racial anthropology were closely related, and most, if not all, physical anthropologists converted to eugenics.

Eugenics influenced German physical anthropology in a number of ways. It accentuated the interest in human heredity and the conversion from nineteenth-century skull measurement (craniometry) to human genetics, and bestowed a therapeutic impulse to cure the nation as a whole from its ills—even if that meant sacrificing individual rights. This notion became widespread within the medical discussion of the time (not only in Germany) and impregnated a broad spectrum of the political culture, including the left.[3] Eugenics also turned anthropology into a practical and applied or "useful" science for the German nation. Since the power of nations appeared to emanate from "race," "heredity," and "selection," anthropologists positioned themselves to advise politicians on which heredity traits and racial elements should be supported and which should be eliminated.

THE SCIENCE OF CLASSIFYING HUMAN "RACES"

The Nazis did not invent the concept of race. As applied to mankind in the modern sense of the word, it was created by Western science in the seventeenth and eighteenth centuries. Naturalists decided to include the human species in the zoological sphere and submitted it to the same type of classification used for plants and animals. Human

Abb. 1. Männer, I. Preis
des Preisausschreibens für den besten nordischen Raffenkopf.

Abb. 2. Männer, I. Preis
des Preisausschreibens für den besten nordischen Raffenkopf.

First-prize *(man)* and second-prize winners *(woman)* in the Nordic Head Contest, sponsored by the anthropological journal *People and Race (Volk und Rasse)* in 1926. *USHMM Collection*

beings were reduced to bodily dimensions—the shape of the body (morphology), structure of bones, and color of skin. The search for "human races" changed labels over time, from "natural history of man" in the eighteenth century to "anthropology" (science of man) or "physical anthropology" (as opposed to cultural anthropology or ethnology) in the nineteenth century.

Physical anthropology became institutionalized as an autonomous academic discipline in the second half of the nineteenth century. The first chair and institute for anthropology at a German university was established, in Munich, in 1886. By the time Hitler came to power, 10 out of some 20 German universities had an institute, a chair, or an assistant professorship specializing in physical anthropology. Even before 1933, however, physical anthropology was already taught in most universities, if not by professional anthropologists then often by professors of anatomy.

From the 1920s to 1945, physical anthropology in Germany was also called *Rassenkunde* ("racial science" or "the study of race"), *Rassenforschung* ("racial research"), or *Rassenbiologie* ("racial biology"). Racial science was not invented by the Nazis but came from established academic science and medicine; yet, the name change of the 1920s from *Anthropologie* or *Menschenkunde* ("science of man") to *Rassenkunde* was not insignificant. It reflected a change in political values conveyed by this discipline. "Mankind" no longer mattered—human beings were now defined in terms of race.

In the Weimar Republic, academic racial anthropology was considered a legitimate field and not perceived as a pseudoscience. Even Jewish medical professors taught racial anthropology, although the Nazi regime later removed them all from their posts. Jewish scientists and leftist politicians fully accepted the creation of the

Abb. b. Frauen, Preis II a
des Preisausschreibens für den besten nordischen Rassenkopf.

Abb. c. Frauen, Preis II a
des Preisausschreibens für den besten nordischen Rassenkopf.

Kaiser Wilhelm Institute for Anthropology in 1927.[4] Most countries, including the United States, Great Britain, France, Italy, the USSR, South American countries, Japan, China, and India, had scientific societies, journals, or chairs in universities dedicated to physical anthropology. Foreign scientists contributed to German journals of racial anthropology, and even during the Nazi regime, international scientific connections were not completely severed. Some foreign antiracist scientists even accepted the idea that races had distinct "racial psychology," as when, in 1924, one of Britain's most eminent anthropologists, a Jewish scientist, declared in an address that "the Nordic race excels other races in steadfastness of will and foresight."[5]

The fact that most of the international scientific community of the time considered German racial science a "normal science" does not mean that it was not strongly politicized. During the 1920s, racial science became a favorite field of *völkisch* (racial) nationalism, and most anthropologists were staunch *völkisch* nationalists. They believed race was the key to everything and that politics should be based on race. Racial science spilled out from university laboratories, through popular books and popular journals, and reached a much broader right-wing public. The most famous writer of popular books on racial science, Hans F. K. Günther, published numerous best-selling books that attempted to describe German and European races.[6] The popular illustrated journal *People and Race*, launched in 1926, also testifies to the political craze surrounding racial science. Its editorial board featured some 30 university professors, including several professional anthropologists such as Eugen Fischer.

The frontiers between academic physical anthropology and highly politicized racial science blurred quickly. The same year Fischer was appointed director of the

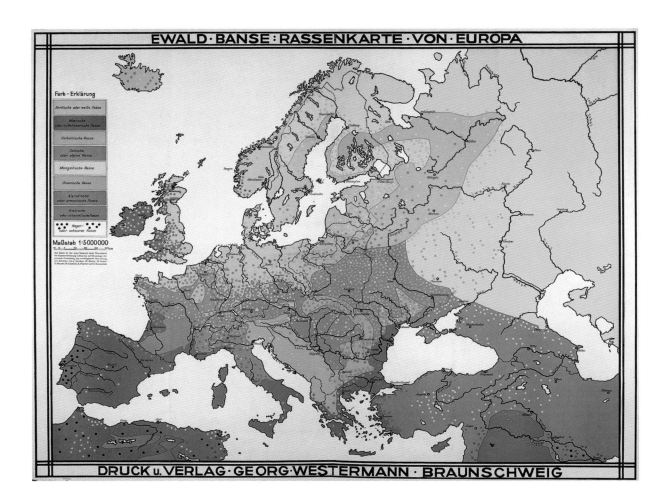

The key at the top left of Ewald Banse's "Racial Map of Europe" (1925) suggests a ranked hierarchy of "races," from the "Nordic or white" *(in red, at the top)* to the "Negro" *(in black, at the bottom). American Geographical Society Library, UW-Milwaukee Libraries*

newly founded Kaiser Wilhelm Institute for Anthropology, he and Günther cowrote an illustrated booklet celebrating *German Heads of the Nordic Race*.[7] Fischer, a shrewd tactician, could pay lip service to the political values of the Weimar Republic while also discreetly advocating his own racist values. More overtly political, Bruno Schultz, a professional anthropologist working at the Munich institute, was also orator for the Nordic Ring (an association founded in 1926, dedicated to promoting Nordic racism), coeditor of *People and Race,* and, from 1932 on, head of the Department of Racial Science in the Racial Office of the SS.

A distinction of German physical anthropology or racial science after 1918 and the loss of Germany's colonies (under the Treaty of Versailles) was its focus on European races—the racial characteristics of the population of Germany, as well as those of Central and Eastern Europe. By comparison, French and British anthropology dedicated research to the indigenous people of their colonial empires, while American anthropology scrutinized its black and American Indian population. German anthropology after World War I often assigned the role of the "superior race" to the tall, blond, and long-headed so-called 'Nordic race," and labeled as "inferior races" the short and roundheaded brunet "Alpine race" (mostly concentrated in the French and Swiss Alps) and the "Eastern European race" found in Slavic countries. Racial hierarchies were repatriated to the European continent.

During the 1920s and 1930s, German racial anthropology was very productive and scientifically modern. To give the race concept more solidity, German racial anthropology looked for the biological foundations of human differences. It focused on comparative anatomy, embryology, blood-group research, and, above all, genetics. Eugen Fischer and

"The Image of Race in the Family Tree," *Illustrierter Beobachter*, July 1933. Pictured are Kaiser Wilhelm Institute scientists Otmar von Verschuer *(top)* and Wolfgang Abel. *Library of Congress, General Collections, Washington, D.C.*

Eugen Fischer *(center)*, director of the Kaiser Wilhelm Institute for Anthropology, Human Heredity, and Eugenics, Berlin, 1934. *Bundesarchiv Koblenz*

his students undertook numerous studies of the genetic basis of human racial traits through "bastard research" (research on racially mixed or "hybrid" populations), twin research, statistical analysis of pedigree collections, comparative embryology of various races, animal experiments, and developmental genetics.

The takeover of power by the Nazis did not cause any significant break in the scientific orientation of German racial anthropology.[8] Jewish or leftist anthropologists were a small minority, and most lost their positions or were marginalized. In general, racial anthropology and human genetics greatly benefited from the Nazi assumption of power. The number of institutes, professorships, and courses increased dramatically, creating more career openings for young anthropologists. The German Research Council *(Deutsche Forschungsgemeinschaft)*, the main German foundation for scientific research, increased budgets for racial research, and institutes for racial anthropology and human genetics received more money. The KWI for Anthropology saw its budget doubled in the first two years of the regime.

Besides dismissing a few of its members and integrating new ones with strong political agendas, the main change in German anthropology and human genetics after 1933 was a radicalization in its style. Politics, discreetly kept out of scientific meetings during Weimar, suddenly erupted in academic halls with political declarations and Hitler salutes. The overwhelming majority of identified anthropologists (90 percent) joined the Nazi Party and carried their Nazi badges when going to their institutes. About one-third joined the SS.[9] Physical anthropology and human genetics became totally oriented toward practical applications of Nazi racial policy. Not only did anthropologists and human geneticists put their science fully at the disposal of

The older boy, Johannes Hauk, was the son of a French-Algerian soldier and a German woman. He was sterilized, in 1937, at the age of 16. *Hans Hauk*

A slide used in lectures on genetics at the State Academy for Race and Health, in Dresden, captioned: "Mulatto child of a German woman and a Negro of the French Rhineland garrison troops, among her German classmates," ca. 1936. *Library of Congress, Prints & Photographs Division, Washington, D.C.*

Germans felt humiliated by the presence of French occupation forces in the Rhineland after World War I. *Musée de l'Armée, Paris*

the regime, they also forgot all ethical boundaries. Many eagerly used any "opportunity" to gain access to corpses and "human material" from victims of the regime, to carry out research or experiments on unwilling subjects.

"BASTARD RESEARCH" AND THE STERILIZATION OF "RACIALLY MIXED" CHILDREN
After the military defeat of Germany in 1918, the French army occupied the Rhineland region. French troops included some 35,000 colonial soldiers from Northern Africa, black Africa, and Indochina. Between 1918 and the mid-1920s, several hundred children were born from relationships between German women and "colored" colonial soldiers. Public health officials and doctors warned that these hybrid, or "bastard," children posed a serious danger, in that they were afflicted with syphilis and all sorts of "inferiorities" resulting from racial mixing. A number of doctors suggested sterilizing the children, but because the law protected individual rights during the Republic, no steps were taken against these so-called Rhineland Bastards.[10] Nine weeks after the Nazis came to power, however, Hermann Göring, Minister of the Interior in Prussia, requested a statistical survey to evaluate the number of racially mixed children and called on racial anthropologists to help identify them. Eugen Fischer assigned the task to his assistant, Dr. Wolfgang Abel, an anthropologist and specialist in human racial characteristics.[11]

Eugen Fischer's 1913 pioneering study on the mixed population in the German colony of South-West Africa inaugurated hybridization research *(Bastardforschung)* in

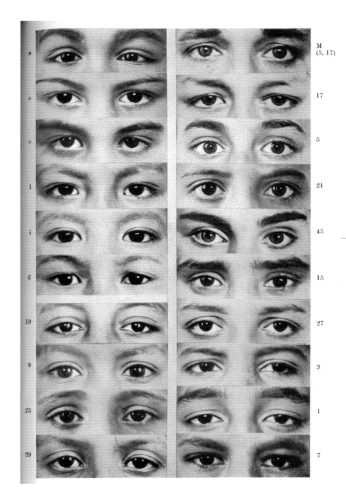

Plates from a 1937 scholarly article by Wolfgang Abel, who studied the *Mischlinge* (racially mixed) offspring of Moroccan-German and Vietnamese-German parents. Abel concluded that the so-called bastards ("hybrids") were physically and mentally "degenerate": "It is the mixing of European with Negroid and Mongoloid races wherein lies the primary reason for the poor condition of the Rhineland bastards found in our population." *National Library of Medicine, NIH, Bethesda, Md.*

German physical anthropology as a new method to determine genetic transmission of human racial traits.[12] Fischer determined that mixing an "inferior race" with a "superior race" meant decline for the latter and, therefore, must be avoided. Abel, a totally reliable Nazi Party member, as well as a member of the SS, believed racial crossing created "disharmonies" in the offspring.[13] He conducted the survey of the mixed-race children in the summer of 1933. The following year, he published an article in the journal of the Racial Policy Office, *New People (Neues Volk)*, entitled "Bastards on the Rhine," where, in thinly veiled terms, he called for their sterilization.[14] Relying on Abel's finding that the children were inferior, the regime ultimately decided that all "bastard children" should be sterilized.[15] Abel, Fischer, and two assistants served as the anthropological experts evaluating the racial status of the children who, in 1937, under Gestapo guard, were forcibly sterilized in hospitals.

Kaiser Wilhelm Institute anthropologist Dr. Wolfgang Abel, ca 1936. *SV-Bilderdienst, Munich*

"GYPSY RESEARCH" (EUGENIC AND ANTHROPOLOGICAL VIEWS OF CRIME)

Accused of being beggars and thieves, "Gypsies" (Sinti and Roma), from the beginning of the twentieth century, had been subjected to discriminatory police measures in several European countries, including Germany. Bavarian police kept a central register of Gypsies that, from 1911 on, contained their fingerprints and all police information on their deviant behavior. During the Weimar Republic, Gypsies could be sent to a compulsory workhouse if they could not prove regular paid employment in the prior two years. What was new in Nazi policy was both its "scientific" aspect and its radicality in solving the "Gypsy problem."

Students at the Berlin School for the Blind learn Gregor Mendel's principles of inheritance *(left)* and the purported application of those laws to human heredity and principles of race *(right),* ca. 1935. During the Third Reich, Germans born deaf or blind, like those born with mental illnesses or disabilities, were urged to submit to compulsory sterilization as a civic duty. *Deutsches Blinden-Museum, Berlin*

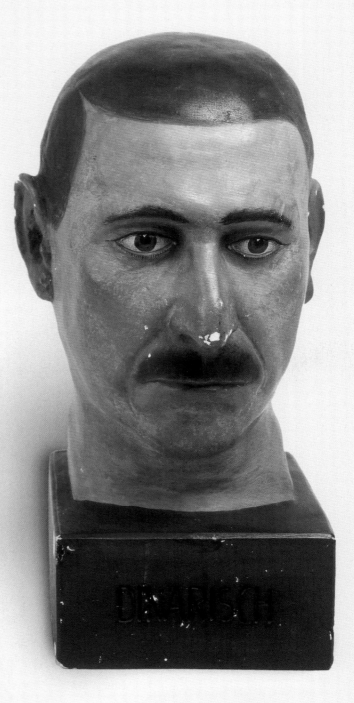

Heads of racial types, created by anthropologists from plaster molds of the faces of living subjects, were mass-produced in Nazi Germany for use in exhibitions and racial hygiene classes. These two heads portray the Dinaric (Balkan) and the Negro type.
Deutsches Blinden-Museum, Berlin

"Gypsies" (*Zigeuner*, in German), historically, have been persecuted, but in the Nazi period, discrimination directed at some 30,000 German Gypsies acquired a biological cast. Research on Gypsies was undertaken by Dr. Robert Ritter, a child psychologist and specialist in juvenile delinquency who believed Gypsies were predisposed to criminal behavior. Here, Ritter conducts field research with the support of German police. Ca. 1938–39. *Bundesarchiv Koblenz*

Anthropologist Sophie Erhardt, Robert Ritter's assistant. *Bundesarchiv Koblenz*

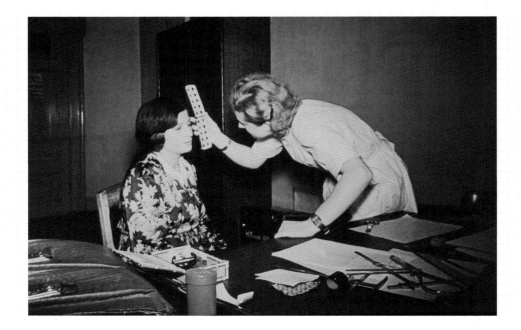

Since the turn of the century, German psychiatrists had developed theories that criminal behavior was the result of "antisocial personality" and "feeblemindedness," and that both characteristics were inherited.[16] Eugenicists collected family pedigrees showing how "degenerate" lineage produced criminals, alcoholics, lunatics, retarded individuals, beggars, hobos, and other antisocials. Because prisons and asylums had to be maintained to house these individuals, they were regarded as a tremendous expense—a direct social cost of their antisocial behavior.[17] Eugenics provided a solution to this social problem: Prevent them from reproducing, through sterilization, castration, lifelong isolation, or systematic "euthanasia." In Germany, this combination of psychiatric theories of crime and eugenic treatment was called "criminal biology." In the Weimar Republic, research foundations and institutions, such as the KWI for Psychiatry, in Munich, financially supported research in criminal biology.

After 1933, Nazi interest in criminal biology led to the establishment of new research institutes, including the Research Institute for Racial Hygiene and Population Biology of the Reich Health Office, headed by Dr. Robert Ritter, a specialist in medical genetics and psychiatry. For his second doctorate, he had conducted a genetic study on ten generations of descendants of "vagrants, swindlers, and thieves." Ritter was also appointed a member of a Hereditary Health Court and was an active member of the Society for the Biology of Crime.[18] A member of the SS, Ritter, in 1942, also became director of the newly created Criminal Biological Institute of the Reich Criminal Police Office. The German police, too, wanted to be "modern" and "scientific."[19]

The first group studied by Ritter's research center was the Gypsies, estimated to be some 30,000 people in Germany and Austria. Helped by a team of medical doctors,

From the data his team gathered, Ritter concluded that most "Gypsies" were "primitive" *Mischlinge*, racially mixed offspring of "highly inferior" habitual criminals.
Bundesarchiv Berlin

Eye color tool, ca. 1937, of the type used by Ritter's research team.
USHMM Collection, Gift of Irmgard Nippert

sociologists, psychologists, human geneticists, and anthropologists, Ritter's aim was to register all Gypsies and Gypsy hybrids *(Mischlinge)* living in Germany, reconstruct their genealogies, and collect information on their social and medical condition. Genealogical registers were necessary to locate all Gypsies and their *Mischlinge* offspring, because a number of them were well integrated in German society, lived in apartments, had regular jobs, and were sometimes highly decorated soldiers. Gypsy research also included taking anthropometric measurements and photographs, analyzing such racial and family characteristics as nostril and ear shapes, collecting blood samples and fingerprints, and making plaster casts of Gypsy heads.

Ritter's research was intended to have direct application for the racial hygienic policy in the Nazi state. His numerous studies concluded that the antisocial and criminal behavior of Gypsies was the result of their genetic endowment and "primitive racial" character. To eradicate this "unwanted" behavior, the regime aimed to stop reproduction, through sterilization or the isolation of men from women in special camps, and to prevent miscegenation by forbidding contact with the German population. Ritter and his assistants produced thousands of certificates for sterilization of "antisocial Gypsy hybrids."[20] Other scientists, such as the blood-group specialist Werner Fischer, received permission from the SS to conduct studies in the Sachsenhausen concentration camp. Analysis of Gypsy blood was carried out at the prestigious Robert Koch Institute, in Berlin, in an attempt to find a serological diagnosis to identify Gypsies and Gypsy *Mischlinge*. Captive Gypsies were also used in other scientific research, including twin studies, and were subjected to deadly

Sophie Erhardt is seen creating a plaster cast that
was the basis for mass-produced busts *(below right)*
used in classrooms and exhibitions. Ca. 1936–40.
Bundesarchiv Koblenz

Alma Höllenreiner, a "Gypsy" of the Sinti tribe, with her three daughters, two sons, nephew, and niece, in the 1920s. The two sons
were forcibly sterilized in the Ravensbrück concentration camp, yet survived the war; the others perished in Auschwitz. Most of
the 30,000 members of the Sinti and Roma tribes in Germany and Austria were killed during the Holocaust. *Dokumentations- und
Kulturzentrum Deutscher Sinti und Roma, Heidelberg*

Idealized Nordic-looking types pervaded Nazi propaganda. *Museum für Kunst und Gewerbe Hamburg*

experimentation. The vast majority of the scientists involved in Gypsy research were never punished.

NORDIC RACISM AND THE SS

The term *Aryan*, although still used by Hitler in *Mein Kampf*, and in the first racial law against Jewish civil servants (April 1933), was rather outdated in the scientific community. Aryan, in Nazi law, was just a positive way of saying "non-Jewish," and "Aryan ancestry" meant having no Jewish ancestor. At that time, scientists talked about "Indo-Europeans" (in linguistics and archaeology) or the Nordic race (in physical anthropology). To anthropologists, the Nordic race was just one of the many races that comprised the European population, like the "Mediterranean race" or the "Alpine race." This anthropological concept of the Nordic race, however, was taken over by other scientists and racial ideologists who attributed to the Nordic race not only the best human qualities but all creativity in the history of civilizations. The Nordic race also became the ideal of many Nazis, in particular those in charge of Nazi policy.

Wedding of an SS official, 1934. SS members and prospective spouses of SS officers both had to pass a "racial" and genetic screening. *Bildarchiv Preussischer Kulturbesitz, Berlin*

Nordic racism, therefore, was a modernized version of the older "Aryan myth." According to Gobineau, the French amateur historian of civilization, in his 1850s work *Essay on the Inequalities of the Human Races*, the Aryan race not only established culture in countries with Indo-European languages but also created the significant civilizations of the world. Gobineau ascribed the decline of civilizations to the mixing of "noble blood" with "inferior races." The turn to Nordic racism in German anthropology came in the period 1890–1914.[21] It was more a "positive" racism, glorifying one race for its superiority, than a "negative" racism, aimed at demonstrating the inferiority of another race. Nordic racism flourished in the Weimar Republic, within the *völkisch* nationalist scene and in the right wing of the eugenics movement. It also appeared in the Scandinavian countries and the United States. The handbook *Foundations of Human Genetics and Racial Hygiene,* by Baur, Fischer, and Lenz, contributed greatly to the spread of Nordic racism.

The handbooks of Fischer and Lenz, or other anthropologists, appealed mainly to a narrow audience of specialists in medical genetics or anthropology, and to medical students. The philologist and amateur anthropologist Hans F. K. Günther popularized Nordic racism, his *Racial Study of the German People* selling 124,000 copies by 1942, while an abridged version sold almost 300,000 copies. The journal *People and Race* played a similar role.

The ideal of the Nordic race was taken over by the SS, the elite Nazi organization molded along the guidelines of Nordic racism and eugenic prerequisites.[22] Jewish ancestry was not tolerated for membership, racial lineage had to be verified, and candidates had to meet political as well as physical and medical standards. Potential

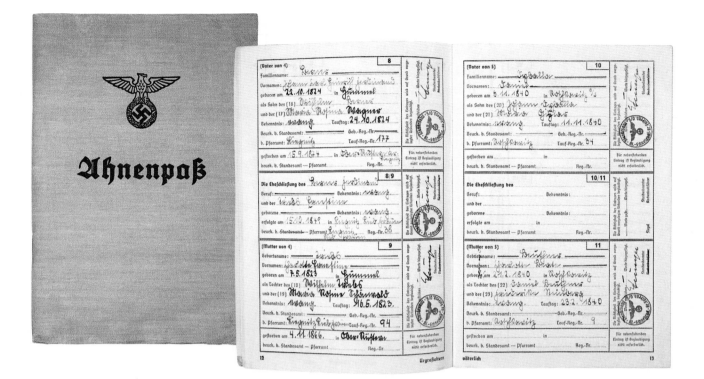

The Nazis created an extensive bureaucracy to collect and register hereditary statistics and family histories from the general population. One of the primary methods used by German citizens to prove "Aryan" (Germanic) heritage was the "Ancestral Passport," which included a family tree to be filled in by each applicant. To become a member of the elite Nazi corps, the SS, one had to trace Aryan lineage back to 1800. *Wolfgang Haney, Berlin*

brides also had to submit to racial, medical, and familial investigations, and marriage authorization was granted or denied on the basis of race and hereditary health. The Race and Settlement Main Office (RuSHA), responsible for the racial selection of new SS members, created some 500,000 personal files for marriage authorizations.

A researcher in a regional Genealogical Research Office established to gather family histories of the local population. Heide, Germany. *Bildarchiv Preussischer Kulturbesitz, Berlin*

RACIAL POLICY IN OCCUPIED TERRITORY

After 1939, the racial experts of RuSHA surveyed the populations of the occupied countries, conducting racial screenings of both "ethnic German" and non-Germanic populations. In October 1939, Hitler appointed the head of the SS, Heinrich Himmler, to the post of Reich Commissioner for the Strengthening of Germandom, making him responsible for implementing "ethnic policy," settlement policy, and "repopulation" policy in the newly occupied countries.[23] Himmler announced that he planned to "create a blond-haired country" in the new territories. Ethnic Germans *(Volksdeutsche)*, mainly from the USSR, Soviet-occupied Poland, the Baltic countries, and southeastern Europe, had to be repatriated into the German Reich and then sent as colonists to the annexed territories. Before being given German citizenship and a piece of land to farm, they were screened by RuSHA racial experts. In occupied Poland, the local population was divided into several groups. The local ethnic Germans, in particular the two million with unclear German ancestry, had to be screened for acceptance on the so-called "German People's List." "Racially valuable" Poles (with Nordic features) could be sent to the Reich for "re-Germanization." Approximately four million Poles, Czechs, Slovenes, French, and ethnic Germans from abroad had their fate determined by SS "racial experts."

A curator from the German Hygiene Museum leads a tour of German army and SS officers through an exhibition in German-occupied Cracow, Poland. Ca. 1940.
Deutsches Hygiene-Museum, Dresden; (chart) USHMM Collection, Gift of Deutsches Hygiene-Museum, Dresden

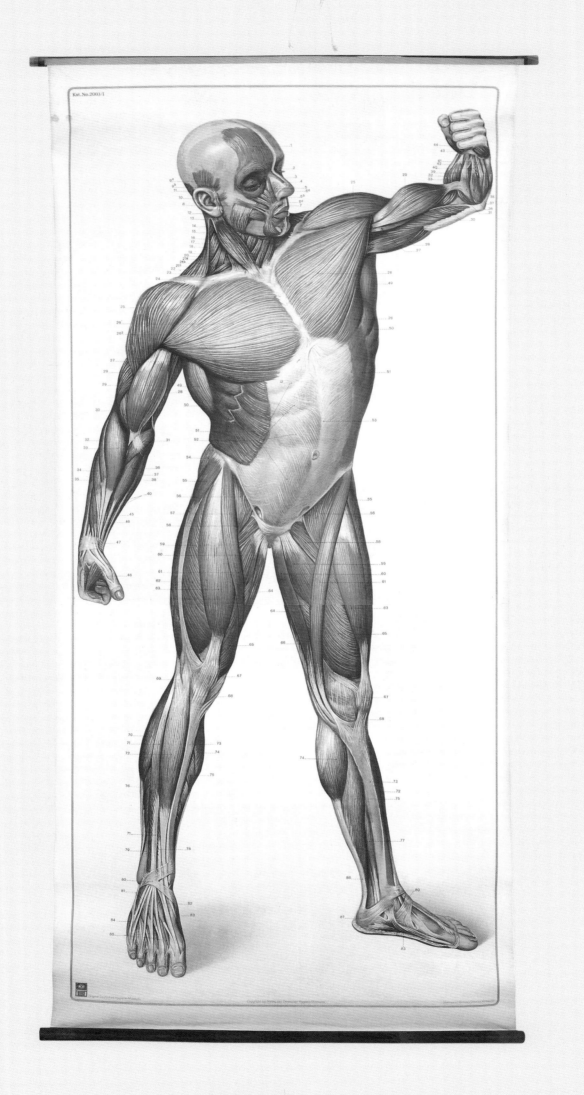

Polish-born Barbara Geisler, seen in a postwar photograph, was adopted by a German family through an SS *Lebensborn* institution in Munich, where she had been held. *Instytut Pamieci Narodowej, Warsaw*

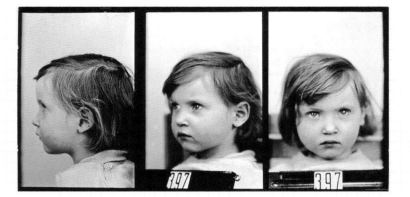

German medical staff examines a Polish boy for Germanic traits in a Lodz holding center. Children rejected for adoption often ended up in special children's camps, where many died from the harsh conditions. Ca. 1940. *Instytut Pamieci Narodowej, Warsaw*

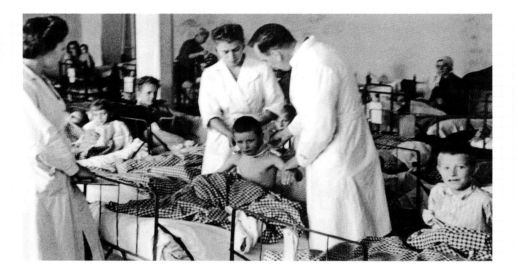

RuSHA counted about 500 such racial experts. Approximately one-fourth of higher-ranking officials were trained "racial scientists," a number of them professional anthropologists with university positions. Before taking over their position, each racial expert of RuSHA had to be trained in racial science, human genetics, and eugenics.[24] From 1934 on, at least 20 SS doctors were sent every year for a ten-month training course at the KWI for Anthropology.[25]

Some anthropologists worked directly for RuSHA as racial experts, training other such experts or offering advice for racial policy in Eastern territories. Dr. Josef Mengele, whose first doctoral degree was in anthropology, worked for RuSHA's screening center in Posen before being posted to Auschwitz.[26] Fritz Lenz, head of the Department for Racial Hygiene at the KWI for Anthropology, advised RuSHA, in January 1940, on racial and settlement policy in the conquered Eastern territories. Lenz recommended a rigorous racial selection of new settlers based on physical characteristics, similar to the one already practiced by the SS.[27]

In the fall of 1941, shortly after the invasion of the USSR, the Racial Policy Office met with renowned racial science specialists to discuss the future "treatment" of the Russian population. Wolfgang Abel had conducted an extensive anthropological survey of Soviet prisoners of war (POWs) for the high command of the armed forces *(Wehrmacht)*. At that time, the Soviet POW camps looked very much like primitive extermination camps, where detained soldiers received hardly any food or shelter. Within six months of the June 1941 attack on the Soviet Union, some 3.35 million soldiers of the Red Army were captured, and 60 percent died from their treatment. Abel concluded that Russians possessed a greater component of the Nordic race

Soviet prisoners at Mauthausen concentration camp, September 21, 1944. The entire group was executed five days later. *NARA, College Park, Md.*

A 1943 German high school biology textbook shows Soviet prisoners of war under the caption "Two Examples of the Racial Chaos of the Soviet Union." The POWs above are "eastern Baltic," those below are considered "Mongoloid." Their inclusion in a biology text aimed to legitimize their subjugation and extermination during World War II. Three million Soviet POWs perished while in German custody in executions or by starvation, exposure to cold, and disease. *USHMM Collection*

than assumed, making them a dangerous opponent and threat for the future. Abel suggested two solutions for this "problem"—either extermination of the Russian people or Germanization of its Nordic elements.[28]

Besides racial policy in Eastern territories, RuSHA racial experts also conducted racial examinations in cases of forbidden sexual intercourse between Slavic forced laborers or nationalities of "alien blood" and German women. In most cases, the foreign worker faced the death penalty, unless deemed "racially valuable"; then, he might be allowed to obtain German citizenship and marry the woman, after "reeducation" in a special SS camp. The pregnant woman also had to undergo a similar racial examination to decide the racial value of the unborn child, whereupon the racial expert decided if she should carry to term. Babies of "high racial value" were taken away from the mother and placed with German foster parents or put in a Nazi orphanage. "Unwanted population additions" were either aborted or sent to special institutions, where many starved to death.

RACIAL ANTHROPOLOGY AND THE "JEWISH QUESTION"

In the late nineteenth century, German anthropologists thought that a "Jewish race" did not exist. Anthropologists viewed Jews as a heterogeneous group with various racial characteristics, and until World War I, German physical anthropology opposed political antisemitism.[29] Even when the German medical profession showed quite strong antisemitic tendencies during the Weimar Republic, very little literature was produced on the racial anthropology of Jews.[30] The introduction of eugenics,

SS chief Heinrich Himmler inspecting a Soviet prisoner of war camp in Minsk. August 1941. On September 3, 1941, several hundred ill prisoners were killed at Auschwitz in a test of newly built gas chambers. *NARA, College Park, Md.*

Nordic racist anthropology, and genetics into physical anthropology ushered in a change of style. Race was not just physical characteristics but, above all, heredity, and heredity also included psychological traits. Thus, the new science of race, which began discreetly in Germany after 1900 and became stronger after 1920, included the "study of human heredity" *(menschliche Erblehre)*, the "study of racial psychology," and the inheritance of psychology and behavior *(Erbpsychologie)*.

In the new racial typologies, racial psychology was added to the physical portrait of each race. When these racial anthropologists and human geneticists wrote about the psychology of the two major races (the "Near East race" and the "Oriental race") composing the "Jewish people," they mixed compliments ("highly intelligent," "greatly gifted," "dynamic") with negative or threatening qualities ("cunning," "calculating," "critical mind," "aptitude for understanding the minds of others and for taking advantage of people and situations"). During the Weimar Republic, scientists such as Fischer and Lenz, living in a country where a great number of influential medical scientists were Jews, had to be careful not to lose their international scientific credibility by what might be perceived as crude antisemitism. Their social value as scientists was based on what had to appear as "serious science" and nonbiased "objectivity." Consequently, they avoided purely derogatory judgments of Jews and tried to present a "balanced" view. At the same time, this apparent objectivity made their theories look more "scientific" and, therefore, made them more powerful. Their standard work, the Baur-Fischer-Lenz, influenced a whole generation of medical students who became doctors and anthropologists in the Nazi regime.

No non-Jewish, academically trained anthropologist ventured to write a full-length book on the racial anthropology of Jews during the Weimar Republic. The main book on the racial characteristics of Jews, *Racial Study of the Jewish People*, was published by Günther in 1929. His description of the racial history and racial composition of the Jewish people was laced with value judgments. Günther insisted on the "foreign" nature of Jews, that racially they were not Europeans but "Orientals" and "Near Easterners."[31] Even during the Third Reich, although the "Jewish Question" was omnipresent, the number of published investigations did not increase dramatically. Almost every handbook for racial science or racial hygiene mentioned the Jewish Question, but new research was rare.

Anthropologists and human geneticists, nonetheless, provided their scientific backing to Nazi antisemitism in speeches, popular articles, and handbooks. Otmar von Verschuer wrote on the Jewish Problem, "racial care," and racial policy in his handbook *Principles of Racial Hygiene*.[32] He explained to medical students that all previous attempts to solve the Jewish Problem had failed and that only a "global solution" *(Gesamtlösung)* based on "racial biology" could be successful. Verschuer also collaborated with Nazi officials of the Research Department for the Jewish Question, lecturing on Jews (and convincing Fischer to join him), despite the possible risk to his scientific reputation:

International Jewry is perfectly aware of what side we are on; taking part or not taking part in such a meeting will not make a difference. It is important that our racial policy—also in the Jewish Question—receive an objective scientific grounding, which can also be accepted by wider circles.[33]

In *Racial Study of the Jewish People* (1930), Hans F. K. Günther, like many anthropologists, viewed Jews as non-European "racial mixtures." Foreshadowing tactics of the Nazi regime, Günther used scientific-looking material to legitimize racist views. With the examples of Archbishop Cohn *(right, second row)*, "a Jew from Poland," and Charlie Chaplin *(left, second row)*, a non-Jewish actor known for his liberal views, Günther implied that "Jewishness" was both innate and politically leftist rather than a matter of religious belief or cultural identity. *USHMM Collection*

Dr. Otmar von Verschuer in his lab at the Kaiser Wilhelm Institute, undated. *Archiv zur Geschichte der Max-Planck-Gesellschaft, Berlin*

In 1937, Verschuer explained that a racial state must preserve its own ethnicity and resist any threat to this ethnic principle. Germany's fight was against Jewry, he asserted, "because the German ethnic principle is especially threatened by the Jewish invasion." To integrate Jews would mean to integrate a racial group totally foreign to Europe. Scientific research on the consequences of intermarriages between Jews and pure Germans could provide a sound basis for policy concerning "Jewish *Mischlinge*."[34] At another meeting, Fischer lectured on the racial composition of Jews. He argued that they were a mixture of several races, mostly foreign to Europe, and that they possessed a "Jewish mind" equally foreign to Europeans—especially to the Nordic race, which felt an "instinctive" antagonism toward Jews.[35]

VIENNA AND ANTHROPOLOGICAL RESEARCH ON JEWS

Vienna became one of the main centers for research on Jews, following the incorporation of Austria into Nazi Germany in 1938, with scientists from the University of Vienna and the city's Natural History Museum launching new studies. A study of 99 Jewish men and women from a welfare home in Vienna—most of them between the ages of 74 and 84—was carried out by Dora Maria Kahlich, from the Anthropological Institute at the University of Vienna.[36] A much larger survey, in 1939, by anthropologists from Vienna's Natural History Museum, studied 440 Jews born in Eastern Europe who had migrated to Vienna. With the start of the war, the Gestapo rounded up and detained these men in Vienna's Prater stadium, where anthropologists photographed them and took anthropometric measurements. Keen to find

307

Posen, den 4.März 1942

An
Herrn Dr.Josef W a s t l ,
Leiter der Anthropolog. Abt.
des Naturhistorischen Staats-
museums in Wien.

Sehr geehrter Herr Doktor !

Auf Ihr Schreiben vom 25.2.42 offeriere ich Ihnen Polenschädel /♂ u. ♀/ zum Preise von je RM 25,- . Die Lieferung kann
etwa im Mai oder Juni d.Js. erfolgen. Ich kann Ihnen aber nur das
Geschlecht , auch das schätzungsweise Alter der Individuen angeben,
aber nichts Näheres über die Person mitteilen, da es sich um hinge-
richtete Polen handelt, die wir durch die Staatsanwaltschaft erhalten.
Ich würde noch gern Ihre besonderen Wünsche wissen, wel-
che Altersstufe Sie hauptsächlich brauchen. 30-40 jährig
Polenschädel von Kindern und Jugendlichen kann ich Ihnen
vorläufig nicht liefern, 20 - 25 jährige Männer erhalte ich weniger,
25 - 50 und 50 - 80 jährige viel, weibliche recht selten. An dem
polnischen Leichenmaterial ist Hyperbrachykephalie sehr selten,
Brachykephalie häufiger , Mesokephalie und Dolichokephalie sehr viel,
Hyperdolichokephalie selten.Plagiokephalie häufig . alle Termen
Judenschädel ♂ / 20-50 jährige kann ich Ihnen auch zum
Preise von RM 25,- offerieren, bei denen das genaue Alter und der
Geburtsort angegeben werden kann. Letzterer besagt allerdings bei
Juden nur wenig. Ich kann Ihnen zu den Judenschädeln auch Toten-
masken der betreffenden Individuen aus Gips liefern im Preise von
RM. 15,- . Von besonders typischen Ostjuden könnte ich Ihnen auch
Gipsbüsten anfertigen, damit man die Kopfform und die oft recht
eigenartigen Ohren sehen kann.Der Preis dieser Büsten würde sich
auf

Posen, March 4, 1942

To

Dr. Josef Wastl,
Director of the Anthropology Department
of the Natural History Museum in Vienna

Dear Doctor,

In response to your inquiry of February 25, 1942, I am offering you skulls of Poles /♂ and ♀/ for the price of 25 reichsmarks each. Delivery can take place in May or June of this year. I can only tell you the sex and approximate age of the individuals but nothing more about the person, because these are executed Poles whom we acquired from the public prosecutor's office.

I would still be interested in knowing which age group you mainly need.

For the time being, I cannot supply you with skulls of Polish children and teenagers. I receive fewer men 20–25 years old, more 25–50 and 50–80 years old, and women very rarely. Among the Polish corpses, hyperbrachycephaly is very rare, brachycephaly more common, mesocephaly and dolichocephaly very common, hyperdolichocephaly rare. Plagiocephaly common.

I can offer you Jewish skulls ♂/ 20–50 years old for the price of 25 reichsmarks and give you the exact age and birthplace, though the latter signifies little for Jews. In addition to the Jewish skulls, I can also provide plaster death masks of the respective individuals for a price of 15 reichsmarks. I could also make plaster busts of the quintessential eastern Jews for you so that you can see the form of the head and the often very peculiar ears.

"typical Jews," they made plaster casts or whole busts of "Jewish faces" and took hair samples. On completion of the project, the SS deported most of the Jews to Buchenwald, where many died.[37]

Physical anthropology also legitimized Nazi racism through racial exhibitions. In May 1939, the Natural History Museum opened a special exhibition, prepared by the anthropologist Josef Wastl, entitled *The Mental and Racial Phenotype of the Jews.* Wastl received assistance from the SS, who provided him with Jewish artifacts seized from the Jewish Museum of Vienna, and from Vienna's Central Police, who supplied him with mug shots of Jews. The exhibition sought to illustrate the physical characteristics of Jews, their foreign features, and, therefore, their foreign mentality. The look of the display, with numerous maps and charts, imparted a scientific seriousness to accompanying political posters, such as "The Jewish Question can only be solved through a clear separation of the non-Jews from the Jews."[38]

Wastl later collected other "anthropological materials." In 1942, he purchased a series of "Jewish skulls," plaster death masks, and "Polish skulls" from the Anatomical Institute at the Reich University of Posen (in annexed Poland). The institute's director, Hermann Voss, collected corpses of Polish resistance fighters put to death by the local Gestapo and of Jews from concentration camps. He even attended guillotine executions in order to conduct scientific experiments the moment the individual died.[39] Between 1942 and 1943, Wastl also obtained 220 Jewish skeletons exhumed from a Jewish cemetery in Vienna. He collected 350 plaster-cast masks, 7,000 anthropometric questionnaires, and more than 300,000 black-and-white pictures, color slides, and photographs.[40]

In March 1942, anthropologist Josef Wastl purchased skulls and plaster death masks of Poles and Jews, executed by the Gestapo, from the Anatomical Institute of the Reich University of Posen, for study at the Natural History Museum, in Vienna. *Naturhistorisches Museum, Vienna*

The Vienna Stadium Study

In September 1939, in Vienna, anthropologists of the Natural History Museum performed a racial study on Jews imprisoned in a city stadium.

Soon after war began, on September 10 and 11, some one thousand stateless Polish Jews were arrested in Vienna on the order of Reinhard Heydrich, chief of the Security Police, within the framework of a Reichwide action. A name registry was created simultaneously, to include their wives and any children under 16. Because of overcrowded jails, the prisoners were interned in Vienna's Prater stadium; in addition, 124 residents from rest homes that belonged to Vienna's Israelite Cultural Association were rounded up, men ranging in age from 74 to 84.

During the week of September 24, an eight-member anthropological commission from the Natural History Museum, under the leadership of Josef Wastl, came to the stadium. They measured 440 of the more than one thousand imprisoned men, recorded individual data, and filled out detailed survey sheets. Almost all of the men were photographed. The anthropologists took hair samples from 105 and made face masks of 19.

Gershon Evan, formerly Gustav Pimselstein, was 16 when chosen as a research subject in the stadium. In his memoir, *Winds of Life,* he described the research procedure.

I was taken to a room whose furniture consisted of a chair and two tables. Tools covered one tabletop; the other one had just one small pillow. A camera mounted on a tripod stood in front of a wall that was partly covered by a large, white sheet.... A man in a white coat, the only person in the room, received me in a friendly manner, and throughout the performing of his work tried to set my mind at ease. Against the white sheet as a background, my face was photographed from the front and side; then my name, age, and additional background information was recorded. Subsequently the man entered the color of my hair, eyebrows, and eyes as well as the complexion of my skin. While he picked the tools to measure the length and width of my nose, ears, lips and eyebrows, I glanced at the cluttered table. Among the calipers, rulers, and unfamiliar things were a metal bowl, spatulas of different sizes, narrow flat sticks, a jar of water, and towels. A bag of plaster of Paris, its top torn open, leaned against the leg of the table.... My head on the pillow, I stretched out on the table and closed my eyes. The man advised me to relax, while he coated my face with a greasy substance. He applied it from the top of my forehead down to the throat and from ear to ear. The lubricant, he explained, was to prevent the hardened plaster of Paris from sticking to my skin. He instructed me to breathe naturally through my nose and not move once he started to apply the mixture. I heard scraping sounds as he stirred powder and water to the right consistency in the bowl, and then felt the creamy paste being spread over my face. From time to time he used the narrow, flat stick to keep the passage to my nostrils open. Eerie emotions and thoughts passed through my head as I waited

Chaim Chiel Aron, one of the subjects of the Vienna study, died in Buchenwald concentration camp in February 1940. *Photo: ca. 1920s.* Henry Aron

for the plaster to harden. Perhaps I imagined it, but the soft mixture seemed to get heavier as it turned into a mask. After quite a while the man loosened the hardened cast by wiggling it from side to side. When he lifted it carefully off my face, it did not hurt. The only sensation was a suction-cup effect.... Before I left, he smilingly handed me a cigarette. A precious gift for a smoker, but hardly one for me. At least I made one fellow prisoner happy.

The research ended midday on September 30. That same day, the measured prisoners as well as the others were taken from the stadium to the Vienna West train station and, except for a few released after a medical examination, were deported to the Buchenwald concentration camp. The next day, it was business as usual again at the stadium. There was a soccer match between a Viennese and a Budapest club.

The prisoners arrived in the city of Weimar on October 2. After marching by foot from the train station to the overfilled Buchenwald concentration camp, a march marked by severe abuse from the guard personnel, they were crammed together in a specially built camp. It consisted of one barrack and a few tents.

In the first weeks and months of imprisonment, 318 of the 440 surveyed men died from a dysentery epidemic, the result of hunger, deplorable hygiene, and inadequate medical care. This must be seen as one of the first mass-murder actions of the Nazi regime on German Reich territory. After the breakup of the special camp in January and February 1940, because of the risks of further epidemics, the few survivors from Vienna were placed in various blocks of the main camp. The fate of the surviving 122 men measured in the stadium can be partially reconstructed. Sixteen, including Pimselstein, were released in February 1940. Thirty were murdered in early 1942, in the so-called Operation 14f13, in the "euthanasia" murder facilities at Bernburg, Sonnenstein, and Hartheim. Twenty-six were deported to Auschwitz in October 1942, on an order by Himmler to make all the concentration camps on German soil "free of Jews." Eleven were liberated from the Buchenwald concentration camp, and an additional 15 from other camps. The wives and children of many of the measured men were deported from Vienna to ghettos and concentration camps—and murdered there. Some children survived; they were sent abroad with the help of a *Kindertransport*.

— by Margit Berner and Claudia Spring

Pimselstein's passport photo, 1940. *Gershon Evan*

Plaster casting of Gustav Pimselstein, September 1939. *Naturhistorisches Museum, Vienna*

Calipers used by Dr. Josef Wastl, who, along with Eugen Fischer and other anthropologists in the Reich, provided expert opinions on individuals' "racial" origins. The determination became a matter of life and death for those they studied. *Naturhistorisches Museum, Vienna*

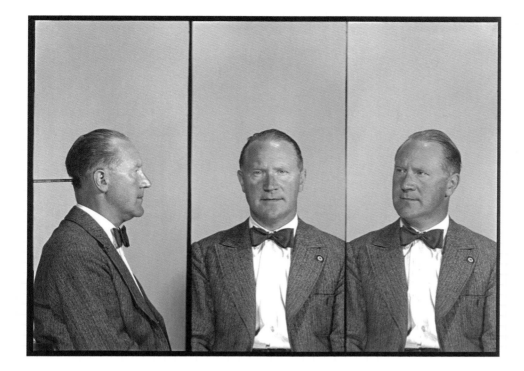

Anthropologist Dr. Josef Wastl, photographed in his laboratory, ca. 1939. *Naturhistorisches Museum, Vienna*

Another major racial investigation of Jews was undertaken by Elfriede Flieth-mann, assistant at the section for Racial and Ethnic Research of the Institute for German Work in the East (*Institut für deutsche Ostarbeit*, or IdO), and Dora Kahlich, from the Vienna Anthropological Institute, who, in June 1942, studied the Jews of the Tarnow ghetto, in occupied Poland. The IdO, located in Cracow, in the General Government of occupied Poland, was a research institute established in 1940 to assist the Nazi regime in policy making.[41] IdO anthropological teams investigated villages, ghettos, POW camps, and concentration camps, making extensive ethnographic and anthropometric evaluations. IdO researchers also surveyed the local population, seeking to detect Polish families suitable for re-Germanization.

Prior to World War II, 55 percent of the population of Tarnow was Jewish. The ghetto was established by the Nazis in spring 1942. Shortly after Fliethmann and Kahlich's investigation was completed, a first convoy of several thousand Jews was deported to the death camp of Belzec. At the same time, a significant number of Jews in Tarnow were Viennese Jews who had been deported there. By late 1943, Tarnow was declared "*Judenrein*" ("free of Jews"). The two anthropologists were protected by armed SS squads during their survey. In less than two weeks, the team examined 106 families, representing 565 persons. For each person, they recorded 18 head and 13 body measurements, made fingerprints and palm prints, and took four pictures of the head and three pictures of the full, naked body. The scientists were perfectly aware of the situation of the Jews, and they knew they had little time to carry out their survey before "this valuable material [was] lost." Fliethmann wanted to ascertain if the psychological characteristics of the Galician Jews ("sense for acquisition

Hans Frank *(center)*, the Nazi administrator of occupied Poland, views a Torah scroll seized from Jews for study at the Institute for German Work in the East, Cracow, September 23, 1941. *Records of the Institut für Deutsche Ostarbeit, Box 56.2, #4A, National Anthropological Archives, Smithsonian Institution, Washington, D.C.*

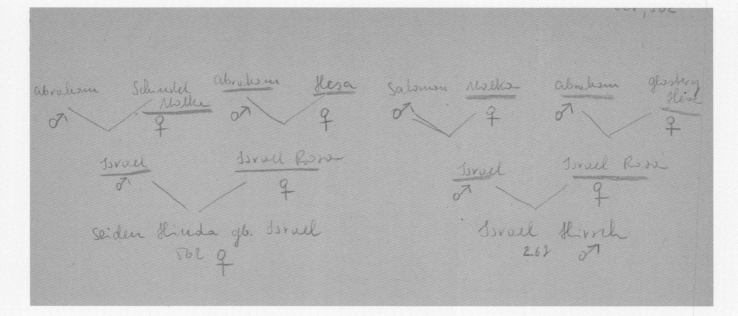

In spring 1942, anthropologists from the University of Vienna, assisted by the SS, studied 106 Jewish families in Tarnow. Funded by the Institute for German Work in the East, the research included a genealogy *(above)* of Hinda Seiden and her brother, Hirsch Israel, and photographs of Hinda Seiden's family: her husband, Elias, and their three children, Majta, 18, Abraham, 16, and Jakob, 10. None of the Seidens survived the Holocaust; all perished at Belzec ca. 1942. *Records of the Institut für Deutsche Ostarbeit, Box 30, folder 1, National Anthropological Archives, Smithsonian Institution. Washington, D.C.; Naturhistorisches Museum, Vienna*

Hinda Seiden   Israel Hirsch

Hinda Seiden   Elias Seiden

Majta Seiden   Abraham Seiden   Jakob Seiden

Views of streets and the Jewish inhabitants of Tarnow and Nowy Sacz, in occupied Poland, taken in April and May 1942 by researchers from the Institute for German Work in the East (IdO) interested in documenting for posterity this rapidly "disappearing" population.
Records of the Institut für Deutsche Ostarbeit, Box 56.2, strip 25, National Anthropological Archives, Smithsonian Institution, Washington, D.C.

V. Brauner, a Jewish artist, sculpted this head for German officials in Lodz. Brauner died, at Auschwitz, in 1944. *Zydowski Instytut Historyczny, Warsaw*

The head of a Jewish youth was sculpted from wood by the Jewish artist M. Winiarski for German officials in the occupied Polish city of Lodz. *Zydowski Instytut Historyczny, Warsaw*

and business," "unscrupulousness") could be associated through correlation statistics with the physical traits of the Near Eastern race (prominent nose, and so on).[42]

Three doctoral students of Eugen Fischer, under supervision of one of his assistants in late 1939 or early 1940, also conducted research on Jews in the ghetto of Lodz.[43] No trace is left of this research, however, except some pictures of Jews of the ghetto that were published, in 1943, in an antisemitic book by Fischer.[44]

IDENTIFYING THE JEWS

A major challenge for Nazi bureaucracy was to locate its victims.[45] Racial anthropology was unable to diagnose who was a member, in the Nazi sense, of the "Jewish race." The 1935 Nuremberg racial laws defined "Jews" in Nazi Germany based on family genealogy; the laws included two categories of mixed German-Jewish lineage *(Mischlinge)*. In the overwhelming majority of cases, Jewish origin was proven through official and family documents. Therefore, the Nazis attempted to collect all birth and marriage certificates and seize all registers from the Jewish community in Germany and in occupied countries. Although an army of genealogy specialists gathered documents, proving descent could be disputed and often was unclear; up to 750,000 individuals fell into various *Mischlinge* categories. Since each category had different status and rights, distinctions ultimately became critical.

Settling unclear or disputed ancestry was the work of a special agency, the Reich Genealogical Office *(Reichssippenamt)*. This office made copies of 350,000 church-register books and created a huge card-index system, which had one million

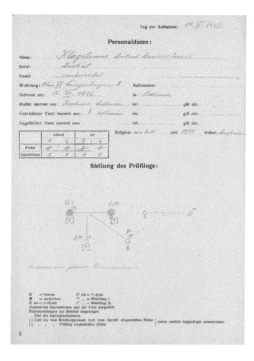
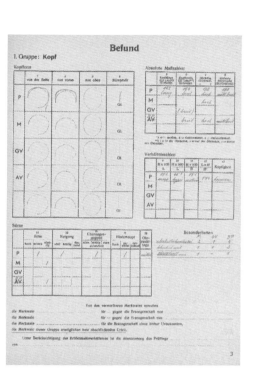
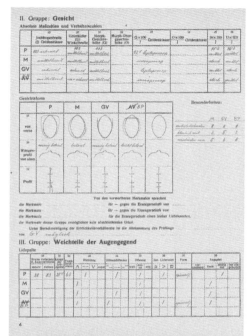

personal cards by 1936. But if such documents were missing or in case of unclear paternity (illegitimate birth), the Reich Genealogical Office turned to "genetic and anthropological certificates" issued by appointed experts—anthropologists, human geneticists, and serologists (specialists in blood serum research).[46]

Because blood-group testing alone was also insufficient to establish paternity, anthropologists were asked to produce paternity certificates that could positively identify the biological father.[47] A biometric method was used to determine the degree of morphological similarity between the child and the mother and the potential biological father, based on comparative analysis of fingerprints and palm prints, color of hair, skin, and iris, shape of the head, face, nose, and ears, and other morphological characteristics. Yet, the real boom in "genetic paternity certificates" began with the Nazi enactment of the racial laws against Jews. Frequently, German citizens were required to bring proof of Aryan ancestry; they needed to produce an official document—the "certificate of origin." Between 1933 and 1940, the Reich Genealogical Office issued some 150,000 certificates of origin. From 1941 on, "genetic certificates of race and origin," according to the result, meant life or death for the individual. None of the anthropologists or human geneticists was forced to issue those certificates, yet they produced thousands of them.

Anthropologists from RuSHA were also involved in the "Final Solution of the Jewish *Mischlinge* Question."[48] RuSHA's Genealogical Department collected information about "quarter Jews," "half Jews," and baptized Jews. In March 1943, RuSHA chief Otto Hofmann wrote to Himmler about the "Final Solution of the Jewish *Mischlinge* Question," adding to his letter a report made by the anthropologist and head of the

Excerpts from an expert anthropological study of "racial" descent, prepared in 1942. *Naturhistorisches Museum, Vienna*

Josef Mengele was the last in a long chain of experts, all physicians by training, who promoted a biological or scientific racism that helped make the Holocaust possible. Several of these men attended an anthropology conference in Tübingen, Germany, in mid-September 1937: Mengele *(second row, far left)*; his academic mentor, geneticist Otmar von Verschuer *(second row, seventh from right)*; and Verschuer's mentor and later colleague, anthropologist Eugen Fischer *(on Verschuer's right)*. Alfred Ploetz, the elderly founder of German racial hygiene, was also present *(second row, center)*. *Archiv zur Geschichte der Max-Planck-Gesellschaft, Berlin, Courtesy of Benoit Massin*

Racial Office of RuSHA, Professor Bruno Schultz. Schultz proposed the racial screening of the quarter Jews (one Jewish grandparent out of four) to decide their status. Those with too many "Jewish traits" would be put in the same category as the half Jews and subjected to the same "treatment" (sterilization or deportation). They would also lose their German citizenship, a policy that was already applied in the Protectorate of Bohemia and Moravia. Although it was never formally adopted, Himmler was enthusiastic about Schultz's idea of systematic racial screening.[49]

THE SEARCH FOR A RACIAL DIAGNOSIS

Much scientific research in racial science, human genetics, and serology during the Third Reich dealt with discovering diagnostic techniques to determine a person's race. The search focused on the genetics of blood groups, fingerprints, and numerous physical and racial characteristics, from the shape of nostrils to the structure of the iris of the eye. The KWI for Anthropology led in research in racial genetics and dermatoglyphics (the genetics of fingerprints and palm prints). A major thrust of blood-group research attempted to identify differences in the blood serum of human races, seeking to locate specific markers, or characteristics, unique to each race.

As scientists were particularly keen to find blood markers for Jews and Gypsies, serological tests were conducted on these groups in concentration camps. One of the most significant research projects on blood for the purpose of racial identification was conducted by Verschuer in Berlin with Mengele in Auschwitz, who sent collected blood samples for processing to the KWI for Anthropology laboratory.[50] In October 1944,

"Gypsy" children who were subjects of Mengele's research at Auschwitz between 1943 and 1945. The original photograph was found in Mengele's files after the war. *Panstwowe Muzeum Auschwitz-Birkenau w Oswiecimiu*

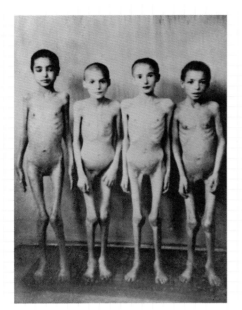

Hyg.-bakt. Unters.-Stelle der Waffen-SS, Südost   Auschwitz OS., am **29.Juni 1944.**

Anliegend wird übersandt :   **(12-jähriges Kind)**
Material: **Kopf einer Leiche** entnommen am
zu untersuchen auf   **Histologische Schnitte**
Name, Vorname :
Dienstgrad, Einheit :   **siehe Anlage**
Klinische Diagnose :

Anschrift der einsendenden Dienststelle :   **H.-Krankenbau**
Zigeunerlager Auschwitz II, B II e

Bemerkungen :   **Der l.Lagerarzt**
K.L.Ausohw tz II

SS-Hauptsturmführer.
(Stempel, Unterschrift)

Receipt, signed by Mengele, authorizing the transfer of the head of a 12-year-old Gypsy as "research material," June 29, 1944. *Panstwowe Muzeum Auschwitz-Birkenau w Oswiecimiu*

Verschuer, by then director of the Anthropology Institute in Berlin, reported that "blood groups of over 200 persons of various racial types have been processed."[51]

Dermatoglyphics comprised a second thrust of racial identification research. Specialists in fingerprints tried to pinpoint races using the skin relief on fingertips. Abel collected 5,000 fingerprints and palm prints from various regions of Germany and other European countries, and, later, in his racial survey on Soviet POWs, he collected another 20,000 prints.

The third area of research, racial genetics, studied such morphological characteristics as the skeleton, muscular system, and shape of the head and face, including skin, hair, and eye color. The inheritance of every bodily detail was investigated—eyelids, eyebrows, ears, nostril shape, hair color, spinal column, and so on. Among the methods researchers relied on were "bastard" research, genealogical analysis, twin research, and embryology. The KWI for Anthropology had one of the largest twin registries in Europe, if not the world, with 4,000 pairs of twins in its data bank. Verschuer used twins to study the inheritance of various human pathologies—tuberculosis, for instance—but also of such racial characteristics as hair color or anthropological dimensions. Dead human embryos, collected by the institute from hospitals and women's clinics, were also used to study inherited pathologies, as well as to determine at what stage racial differences appeared in humans.[52]

Dr. Karin Magnussen, of the KWI for Anthropology, interested in the genetics of eye pigmentation, gained access to "human material" from Auschwitz through Mengele, cooperating with him on a research project involving experiments on children. Magnussen received packages from Auschwitz containing the eyes of camp inmates,

Mengele studied the inheritance of dwarfism, using as subjects members of the Ovitz family. This photo was taken prior to the Jewish family's deportation to Auschwitz in spring 1944, when they were under the guard of Hungarian police. *Ovitz Family, Haifa, Courtesy of Yehuda Koren and Eilat Negev*

murdered in order to obtain the genetic material. Each shipment was accompanied by an anthropological evaluation of eye color on the living person, a personal file with genealogical and medical data, and the autopsy report. She intended to publish her findings in a scientific journal, but the course of the war prevented publication.[53]

The image of racial science that emerges from these various research projects is not only of a pseudoscience based on speculation and prejudices, such as the racial psychology of the amateur Hans F. K. Günther, but also of a discipline with all the characteristics of a "hard" biomedical science, based on observation, measurements, laboratory instruments, experiments, and genetics. Blood-group research or racial genetics in Nazi Germany used what were then the most modern methods in human genetics, including twin research, statistical models in population genetics, embryology, and developmental genetics. In the case of German physical anthropology and human genetics, Nazism did not destroy science. On the contrary, Nazism strongly supported science and gave it a central relevance for politics and for the daily life of citizens in German society. It also empowered a scientific clan— the racist and hard-line eugenics advocates of "human selection"—who already held a hegemonic position in the scientific community. Actually, one can even consider that Nazism gave the scientific community the possibility of imposing its own worldview on the rest of society. Racial anthropologists and medical geneticists intervened in almost every aspect of Nazi racial policy: the sterilization of colored "mixed-race" children, the "solution of the Gypsy Problem," SS racial policy (particularly in Eastern occupied territories), and the "Jewish Question." Not only did these scientists help the regime, sometimes they directly inspired its murderous policies.

A group of children, including twins who were subjects of Mengele's experiments, at Auschwitz after the liberation of the camp by Soviet forces in January 1945. *Belorusskiy gosudarstvennyy arkhiv, Dzerzhinsk*

NAZI "EUTHANASIA" PROGRAMS

BY MICHAEL BURLEIGH

In pursuing its goal of a cohesive, racially pure society, National Socialism sought to cleanse the German "national community" *(Volksgemeinschaft)* of people deemed racially "alien" and eugenically "unfit." The Nazi regime attempted to turn utopian theory into practice by inaugurating a number of eugenics-based programs. In addition to positive eugenic strategies, such as the promotion of healthy diets and lifestyles, and the encouragement of racially pure and genetically healthy couples to have large numbers of children, the regime also launched brutal, negative eugenic programs, including compulsory sterilization and the systematic mass murder of disabled and mentally ill people. Euphemistically referring to it as "mercy death," this latter Nazi "euthanasia" program provided both the effective methods and the trained personnel that were subsequently deployed to liquidate millions in the extermination camps of the Holocaust.

The notion of a dignified, "gentle death" is an ancient one, and discussion of voluntary euthanasia has been common to many modern societies, including Germany. World War I seems to have been the time when this issue became entwined with eugenicists' goals to reverse modern medicine's "counter-selective" process, which, by keeping the weak and sick alive, was promoting survival of the unfit.

"You Are Sharing the Load! A Hereditarily Ill Person Costs 50,000 Reichsmarks on Average Up to the Age of Sixty," reproduced in a high school biology textbook, by Jakob Graf. *USHMM Collection*

In *Authorization of the Destruction of Life Unworthy of Life*, published in 1920, legal scholar Karl Binding and psychiatrist Alfred Hoche argued that killing incurable "idiots" and other "worthless" life would be a defensible form of healing the state organism. *USHMM Collection*

The massive wartime loss of young males and the subsequent chronic economic problems of the Weimar Republic led some experts to contrast this with the ways in which the modern welfare state was keeping alive so-called "unproductive" people, institutionalized and under custodial care.

In 1920, the legal scholar Karl Binding and the psychiatrist Alfred Hoche, whose only son had been killed in battle on the western front, published a tract entitled *Authorization of the Destruction of Life Unworthy of Life.*[1] Binding and Hoche began by sketching out many of the arguments used to justify voluntary euthanasia for the terminally ill. These might appear unremarkable to advocates of such measures today; nonetheless, the authors had to adjust traditional notions of right and wrong, and attempted to demonstrate the relativity of such notions as "the sanctity of human life" by simply pointing to what was practiced in ancient Sparta or among contemporary primitive peoples. Next, they assessed the human personality of people they described as "incurable idiots," arguing that sympathy for such people was misplaced: "Where there is no suffering, there can be no pity." The authors made a number of economic arguments, designed to highlight the allegedly exorbitant costs of caring for disabled or mentally ill people. The latter were "ballast existences," a deadweight that represented so much "life unworthy of living." The measure of relative value to the nation was underscored with a poignant, patriotic contrast to the devastating losses of "fit" Germans during the war: "If one imagines...a battlefield covered with thousands of dead youths...and then our institutes for idiots and their care...one is most appalled by...the sacrifice of the best of humanity while the best care is lavished on life of negative worth." At no time did the authors mention race.

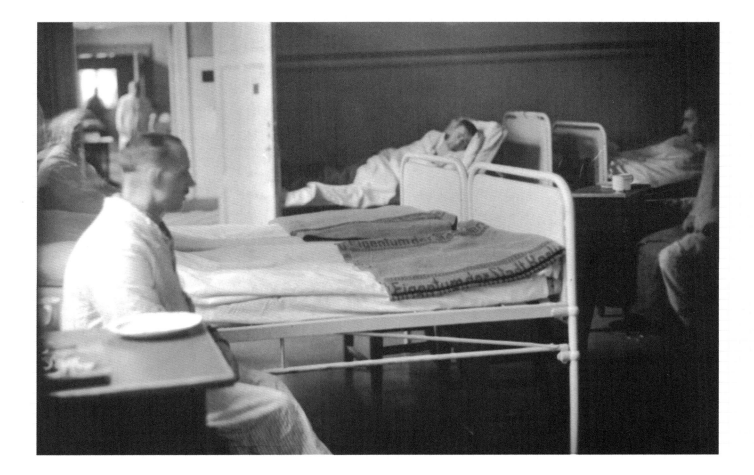

Ironically, the very sacrifice Binding and Hoche demanded of such people had already been made by 70,000 inmates of psychiatric hospitals who had starved to death as a result of the Allied blockade in the 1914–18 war and German rationing policies.

Although this tract sparked much controversy at the time, it provided many of the rationalizations employed by the Nazis nearly 20 years later for killing psychiatric patients and other institutionalized individuals. So, too, did a 1923 poll conducted by an asylum director in the state of Saxony, which claimed that 73 percent of the parents of his handicapped charges felt so overburdened by their responsibilities that they wished the children had died.[2] A smaller number even said that, in theory, they would not object to the state covertly killing their children, ironically fore-shadowing later Nazi practice. This poll may have influenced the decision that made infants the first group of victims in the regime's "euthanasia" program.

Beginning with small clusters of enthusiastic supporters of eugenic ideas, many countries spawned organizations promoting eugenics that attracted medical professionals and welfare experts. In Germany, their ranks often included socialist as well as conservative orientations and usually represented Protestants as well as a smattering of dissident Catholics, since both churches operated large health and welfare networks. Apart from such euthanasia advocates as Binding and Hoche, more positive trends in psychiatric medicine during the 1920s and 1930s contributed to the adoption of radical solutions to social problems. Psychiatry had a poor image, whether for merely warehousing the chronically ill in prisonlike institutions or abusing shell-shocked soldiers with crude technologies and therapies in wartime. According to popular folklore, madness often rubbed off on psychiatrists.[3]

Crowding became common in psychiatric hospitals by the early 1930s. Wittenau Psychiatric Clinic, Berlin, 1930. *Landesarchiv Berlin (A Rep. 003-04-04 Nr. 3)*

Doctor with patients diagnosed with "depressive psychosis." *Deutsches Hygiene-Museum, Dresden*

A number of reforms were designed to improve the profession's image and status. These included making asylums resemble hospitals rather than prisons, and fashioning psychiatry into a more scientific branch of medicine that could achieve tangible results equivalent to setting a fractured arm or leg. The introduction of occupational therapy and outpatient provision gave patients a much needed routine and a purpose in life, and brought psychiatry into the wider world beyond the asylums. These reforms were also cost-efficient, an important point at a time of national economic austerity. Up to 80 percent of asylum inmates could be engaged in low or unpaid work within institutions that became almost self-sufficient, while the cost of outpatient facilities for the entire Munich area was less than that of keeping one person in an asylum bed for a year.[4] A new range of drug and shock therapies, eventually including electroconvulsive shock therapy, also appeared to help acutely ill patients. These innovations gave psychiatrists a renewed optimism about the curative powers of their branch of medicine. Psychiatric journals vividly recounted emotionally moving "before and after" accounts of people who had been cured of terrible mental illnesses by concerned psychiatric scientists.

All of these reforms, however, also exposed a wealth of problems to psychiatrists, some of whom were increasingly influenced by contemporary eugenic ideas. Developments in the diagnosis of psychiatric disorders, such as outpatient work and family visitations, revealed a huge incidence of "hidden" mental illness among the population that "required" a correspondingly drastic solution. Occupational therapy (for instance, weaving or gardening) introduced the capacity to work as an indicator of recovery, and the application of new treatment methods to acute cases high-

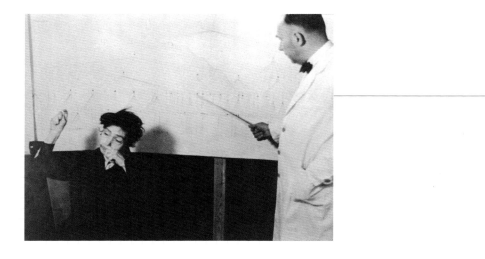

Dr. Kurt Pohlisch, an academic psychiatrist, demeans a patient during a genetics lecture, 1937. *Archiv der Rheinischen Landesklinik, Bonn*

Psychiatric institutions provided "work therapy" for fitter patients, a measure that also helped cut institutional costs. 1930. *Landesarchiv Berlin (A Rep. 003-04-04 Nr. 3)*

NAZI "EUTHANASIA" PROGRAMS

lighted the problem of the chronically ill languishing idly under dire conditions in the neglected back wards of institutions. The years from 1924 to 1929 saw a steady increase in long-term patients: The total number of psychiatric patients rose dramatically from 185,397 to more than 300,000. The advent of the Nazi regime, in 1933, provided a political environment in which advocates of the most extreme eugenic solutions to these problems were given free rein.

In 1933, Hitler's cabinet promulgated the Law for the Prevention of Genetically Diseased Offspring, which introduced a large-scale program of eugenic sterilization. This raised physicians to positions of sentinels watching over the genetic health of the entire nation as it flowed through the generations. They believed there could be a "scientific" quick fix to complex problems. In fact, as British biologist Lancelot Hogben pointed out, these eugenic solutions would take 8,000 years to have much of an impact and, therefore, were irrelevant for practical purposes.[5] Eugenics also involved medical professionals in breaches of every ethical standard in medicine, such as their duty to the individual patient as opposed to the notion of a biological collective (the German people, or *Volk*), or their obligation to respect medical confidentiality. Physicians and psychiatrists not only initiated measures for sterilizations but also sat as judges on the more than 200 Hereditary Health Courts that legitimated them—in flagrant breach of conventional legal practice. Increasingly, the criteria used to sterilize people reflected middle-class prejudices toward perceived antisocial behavior and lifestyles of poor people rather than medical or psychiatric criteria. Even the latter were highly arbitrary, exempting, for instance, Nazi Party members of obviously low intelligence who otherwise might have been defined as feebleminded and subject to sterilization.

"Germany was Proud of Having the Best Lunatic Asylums." Photograph of a display from a Nazi eugenics exhibition that briefly appeared at several venues in the United States in 1934 and 1935. Growing anti-Nazi sentiments stopped its circulation.
Buffalo Museum of Science

The sterilization program was backed with a massive propaganda campaign, consisting of film as well as printed materials, about the new role of the "genetic doctor" *(Erbarzt)* or the cost savings that would result from stemming the flow of eugenic damage through the generations. Extremely vulnerable people were transformed by this propaganda into a growing, menacing threat to German society. Illustrations in Nazi publications, for instance, demonstrated how, over time, a "normal" person literally shrank next to an ever-larger image of a "moron." Some of this German propaganda simply plagiarized U.S. eugenic prototypes regarding the long-term costs of such white-trash families as the Jukes, whom American eugenicists were similarly keen to sterilize. Propaganda also sought to foment mass resentment against persons in custodial settings. It distorted and decried the allegedly luxurious conditions enjoyed by the inhabitants of Germany's asylums—some were indeed converted baroque palaces—contrasting them to the dark slums where the healthy children of "honest" German workers had to play. This was a travesty of the truth. The Nazis deliberately starved asylums of

BERLIN, 1.Sept.1939.

ADOLF HITLER

Reichsleiter B o u h l e r und

Dr. med. B r a n d t

sind unter Verantwortung beauftragt, die Befug -

nisse namentlich zu bestimmender Ärzte so zu er -

weitern, dass nach menschlichem Ermessen unheilbar

Kranken bei kritischster Beurteilung ihres Krank -

heitszustandes der Gnadentod gewährt werden kann.

Hitler's note authorizing "mercy death" for "incurable" patients, September 1, 1939. *NARA, College Park, Md.*

Hitler greeting Philipp Bouhler, head of his private chancellery and coadministrator of Operation T-4, October 1, 1938. *Bundesarchiv Koblenz*

NAZI "EUTHANASIA" PROGRAMS

resources, with doctor to patient ratios worsening to 1:500 in some institutions.[6] Many asylums were headed by psychiatrists (sometimes, members of the SS) more interested in economy measures than in patient welfare, subjecting patients to unhygienic living conditions and providing little actual treatment or care. This atmosphere of pervasive neglect only encouraged some psychiatrists to think in terms of policies that went beyond sterilization. War provided the opportunity.

Several interrelated factors explain why the Nazi leadership opted to launch the euthanasia program on the outbreak of war in the fall of 1939. As in the case of the Jews, Hitler seems to have regarded war as a pretext and cover for policies that would have been more difficult to implement in peacetime. Conditions of secrecy are easier to impose in a national emergency, and people can be mobilized behind the language of sacrifice and struggle. On two occasions, in 1929 and 1935, Hitler expressed the general intention of using a war to decimate the ranks of the eugenically unsound.[7] In late 1939, he issued a perfunctory note on his private letterhead that licensed both Philipp Bouhler, the head of the Chancellery of the Führer, and Dr. Karl Brandt, Hitler's personal physician, to authorize designated doctors to carry out "mercy killings." It is worth emphasizing that this document had no legal status whatsoever, and that throughout the Third Reich, euthanasia remained a crime of manslaughter and murder.

Yet, even before the killing of adult patients officially began, a special children's euthanasia program had already been initiated. On August 18, 1939, the Reich Ministry of the Interior circulated a decree ordering midwives and physicians to report all cases of infants born with such physical deformities or mental conditions as idiocy, microcephaly, hydrocephaly, missing limbs or cleavages of the head and

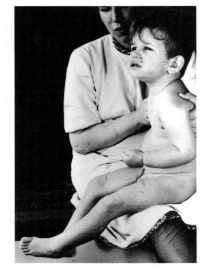

Norbert P. was killed at
the Wittenau Psychiatric
Clinic, Berlin. Infants
and children up to three
years old were the initial
victims of the children's
"euthanasia" program.
*Karl Bonhoeffer-
Nervenklinik, Berlin*

This decree ordered mid-
wives and physicians to
report infants born with
specified medical condi-
tions. Reflecting the
regime's need for discre-
tion, it did not appear in
the official publication
of decrees of the Ministry
of the Interior. *Bundesarchiv
Berlin*

The methods of killing children ranged from
overdoses of the sedative Luminal to starvation, deadly injections of morphine, and
gassing. *Unternehmensgeschichte/Archiv
der Bayer AG, Leverkusen*

spinal cord, and paralysis.[8] Hitler's brief authorization mobilized the bureaucratic structures to then act on the reports—to assess and kill these malformed infants. These children were selected as the initial target group since it was anticipated that here would lie the least line of resistance should news of these measures become public. The parents of children selected for murder were then offered the most up-to-date treatment in more than 30 specially designated "pediatric wards." In reality, these clinics, or wards, were operated by handpicked and volunteer physicians and nurses whose function was to kill the infants. Various medications were used for this purpose—injections of morphine, overdoses of the sedative Luminal or the sleeping pill Veronal, usually dissolved in liquid or food. Sometimes, these drugs did not kill immediately but did precipitate deadly medical compli-cations, such as pneumonia, allowing physicians to list "natural" causes of death. Additionally, some children were murdered simply through starvation.[9] The methods were devised, and the children's fates evaluated, on the recommendation of a small team of experts—Werner Catel, Hans Heinze, and Ernst Wentzler—all pediatricians in charge of their own clinics in the Berlin area. More than 5,000 children, from toddlers to juveniles as old as 16, were killed in this first euthanasia program.

In targeting Germany's adult asylum population—authorized by Hitler's letter— a planning team of civil servants and psychiatrists was established within the Chancellery of the Führer, but physically based at a Berlin villa at Tiergartenstrasse 4, from which the operation derived the code name Operation T-4. Brandt, Bouhler, and his deputy, Viktor Brack, organized both scope and methods of the euthanasia program. These men used a simple ratio to identify the proportion of people to be killed. If ten persons in every

"Light and Air in the Home." This poster reflects Dr. Wentzler's interest in developing treatments for rickets, a bone disease afflicting children who lack vitamin D from underexposure to sunlight. 1926. *Deutsches Hygiene-Museum, Dresden*

Ernst Wentzler's pediatric clinic, in Berlin, served many wealthy families, as well as such high-ranking Nazi officials as General Field Marshall Hermann Göring. Although Wentzler had developed methods to treat premature infants or children with severe birth defects (including an incubator dubbed the "Wentzler warmer"), he also supported ending the lives of the "incurably ill." From 1939 to 1945, Wentzler served as a primary coordinator of the pediatric "euthanasia" program, evaluating patient forms and ordering the killing of several thousand children. *National Library of Medicine, NIH, Bethesda, Md.*

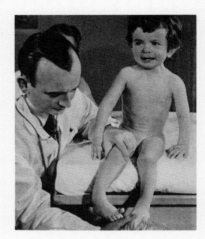

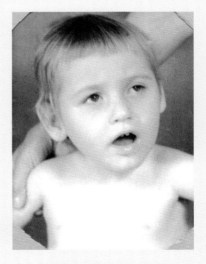

Edith F., a victim of the children's "euthanasia" program. *DÖW, Vienna*

Tiergartenstrasse 4, Berlin, headquarters
for the secret "euthanasia" (murder)
program. The villa was confiscated earlier
from a Jewish family. *Landesarchiv Berlin*

Most of the girls shown in this 1938 photo, taken at the Alsterdorf institution for the care of the "feebleminded"
in Hamburg, were transported during the war to the special children's ward, Spiegelgrund, at Steinhof Hospital,
in Vienna, where many were killed. *Evangelische Stiftung Alsterdorf, Hamburg*

Wheelchair, ca. 1920, from the Kork
Institution for Epileptics. In 1940, two
T-4 bus transports took 113 patients
from Kork to the Grafeneck "euthanasia"
center, where they were gassed.
*Diakonie-Kork Epilepsiezentrum,
Kehl-Kork*

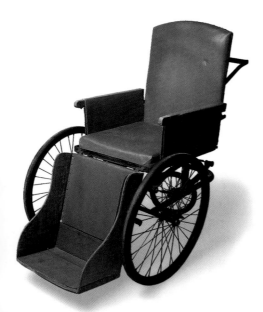

thousand people required psychiatric treatment, then five of these were inpatients; if one in five of these were killed, then, according to the ratio, the total number of victims would be 65,000 to 70,000—reflecting the percentage of the overall German population.[10] Using this formula, the most incapacitated patients—those who lacked the ability to work or were completely bedridden —were then selected for euthanasia.

Having identified "who," the planners turned to "how." Such scenarios as mass train derailments were deemed implausible. Forensic chemists then suggested carbon monoxide poisoning as an efficient mode of killing. Trials involving the delivery of bottled carbon monoxide gas through fake showerheads were soon under way, with supplies of the gas coming from the BASF chemical plant in Ludwigshafen, an I. G. Farben subsidiary. Next, the T-4 planners, through the Ministry of the Interior, introduced a registration system for all asylum inmates, based on forms that inquired into whether or not a person worked, received regular visits, had been institutionalized for five or more years, or had certain psychiatric or neurological diseases. A panel of expert assessors was created, consisting of leading psychiatrists, whose function was to decide whether a patient lived or died by marking these forms with a + or – and ? in doubtful cases. Armed with lists of those to be killed, a separate Community Patients' Transport Service removed patients from their home asylums, either detaining them in a network of transit institutions, which served as temporary holding centers, or sending them straight to the T-4 gassing facilities. These were established in six carefully selected institutions, which combined locations in remote areas with the added advantage of being near good rail or road connections. In addition to Brandenburg, the first site, located in an abandoned penitentiary, five asylums

Euthanasia Centers in Germany, 1940–45

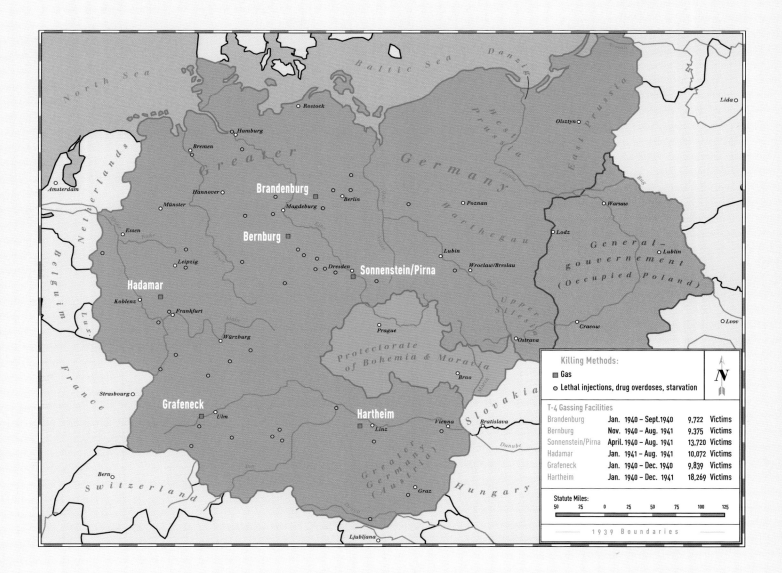

North Sea

Baltic Sea

Danzig

Rostock

Hamburg

Bremen

Amsterdam

Netherlands

Hannover

Münster

Essen

Belguim

Lux

Leipzig

Brandenburg

Magdeburg

Berlin

Poznan

Warsaw

Lodz

Lublin

Wroclaw/Breslau

Bernburg

Dresden

Sonnenstein/Pirna

Lubin

General–gouvernement (Occupied Poland)

West Prussia

East Prussia

Greater Germany

Warthegau

Olsztyn

Lida

Hadamar

Koblenz

Frankfurt

Würzburg

Prague

Upper Silesia

Cracow

Lvov

Lublin

France

Strasbourg

Grafeneck

Ulm

Protectorate of Bohemia & Moravia

Brno

Hartheim

Linz

Vienna

Slovakia

Bratislava

Ostrava

Bern

Switzerland

Greater Germany (Austria)

Graz

Danube

Hungary

Ljubljana

Killing Methods:

▪ Gas

○ Lethal injections, drug overdoses, starvation

N

T-4 Gassing Facilities			
Brandenburg	Jan. 1940 – Sept.1940	9,722	Victims
Bernburg	Nov. 1940 – Aug. 1941	9,375	Victims
Sonnenstein/Pirna	April. 1940 – Aug. 1941	13,720	Victims
Hadamar	Jan. 1941 – Aug. 1941	10,072	Victims
Grafeneck	Jan. 1940 – Dec. 1940	9,839	Victims
Hartheim	Jan. 1940 – Dec. 1941	18,269	Victims

Statute Miles:

50 25 0 25 50 75 100 125

1939 Boundaries

The prominent psychiatrist Paul Nitsche long combined the advocacy of treatment for "fitter" patients, utilizing occupational and electroshock therapy, with support for "mercy death" for "incurables." A member of the Nazi Party since May 1933, he served as deputy, then head, of the T-4 medical office, the division charged with selecting patients for gassing. *Sächsisches Hauptstaatsarchiv, Dresden*

Transport of patients from the Liebenau clinic, August 1940. *Stiftung Liebenau, Meckenbeuren*

Electroshock therapy machine, ca. 1942. In the late 1930s and early 1940s, calls for killing "life unworthy of life" grew stronger as more and more asylums came under the leadership of Nazi administrators or SS doctors. Electroshock therapy was developed and tried with patients deemed treatable. One aim was to cut down hospital stays and reduce the costs of care. *USHMM Collection, Gift of Medizin & Pharmaziehistorisches Museum, Wismar*

were also used to kill people— Bernburg, Grafeneck, Hadamar, and Sonnenstein, in Germany, and Hartheim, in Austria.[11]

The facilities were staffed by specially selected physicians and nurses, although some of these killing centers also continued to employ former staff members. If the senior medical professionals who ran the euthanasia program from its Medical Office (such as Paul Nitsche, who believed mercy killing heightened a doctor's sense of "responsibility," or Werner Heyde, professor of medicine at Würzburg, who was expert in sterilization cases and a fanatical SS officer) were eugenics enthusiasts, they were also very much tantalized by their unaccustomed proximity to real power. They, in turn, used their prestige and influence upon impressionable (and fanaticized) former students, who became the killers in white coats—students being one of the groups in the population converted almost en masse to Nazism. The physicians' presence was only essential to give mass murder a medicalized appearance, since literally anyone could easily turn on a gas valve. These doctors now functioned as intermediary technicians, whose ethical training was perfunctory or nonexistent. Many had become accustomed to regarding patients as an assemblage of malfunctioning mechanical parts or, simply, a nuisance. Many of them were not immune to careerism, greed, or political fanaticism.[12]

This dedicated cohort of killers inevitably interacted with the wider institutional framework, which included institutions run by the charitable networks of both Protestant and Roman Catholic churches. Asylum directors throughout Germany and Austria received the patient registration forms sent from the Ministry of the Interior; they were given between three and ten weeks to

Name of institution: ....

In: ....

First and last name of patient: .... Maiden name: ....

Date of birth: .... Place: .... District: ....

Last residence: .... District: ....

Single, married, widowed, divorced: .... Religion: .... Race:*] ....

Former profession: .... Nationality: .... War veteran: yes/no ....

War casualty (even if not in connection with mental illness): yes/no ....

How was war casualty proven and what does it consist of? ....

Address of nearest relative: ....

Regular visits and by whom (address): ....

Guardian or caregiver (name, address): ....

Cost-bearer: .... How long at that institution: ....

From where and when admitted: .... Since when ill: ....

Has been in other institutions, where and how long: ....

Twin yes/no: .... Mentally ill blood relatives: ....

Diagnosis: ....

Clinical description (previous history, course, state; in every case sufficient specifications on mental state!) ....

Very restless? yes/no .... Bedridden? yes/no ....

Incurable physical suffering: yes/no (which?) ....

For schizophrenia: Recent case .... Final condition: .... good remission ....

For feeblemindedness: subnormal .... imbecile .... idiot ....

For epilepsy: psychologically changed: .... Average frequency of seizures ....

Therapy (insulin, Cardiazol, malaria, Salvarsan, etc., when?) .... Long-term success: yes/no ....

Admitted on the basis of §51, §42b of the Penal Code, etc. .... by ....

Crime: .... Previous offenses: ....

Type of occupation (detailed description of work): ....

Constant/occasional occupation; independent worker yes/no: ....

Value of work performance (when possible compared to average healthy individual): ....

Do not mark in this space

.... Place, Date ....

Signature of the head physician or his representative (Physicians who are not psychiatric-neurological specialists must note this)

*German or related blood (German-blooded), Jew, Jewish Mischling 1st or 2d degree, Negro (Mischling).

return them. At first, many mistook this for a survey of untapped labor reserves and so deliberately underestimated patients' work capacities, which proved fatal to them. Others had no qualms in writing off the chronically ill residuum that had been marginalized by their own progressive psychiatric reformism.[13] The completed forms were either scrutinized by the central assessors themselves or were contracted out on a piecework basis to individual physicians, some of whom performed enormous feats of paper processing, handling up to 15,000 forms per month in an utterly mechanical manner. Payment per number of forms handled provided an extra incentive for speed.[14] Specially adapted postal buses then descended upon asylums, armed with alphabetical lists of patients allegedly subject for transfer to other institutions.

There were also instances of concerned asylum staff discharging vulnerable patients into the care of their families, finding them local employment, or desperately rewriting their medical records to exempt them from these policies. Tense scenes sometimes resulted when long-term patients were torn from the hands of compassionate and dedicated caregiving staff. Cunningly, the T-4 personnel anticipated how to deal with such opposition by allowing asylum directors to haggle over a small percentage of patients, whose lives they could then claim to have rescued, while the majority of their charges were killed. Enormous care was taken to keep these measures secret. The asylums where patients were killed were ringed with fences and signs warning of "danger of disease." Relatives of the victims were only notified of a person's transfer weeks after it had happened. In order to make inquiries more difficult, patients were often shipped to transit institutions, kept there for several weeks, and only then sent to a euthanasia facility.

Forms like this were submitted by institutions throughout Greater Germany, and were used by the medical experts of Operation T-4 to select patients to be killed in gassing facilities. *Landesarchiv Berlin (A Rep. 003-04-04 Nr. 16)*

Franz Karl Bühler
1864–1940

Bühler was an award-winning metalwork-er and a teacher at an artisan school in Strasbourg until he became afflicted with symptoms diagnosed as schizophrenia. He spent nearly 40 years in the Emmendingen Hospital in southern Germany. Bühler painted portraits of many inmates, believ-ing he was commissioned by the govern-ment to do so. On March 5, 1940, he was gassed at the Grafeneck killing center. His death notice claimed that he died of acute weakness of the heart muscle. *Stadtarchiv Offenburg*

TRANSPORTLISTE

ANSTALT: Heil- und Pflegeanstalt Emmendingen.

Durchgeführt am: 5. III 40

Nr.	Name	Vorname	Transp.Nr.	Krank.Nr.	Geburtstag	Geburtsort
1.	Schmutzler	Erich			24.1o.89	Meerane/Kr. Zwickau
2.	Duffner	Anton			8. 4. 84	Schönwald
3.	Ebling	Peter			11.12.69	Nierstein
4.	Frietsch	Erhard			11.2. 83	Stollhofen
5.	Fischer	Karl			11.12.9o	Neustadt i.Schw
6.	Gengenbach	Gottlieb			28.5. 81	Schellbronn
7.	Haas	Michael			1o.9. o1	Hepberg b. Ingolstadt
8.	Hochheim	Gottfried			8. 2. 8e	Koblenz
9.	Huber	Josef			2.3. 79	Ohlsbach
1o.	Walter	Otto			3. 3. 97	Sulz/A.Lahr
11.	Kohl	Michael			23.9. 96	Unterschneid-heim/Württ.
12.	Meier	Wilhelm			6. 5. 9o	Burgheim/A-Lahr
13.	Tiefbrunn	Valentin			25.11.8o	Gengenbach
14.	Wolfheim	Friedrich Israel			2o.7. 92	Berlin
15.	Bühler,	Franz Karl			28.8. 64	Offenburg
16.	Huber	Emil			12.2. 71	Basel
17.	Wellasch	Erich			2o.9. 96	Hamburg
18.	Hatz	Amalie			2. 1o.7o	Oberweiær
19.	Noll	Anna Maria			31.8. o1	Hugsweier
2o.	Hofeler	Leo,Isr.			17.2. 97	Eichstetten
21.	Scherle	Hermann			13.9. 98	Mannheim
22.	Wurmser	Max,Isr.			13.7. 77	Breisach
23.	Bausch	Marie			2o.1. 95	Litzelstetten

Transport list with Bühler's name *(line 15)*, March 5, 1940. Upon arrival at the Grafeneck "euthanasia" center, Bühler and the other patients were forced to undress, then shown into a sealed chamber disguised as a shower room, where they were killed by poisonous carbon monoxide gas piped in from outside tanks. *Staatsarchiv Freiburg*

Untitled, 1898–1900, pen and ink, with pencil, on paper. *Sammlung Prinzhorn, Heidelberg*

Lamentable Things, 1899, pen and ink, with pencil, on paper. *Sammlung Prinzhorn, Heidelberg*

Untitled, 1906, chalk with wash, on paper. *Sammlung Prinzhorn, Heidelberg*

Heretical Blasphemy, ca. 1906, chalk with wash, on paper. *Sammlung Prinzhorn, Heidelberg*

Untitled (Self-Portrait), September 1918, color pencil and chalk with wash, on paper. *Sammlung Prinzhorn, Heidelberg*

Untitled, undated, watercolor with gouache, on paper. *Sammlung Prinzhorn, Heidelberg*

Gertrud Fleck
1870–1940

Gertrud Fleck studied drawing and painting in school. After failing to find work, she returned to her childhood home in Dresden, where she began to suffer depression and show signs of serious mental illness. In 1901, Fleck was institutionalized. Initially, she was a violent patient who had to be sedated. One activity that kept Fleck occupied was painting. Her work drew the attention of doctors and nurses, who, by 1939, were describing her as a friendly patient. She was gassed at the Sonnenstein killing center in November 1940. *Bundesarchiv Berlin*

Untitled, 1911, watercolor, on paper. *Sammlung Prinzhorn, Heidelberg*

Untitled, 1915, watercolor with gouache, on paper. *Sammlung Prinzhorn, Heidelberg*

Alois Dallmayr
1883–1940

Born in Bavaria, Alois Dallmayr wanted to study natural history and medicine, but he could not because of a mental illness that originated from a concussion he suffered as a boy. Diagnosed with dementia praecox, Dallmayr was admitted to the Eglfing clinic in 1916; he remained there until his murder, by gassing, in the Hartheim killing center, in 1940. His paintings demonstrated his delusions (he portrayed himself as God), sexual confusion, and resentment toward his mother.

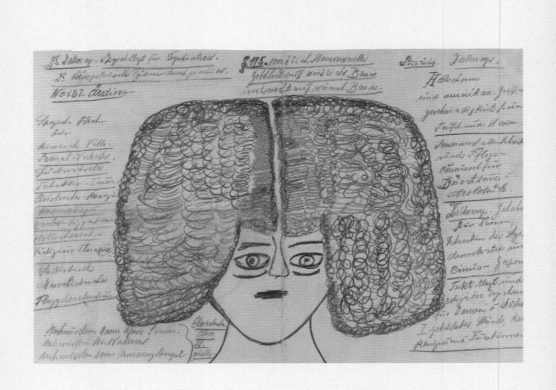

Dr. Dallmayr, Special Doctor for Psychiatry, undated, pencil on paper. *Sammlung Prinzhorn, Heidelberg*

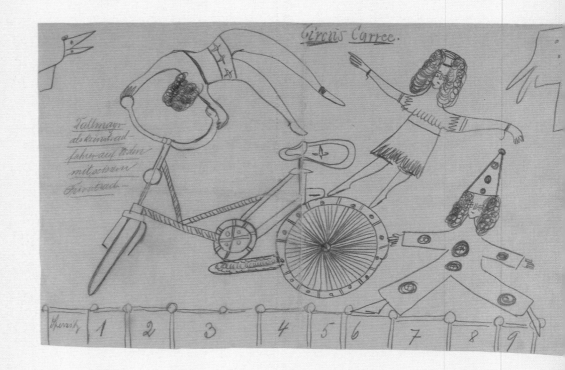

Square Circus, undated, pencil on paper. *Sammlung Prinzhorn, Heidelberg*

Alois Dallmayr as a Russian God, undated, pencil on paper. Sammlung Prinzhorn, Heidelberg

Anna Wödel and her son, Alfred. On February 22, 1941, he was killed, at the age of six, in the euthanasia program, despite her efforts to save him. Although the Nazis attempted to shroud the euthanasia killings in secrecy, it was difficult to hide a program occurring in the Germans' midst. *DÖW, Vienna*

This frequently coincided with notification of their death, from a preselected list of appropriate illnesses. Strokes were not recommended for adults under 40, but blood poisoning became a frequently listed killer of all age groups. Relatives were invariably told that the body had already been cremated; this avoided any embarrassing postmortems that would have revealed every death was the result of carbon monoxide poisoning. Special registry offices inside the killing centers were occupied, with the aid of maps and pins, distributing the deaths around Germany, so that not too many people would appear to have died in places with very modest populations.[15] About 5,000 Jewish patients were included in Operation T-4, many of them killed at Brandenburg, in the spring of 1940, when the Nazis began murdering Jewish patients. Nazi officials fabricated accounts, claiming that Jewish patients had been sent to hospitals in occupied Poland.

Inevitably such an elaborate system of deceit resulted in human error. Families with one relative in an asylum received two urns of ashes. People died of appendicitis even though that organ had been removed years earlier. Brooches and hairpins turned up in the ashes of males. Disturbed by such discoveries, families turned to lawyers, pastors, and priests for guidance. Where patients were wards of the court, guardianship judges were responsible for their affairs and had oversight over such matters as their detention for psychiatric observation. Upon realizing that patients from the Brandenburg-Görden asylum—for whom he was responsible—were being murdered, the Brandenburg provincial judge, Lothar Kreyssig, complained all the way up to the highest legal authority, Minister of Justice Franz Gürtner. Kreyssig's threats to prosecute T-4 personnel

Clemens August von Galen, Bishop of Münster, courageously condemned the "euthanasia" killings in sermons delivered to his parish in the summer of 1941. Excerpts were reproduced and distributed clandestinely. *Katholische Nachrichtenagentur, Bonn*

for murder, however, resulted instead in his own removal from the judiciary by forced early retirement.[16]

Some clerics were involved in protesting these policies, too. The Protestant pastor Gerhard Braune bravely collated the bits of information he was receiving from distressed relatives, incorporating them into a memorandum he sent to Hitler. This raised an awkward question: How was it possible for more than 2,000 people to have died in a 40-day period at the Grafeneck asylum—an asylum that had only 100 available beds? Individual Protestant bishops, notably Theophil Wurm, of Württemberg, also distinguished themselves by raising the issue of what was happening with members of the government who they thought had a religious conscience. On the Roman Catholic side, Gestapo interference with religious orders in his diocese, and outrage at a program whose victims could be limitless, prompted Bishop Clemens August von Galen to denounce "euthanasia" killings in a vivid sermon on August 3, 1941, in Münster. Here, von Galen courageously asserted:

If you establish and apply the principle that you can kill unproductive fellow human beings then woe betide us all when we become old and frail! It is impossible to imagine the degree of moral depravity, or general mistrust that would then spread even through families if this dreadful doctrine is tolerated, accepted, and followed. Woe to mankind, woe to our German nation if God's holy commandment "Thou Shalt not Kill," which God proclaimed on Mount Sinai amidst thunder and lightning, which God our Creator inscribed in the conscience of mankind from the very beginning, is not only broken, but if this transgression is actually tolerated and permitted to go unpunished.[17]

200,000 "Useless"

The Vatican and a German bishop confirm the dark rumors that have been disturbing Germany for months.

Last fall frightening rumors began floating around Germany. The elderly, residents of nursing homes, infirmaries, and hospitals, suddenly started to disappear, and instead of an explanation, their relatives received an urn with ashes.

Infirm and feebleminded children, the insane and incurably ill were dealt with the same way.

The importance that the Vatican has attached to this matter is clear from a December 13, 1940, Vatican Radio broadcast. "The Highest Congregation of the Holy See," the report said, "has issued a decree stating that secular authorities are acting against natural and divine law when they take the lives of those who are guilty of no crime but because they suffer from mental or physical affliction and can no longer serve the nation and have become a public burden."

In Berlin they say that [Pastor Friedrich von Bodelschwingh] was threatened with concentration camp for refusing to give consent to the killing of the elderly living in Bethel [a vast hospital complex] under his care. From Grafeneck in Württemberg, it was reported that special block houses have been erected in which the insane have been killed with poison gas.

In Augsburg, they say, 100 children and two attendants disappeared from the state insane asylum. And similar reports have come from Austria: they refer to the occupants of the Steinhof facility near Vienna and the Lainz facility. All over the country, Hitler has been given the nickname "urn dealer."

Thoughtless Confessions

Several German authorities have substantiated these reports, either inadvertently or deliberately. For example, Professor Reiter, president of the Reich Health Office, wrote in the *Frankfurter Zeitung*: "The burdens of public welfare for the feebleminded, cripples, epileptics, even the work shy and psychopaths, should be significantly reduced."

And similarly significant statements were made by the leader of the Tuberculosis Department of the Public Health Service in Berlin in a conversation with an American journalist and Dr. Kurt Nissel on Radio Luxembourg on May 28.

Soldiers, too?

The rumor provoked extreme disquiet that even some of those severely wounded in the war will be put on par with the "useless..."

A German bishop claimed that 80,000 people in Germany—the elderly who lived in homes or from public support, infirm and feebleminded children, the insane, etc.—were at the mercy of euthanasia (as one in the Third Reich calls the murder of the "useless"). News from Catholic priests that has reached Switzerland and Rome suggest that since that bishop's declaration, the number of victims has risen to at least 200,000.

The British Royal Air Force dropped copies of this flier reporting the "euthanasia" crimes, dated June 23, 1941, over Hamburg, Germany. *Evangelische Stiftung Alsterdorf, Hamburg*

Angered by the sermon, Nazi leaders discussed whether or not they could get away with arresting and executing the bishop, but nothing was done. Many priests and others who dared to disseminate the sermon, however, were sent to concentration camps or were executed.[18]

Galen's sermon coincided with the first attempt to sell eugenic euthanasia to the general population. This took the form of a 1941 feature film *Ich klage an (I Accuse)*, which starred many of the most familiar and beloved stars of the day. It skillfully blended the issue of voluntary euthanasia—telling the story of a young woman who wants to die because she has multiple sclerosis—with the entirely separate issue of whether or not to kill seriously handicapped children, represented here by an unseen, but deformed, child whose life a kind doctor once saved. The young woman's professor-husband eventually kills her. He is brought to trial, enabling the issues to be reviewed yet again by a jury. The film's audience is invited to decide the verdict. SS audience-monitoring found that many people regarded the film as an unconvincing response to Galen's sermon, whose text the British air force was dropping in leaflet form all over Germany.[19]

Popular unrest in parts of the country, combined with the fact that Operation T-4 had already achieved its statistical objectives, partially halted the program of mass gassing. At this time, SS concentration camps, such as Buchenwald, Dachau, or Mauthausen, lacked the capacity for mass killing. In April 1941, the SS struck a deal. Camp inmates they denoted as being ill could be murdered at T-4 facilities. This operation was designated "14f13": "14f" represented the internal filing code used by concentration camp officials to indicate the death of an inmate, "13" meant

A doctor performs an autopsy on a child killed at the Wiesengrund Clinic, Berlin, ca. 1940–44. *Archiv der Klinik Wiesengrund, Berlin*

transfer to a T-4 facility. Physicians, many of them members of the SS, like Friedrich Mennecke of the Eichberg asylum, were unleashed upon the unfortunate camp inmates. Mennecke's letters to his wife, Eva, vividly chronicled his experiences; he seemed to relish his task, boasting, for instance, about evaluating, or "examining," 470 patients on one particular day at Buchenwald—patients, or inmates, he utterly degraded as "portions of Aryans." In the process of filling out forms—making life and death selections—these Nazi racial zealots arrived at such totally ridiculous nonmedical diagnoses as "antisocial Communist psychopath," "fanatical Germanophobe," or, in the case of Jews, "parasite on the nation." It has been estimated that as many as 20,000 camp inmates perished during the two-and-one-half-year course of this program, from spring 1941 to the close of 1943.[20]

The next extension of medicalized killing began when the T-4 apparatus subcontracted about 90 personnel, including the T-4 physician Irmfried Eberl, to run the Operation Reinhard death camps in occupied Poland—Belzec, Sobibor, and Treblinka. This operation, commencing in spring 1942 and ending in fall 1943, eliminated the populations of the major Jewish ghettos in Poland and proved an intrinsic link between T-4 and the "Final Solution." Physicians were omnipresent at the Auschwitz camp complex in Silesia, medicalizing the procedure by taking charge of the initial selections of people who arrived by the trainload. They literally acquired the power of life or death. As in the euthanasia programs, physicians availed themselves of both the human materials and the transgressive moment to conduct so-called scientific research, either at the behest of such agencies as the armed forces or purely to further their own scientific careers. Julius Hallervorden,

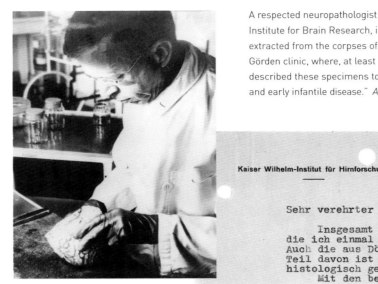

A respected neuropathologist and head of the Histopathology Department of the Kaiser Wilhelm Institute for Brain Research, in Berlin, Dr. Julius Hallervorden received hundreds of human brains extracted from the corpses of "euthanasia" victims. Many were children killed at the Brandenburg-Görden clinic, where, at least on one occasion, Hallervorden himself removed the brains. He later described these specimens to a colleague as "wonderful material...feebleminded, malformations, and early infantile disease." *Archiv zur Geschichte der Max-Plarck-Gesellschaft, Berlin*

Kaiser Wilhelm-Institut für Hirnforschung

Berlin-Buch 9.März 1944.
Lindenberger Weg
Telephon: 58 81 36

Sehr verehrter Herr Kollege,

Insgesamt habe ich 697 Gehirne erhalten einschl. derer, die ich einmal in Brandenburg selbst herausgenommen habe. Auch die aus Dösen sind mit einberechnet. Ein erheblicher Teil davon ist bereits untersucht, ob ich sie freilich alle histologisch genauer untersuchen werde, steht dahin. Mit den besten Grüssen

Ihr

127898

Hallervorden acknowledged the receipt of 697 brains from Brandenburg-Görden (the site of a children's "euthanasia" ward). March 9, 1944. *NARA, College Park, Md.*

of the Kaiser Wilhelm Institute for Brain Research, in Berlin, exemplified the close collaboration of Germany's foremost scientists and research institutes with Operation T-4. His department received hundreds of human brains that had been extracted from individuals murdered in various psychiatric clinics and euthanasia centers. Many of the victims were children, and, at least on one occasion, Hallervorden removed their brains himself. Neurological materials derived from these programs were used as recently as the 1990s, to instruct medical students at some leading German universities.[21]

The presence of T-4 personnel in these camps did not mean that their brand of euthanasia ceased in Germany. Although patients were no longer killed with poisonous gas in dedicated centers, killings of huge numbers of inmates continued in a decentralized and larger network of German and Austrian asylums. Although many asylums, in fact, generated food surpluses from their own farms, rations for psychiatric patients were continually cut—so that starvation prevailed in some asylums—with those slated to be killed being finished off with lethal injections. The reasons for killing people had long lost any connection with eugenic criteria. People were killed for being a nuisance, or for such "offenses" as persistent bed-wetting, with the choice of victim being left to the whim of their male and female killers. In addition to Germans and Austrians, hitherto the only victims of the euthanasia programs, victims now included foreign workers from Poland, Russia, or Ukraine who were physically or mentally ill. Having decided that it was incon-venient or counterproductive to repatriate persons whose labor was their sole value, the simpler option proved to be to kill them.[22]

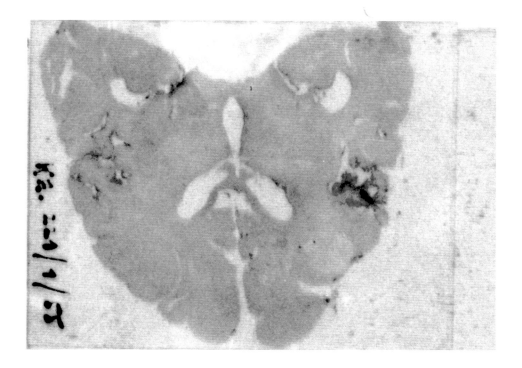

Cross-section of a brain sample from the autopsy of Karlheinz R., who was killed in the Nazi "euthanasia" program implemented between 1939 and 1945. *DÖW, Vienna*

Decentralized euthanasia killings in German asylums sometimes continued for days or weeks after the Allies occupied the surrounding areas. When the troops ventured in, they often brought film crews, as when U.S. Army cameramen filmed in the desolation that was liberated Hadamar. Apart from the people gassed there, more recent killings had resulted in an overflowing asylum cemetery, with mass graves containing 1,000 corpses, crudely stacked in layers. The United States prosecuted a portion of the staff of Hadamar, a number of whom were executed. Of the principal organizers of the euthanasia program, Philipp Bouhler committed suicide, and Karl Brandt was hanged after the Nuremberg Doctors' Trial, one of several cases that the United States used to try a given cross section of German society, such as businessmen or policemen. Assiduous German prosecutors have dedicated an extraordinary amount of effort in prosecuting several of the doctors and nursing personnel involved in the euthanasia program. Trials continued almost to the present, but the results, in terms of convictions and appropriate sentences, have been mixed.[23]

What is clear is that in its effort to cleanse the national community of the alien and unfit, the Nazi medical killers carefully planned and covertly executed an operation with precisely defined objectives—and succeeded in murdering more than 200,000 people. Moreover, in this process the regime also developed the killing techniques and methods that enabled it to undertake the murder of millions in the Holocaust.

Brain specimen jar from the Eichberg Psychiatric Clinic. *Zentrum für Soziale Psychiatrie Rheinblick, Eltville*

FROM "EUTHANASIA" TO THE "FINAL SOLUTION"

BY HENRY FRIEDLANDER

N azi ideology aimed to revitalize and racially purify the Germanic national community. All those who did not belong to the so-called Nordic race, and all those deemed to be inferior or "degenerate" members of society, were to be excluded from the national community. Targeted were three biologically defined groups—Jews, "Gypsies," and the disabled. The Nazi regime sought to eliminate those it regarded as racially "foreign" elements, as well as all those who threatened to dilute the purity and vitality of the national gene pool with hereditary physical and mental disabilities.[1] The Nazis not only carefully defined and excluded these individuals but ultimately moved to murder them.

Upon assuming power in 1933, the Nazis moved rapidly to enact exclusionary laws focusing on the three target groups. Against the disabled, the regime enacted into law the program long advocated by racial hygienists to control a population considered degenerate and inferior. The Law for the Prevention of Genetically Diseased Offspring, or the Sterilization Law, issued on July 14, 1933, served as the cornerstone of the regime's eugenic and racial legislation. This legislation was followed in October 1935 by the Marital Health Law, which mandated screening the entire population to prevent marriages of persons considered carriers of hereditary

Roll call of Jewish men newly arrived at the Buchenwald concentration camp, November 1938. *Kristallnacht* marked the first time that German Jews—the vast majority of them men—were arrested and incarcerated in concentration camps solely because they were Jews. Many were released only on the condition that they leave Germany. *American Jewish Joint Distribution Committee, New York*

Boys in a Hitler Youth camp studying the definitions of "full Jew," "half Jew," and "quarter Jew." 1937.
SV-Bilderdienst, Munich

degeneracy.[2] As racial hygiene had always linked the disabled to criminal and other "antisocial" behavior, the bureaucrats drafting this legislation believed that their eugenic laws should also cover "inherited criminal traits."[3] To accomplish this, the regime enacted, in November 1933, the Law against Dangerous Habitual Criminals. The new provisions of the penal code gave the courts substantial new powers to confine and punish persons considered habitual criminals. The courts were authorized to commit antisocial individuals to state hospitals, to impose protective custody or longer prison terms on habitual criminals, to mandate castration for sexual offenders, and to prohibit defendants from practicing their professions or occupations.

To exclude the Jews, the regime promulgated a large number of laws and amplified them with innumerable ordinances. A listing of these laws and decrees, with brief summaries, occupies a book of more than 400 pages.[4] The first major legislation directed, at least in part, against Jews was the Law for the Restoration of the Professional Civil Service, enacted in April 1933. Breaching civil service law to permit the regime to fire political opponents from the civil service, the law also included provisions for the removal of so-called non-Aryan, mostly Jewish, civil servants. A vast number of regulations followed on both the national and local levels to drive Jews from all positions in government, education, the media, the arts, and, later, the free professions of law and medicine. After 1937, laws and regulations also began to curb the economic activities of Jews, to limit their participation in the social and cultural life of the nation, and to restrict their freedom of movement.

The centerpiece of the anti-Jewish legislation was enacted in September 1935 as the Reich Citizenship Law and the Law for the Protection of German Blood and

August Landmesser with his Jewish fiancée, Irma, and their daughters, Ingrid and Irene, June 1938. The parents were forbidden to marry after the birth of the children, although Irma had been baptized Protestant. Both parents were arrested for "race defilement" (Rassenschande). Irma died in the Ravensbrück concentration camp; August served more than two years in prison. *Irene Eckler*

German Honor, together known as the Nuremberg racial laws. The drafters of these laws rejected the use of the terms *Aryan* and *non-Aryan*, probably because they were imprecise, although these terms continued to be used in numerous other regulations; instead, the laws defined so-called Aryans as persons with "German or related blood."[5] The Law for the Protection of German Blood and German Honor, which was not retroactive, excluded Jews from the German national family by prohibiting marriages, and sexual relations outside marriage, between Jews and citizens with German or related blood. The Reich Citizenship Law did not alter the status of Jews as citizens *(Staatsangehörige),* but did stigmatize Jews as citizens of lesser worth by creating the elevated position of Reich citizen *(Reichsbürger),* which only those with German or related blood could hold. The required Reich citizenship warrants were, however, never issued.[6]

Although the Nuremberg racial laws were primarily directed against Jews as the minority considered most dangerous to German society and the German gene pool, the provisions of the laws were also applied to other minorities. The Reich Minister of the Interior, Wilhelm Frick, who administered the laws, defined "alien blood" as follows: "No Jew can become a Reich citizen, because German blood is a prerequisite in the Reich citizenship code. But the same also applies to members of other races whose blood is not related to German blood, as, for example, Gypsies and Negroes."[7] The Law for the Protection of German Blood and German Honor mentioned only Jews, but the official commentaries prohibited marriage if offspring from such a union would endanger the purity of German blood; the commentators demanded the exclusion of "other racially alien blood," particularly that of "Negroes and Gypsies."[8]

"Protective custody" arrest warrant for Manfred Löwin for the crime of relations with a non-Jewish woman, issued by the Gestapo on September 24, 1938, and signed by SS chief Reinhard Heydrich. *USHMM Collection*

To identify "Jewishness," the Nazi regime relied on family genealogy and religious practice. In 1935, officials identified some 450,000 people as "Jews" and 200,000 as *"Mischlinge."* Germany's total population was 66,870,000. *Stadtarchiv und Landesgeschichtliche Bibliothek, Bielefeld*

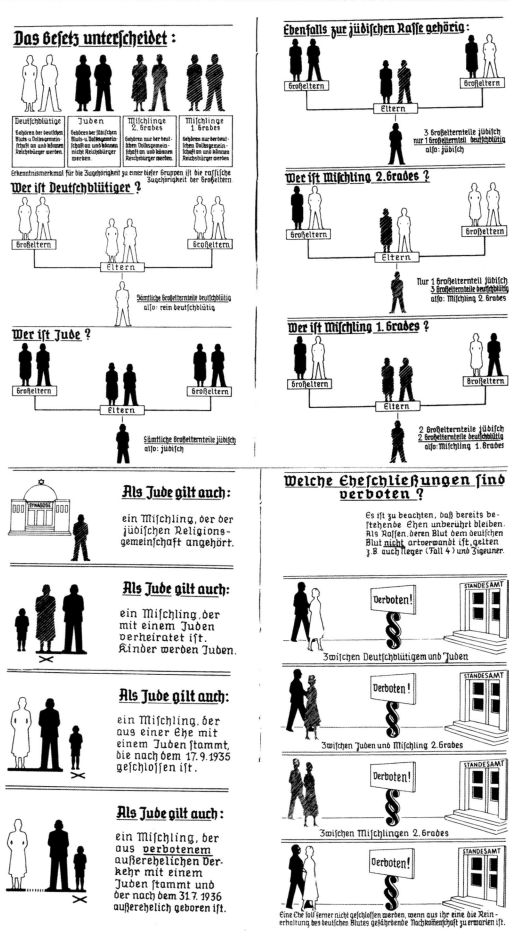

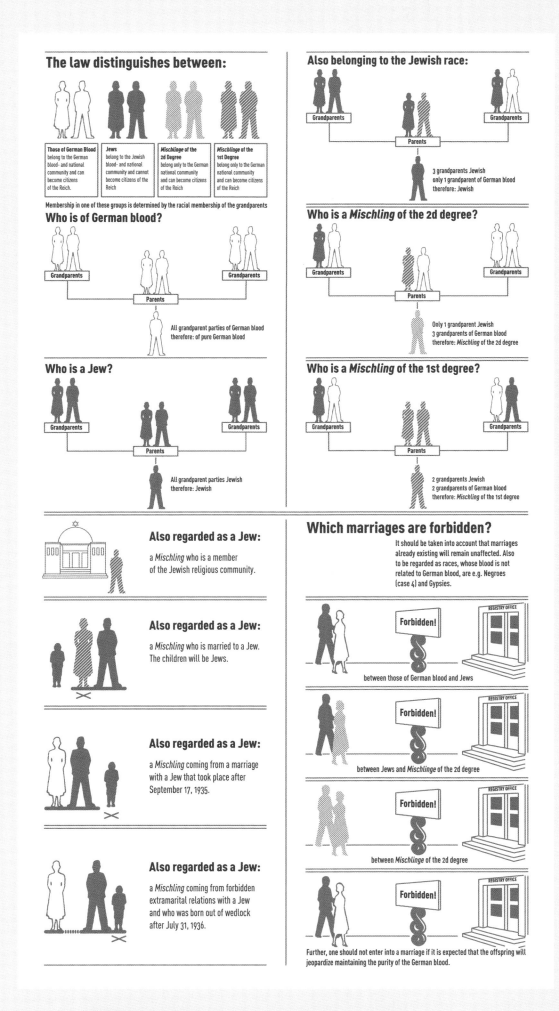

The law distinguishes between:

Those of German Blood belong to the German blood- and national community and can become citizens of the Reich.

Jews belong to the Jewish blood- and national community and cannot become citizens of the Reich.

Mischlinge of the 2d Degree belong only to the German national community and can become citizens of the Reich.

Mischlinge of the 1st Degree belong only to the German national community and can become citizens of the Reich.

Membership in one of these groups is determined by the racial membership of the grandparents

Who is of German blood?

Grandparents — Parents — All grandparent parties of German blood therefore: of pure German blood

Who is a Jew?

Grandparents — Parents — All grandparent parties Jewish therefore: Jewish

Also regarded as a Jew:

a Mischling who is a member of the Jewish religious community.

Also regarded as a Jew:

a Mischling who is married to a Jew. The children will be Jews.

Also regarded as a Jew:

a Mischling coming from a marriage with a Jew that took place after September 17, 1935.

Also regarded as a Jew:

a Mischling coming from forbidden extramarital relations with a Jew and who was born out of wedlock after July 31, 1936.

Also belonging to the Jewish race:

Grandparents — Parents — 3 grandparents Jewish only 1 grandparent of German blood therefore: Jewish

Who is a Mischling of the 2d degree?

Grandparents — Parents — Only 1 grandparent Jewish 3 grandparents of German blood therefore: Mischling of the 2d degree

Who is a Mischling of the 1st degree?

Grandparents — Parents — 2 grandparents Jewish 2 grandparents of German blood therefore: Mischling of the 1st degree

Which marriages are forbidden?

It should be taken into account that marriages already existing will remain unaffected. Also to be regarded as races, whose blood is not related to German blood, are e.g. Negroes (case 4) and Gypsies.

Forbidden! — REGISTRY OFFICE
between those of German blood and Jews

Forbidden! — REGISTRY OFFICE
between Jews and Mischlinge of the 2d degree

Forbidden! — REGISTRY OFFICE
between Mischlinge of the 2d degree

Forbidden! — REGISTRY OFFICE

Further, one should not enter into a marriage if it is expected that the offspring will jeopardize maintaining the purity of the German blood.

Interfaith marriages, like that of the Glücksteins *(center)*, with their son, Fritz, in 1932, were becoming more common in the decade before Hitler took power. *Fritz Gluckstein*

A lecture slide from the Kaiser Wilhelm Institute, ca. 1933–39. Anthropologists examined these brothers to render an "expert opinion on racial origin," based on a detailed study of their measured and photographed physical traits. A notation on the slide reads, "phenotype—suspicion of Jewish descent." *USHMM Collection, Gift of Irmgard Nippert*

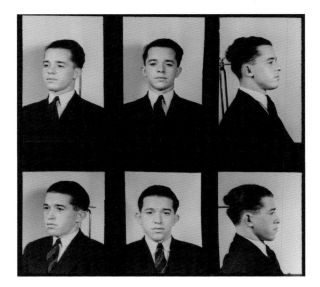

An exact definition of who belonged to the excluded groups was essential for the administration of the eugenic and racial laws. The First Decree to the Reich Citizenship Law thus defined the meaning of the term *Jew*, including the various levels of German-Jewish hybrids *(Mischlinge)*. The scientists provided the definitions. The civil servants drafting the laws and compiling the commentaries based their definitions on the writings of the race scientists; they quoted the anthropologists Eugen Fischer and Hans F. K. Günther, and sat on committees with Fischer, the psychiatrist Ernst Rüdin, and the geneticists Fritz Lenz and Otmar von Verschuer.

The Nazi regime did not incarcerate the excluded and impoverished Jewish minority in Germany and incorporated Austria; the concentration camps were not established for that purpose. Instead, the regime put pressure on Jews to emigrate, and about half of the German and Austrian Jewish communities did leave the country prior to the war. In 1938, the persecution of Jews intensified. In October, all Jews with Polish citizenship, including children born on German soil, were deported across the Polish border. In early November, the regime staged the pogrom known as the Night of Broken Glass *(Kristallnacht).* Thereafter, the desire of the remaining Jews to emigrate increased, but most countries, by that time, had closed their doors to refugees from Nazi Germany.

Against Gypsies, the authorities increased the powers of repression traditionally imposed by the police. In 1936, Reich Leader SS Heinrich Himmler issued detailed regulations for ways in which the police should restrict the freedom of Gypsies to travel and trade, and in 1937, the Reich Ministry of the Interior authorized the police to use preventive arrests to incarcerate Gypsies. Throughout Germany, the local

A Jewish-owned store whose shop windows were smashed during the *Kristallnacht* pogrom. Berlin, November 10, 1938. *NARA, College Park, Md.*

German Jews seeking to leave Germany for British-controlled Palestine, January 1939. SV-*Bilderdienst, Munich*

Austrian Jews Sigmund Freud and his daughter, Anna, on their way to London, 1938. Freudian psychoanalysis had scarcely penetrated Germany before 1933, and after the Nazi takeover, it was regarded as an "un-German" science. Because it empha-sized environmental influences on behavior, Freudianism was antithetical to Nazism's obsession with heredity. *Popperfoto.com*

Sign from Berlin clinic of Dr. Oscar Israel Hirschberg reads: "Authorized to give medical care only to Jews." Note the middle name, "Israel," which, beginning in January 1939, the Nazis forced German-Jewish men to adopt. *Jüdisches Museum Berlin*

"Gypsies" at roll call in the Dachau concentration camp, 1939. *KZ-Gedenkstätte Dachau*

authorities established Gypsy camps to restrict large numbers of Gypsy families.[9] Although these regulations, which increased in number in the late 1930s and early 1940s, categorized Gypsies as antisocial elements that had to be contained by the police, their persecution was based on race. Gypsies as a group were defined as criminal and antisocial, obviously a categorization based on race or ethnicity; therefore, individual Gypsies, as members of that racially defined group, were automatically classified as antisocial criminals.[10] The provisions of the Nuremberg racial laws were applied to them as much as to Jews. Thus, the Reich Ministry of the Interior, charged with the enforcement of the racial laws, decided that "in Europe, only Jews and Gypsies are considered alien races."[11]

As war approached in 1939, the Nazi regime moved to adopt more radical methods of exclusion, targeting not only alien races but also the disabled. As early as 1935, Adolf Hitler had told Gerhard Wagner, the Reich physician leader, that once war began, he would implement a "euthanasia" program. Although its role was to remain hidden, the actual planning and implementation of the euthanasia killings was directed by Hitler's private chancellery—the *Kanzlei des Führers* (KdF). Hitler appointed Karl Brandt, his attending physician, and Philipp Bouhler, chief of the Chancellery, as plenipotentiaries for this "top secret" program. Bouhler assigned the job of organizing the euthanasia killings to the Chancellery's Office II, and made its head, Viktor Brack, the program's day-to-day manager.

The Nazi "children's euthanasia" measures, launched first, ultimately claimed some 5,000 disabled children. Hitler expanded the killing operation to include disabled adults, eventually murdering more than 200,000. Here, too, the KdF administered

Karl Brandt, Hitler's attending physician and coadministrator of Operation T-4. Brandt studied under the prominent Berlin surgeon Ferdinand Sauerbruch and had sterling medical credentials. *Instytut Pamieci Narodowej, Warsaw*

Hadamar "euthanasia" center. *Archiv des Landeswohlfahrtsverbandes Hessen, Kassel*

the adult program alongside children's euthanasia. Also conducted secretly, the adult euthanasia program became known as Operation T-4, after the address of the confiscated Jewish villa housing the offices of the program, in Berlin, at Tiergartenstrasse 4. To gain the cooperation of nervous physicians and bureaucrats, Hitler eventually signed a secret authorization, in the form of a letter to Bouhler and Brandt, to grant mercy death.

Physicians used medication to kill the disabled children, but they had to search for a better method for the far larger group of disabled adults. For them, the T-4 technicians established killing centers, thus creating the unprecedented institution that was to symbolize Nazi Germany and the early twentieth century. The term *killing center* best describes the places where human beings were killed in a process that copied assembly-line factory production.[12] After experimenting with a variety of killing methods, the T-4 managers settled on gas as the killing agent. Karl Brandt discussed the various killing methods with the Führer, and when Hitler supposedly asked him, "Which is the more humane way?" Brandt recommended the use of gas. After giving this account at his trial at Nuremberg, Brandt proudly told his American interrogator, "This is just one case where in medical history major jumps are being made." Thereupon, they agreed on this agent for the mass killings.[13] The bizarre comment was not an isolated statement but only an extreme example of the fascination with technology exhibited by the managers of killing operations. Six killing centers were established—Brandenburg, Grafeneck, Hartheim, Sonnenstein, Bernburg, and Hadamar.

The disabled patients were usually transported to the killing center by a special T-4 bus, but, sometimes, also by train. In the reception area of the center—made to

Gas chamber at the Hadamar "euthanasia" center after the space was renovated for educational tours, 1991. *Archiv des Landeswohlfahrtsverbandes Hessen, Kassel*

look like a hospital—the patients were undressed, then taken one at a time into an examination room. This was not a regular medical examination. The physician only established the identity of the patient on the basis of his or her medical records, through which he hastily "gained a general impression from those people."[14] At this point, a mark was made on the naked bodies of the patients; those possessing gold teeth or gold bridges were identified with a cross on their back or their shoulders. This mark later served to identify corpses with valuable dental work. After the examination numbers were stamped on the patients, or attached with adhesive tape, they entered an adjacent room to be photographed—"sitting, from the front, from the side, and standing." These final pictures, identified by the stamped or attached numbers, were designed to complete the record and to show the physical inferiority of the murdered patients "for scientific reasons"; they were eventually collected and catalogued at T-4 headquarters, in Berlin. After all the examinations and other formalities were completed, the patients, still naked, were assembled so that they could be led into the gas chamber.[15]

Once all patients had entered the gas chamber, the staff closed the steel door and made sure that the door and the ventilation shafts were hermetically sealed. The physician in the adjacent room then opened the valve of the compressed carbon monoxide gas canister—obtained by the killing centers from BASF, the I. G. Farben factory at Ludwigshafen—and the lethal gas entered the chamber. Usually, the gas valve was opened for about ten minutes. In about five minutes, all the patients were unconscious; in about ten minutes, they were all dead. The staff waited one to two hours before ventilating the chamber.[16]

Hartheim Castle, where a gas chamber was installed as part of the Operation T-4 murder program. In the early 1940s, a farmer who lived in the vicinity clandestinely photographed the smoke rising from the chimney of its crematorium.
NARA, College Park, Md.; Wolfgang Schuhmann

After the fans completed ventilating the gas chamber, the physicians pronounced the occupants dead and the bodies were removed. They were dragged, not carried, from the chamber by staff members charged with the task of burning them; these staff members were known as stokers. They had to disentangle the corpses and drag them from the gas chamber to the room, usually known as the death room, where they were piled up prior to cremation. At this point, the staff proceeded to loot and mutilate the corpses to enrich the killing program. Specially selected corpses, often identified by the physicians prior to the gassing, underwent autopsies. This served two purposes: It provided young killing-center physicians with training and academic credit toward their specialization, and it recovered organs, especially brains, for scientific study at medical institutes. Furthermore, all patients with dental work containing gold had been marked earlier with a cross on their backs. The corpses so identified were collected after death, and the stokers broke out all the gold teeth. The teeth were delivered to the killing-center office.[17]

At the end, the stokers placed the corpses in the crematorium. Although they customarily cremated two to eight bodies at once, far more time was required to burn the bodies than to kill the patients; the disposal of corpses proved far more difficult technically than the murder of human beings. The stokers worked in shifts, and frequently they had to work through the night to cremate the murdered patients from one transport.[18]

The killing center was able to "process" living human beings into ashes in less than 24 hours; in the language of T-4, this was called "disinfection." After cremation, the stokers used a mill to grind into a powder the human bones not totally

pulverized by the fire. Ashes were placed in urns for burial, about seven pounds for every human being. The relatives of the murdered patients could obtain such an urn, but they were not told that the ashes did not belong to the person whose name was stamped on the urn; the stokers simply took ashes from a "large pile" to fill the urns.[19]

The work of the killing centers was shrouded in secrecy. To maintain secrecy, the office staff of the centers had to leave a paper trail to hide the killings. The physicians issued fraudulent death certificates. The office sent condolence letters to the relatives. Dates of death and other details were changed. Nevertheless, the truth leaked out. Too many errors were made; too many patients suddenly died. This created unrest, something the regime could not permit in the middle of the war. In August 1941, Hitler ordered a stop to the gassings of the disabled at the killing centers; it had become too public. That did not mean that the killings stopped. The disabled, thereafter, were killed in various institutions and hospitals throughout the country by medication or starvation. It was less noticeable, but just as effective. A statistician employed by T-4 compiled a summary of the numbers of patients killed. In his report, found after the war at Hartheim, he provided monthly figures for each killing center, arriving at a total of 70,273 persons "disinfected." Of these, 35,224 were killed in 1940 and 35,049 in 1941.[20]

The bizarre T-4 statistics found at Hartheim also provided an exact account of future monies saved by killing the disabled. The T-4 statistician figured that 70,273 "disinfections" saved the German Reich 885,439,980 reichsmarks over a period of ten years. Computing future savings of food, he argued that 70,273 murdered patients,

An asbestos mitt, used by stokers in the Hartheim crematorium, was among the hundreds of objects buried with the ashes of the victims in pits dug on the facility's grounds. *OOE Landesarchiv, Linz*

Victims' personal belongings excavated in 2001–2002 from the grounds adjacent to Hartheim Castle, one of the six T-4 killing centers: pocket mirror, fragment of a man's pipe, razor, pocket watch, cup, rosary beads, brooch pin, comb, and jack-knife.
OOE Landesarchiv, Linz

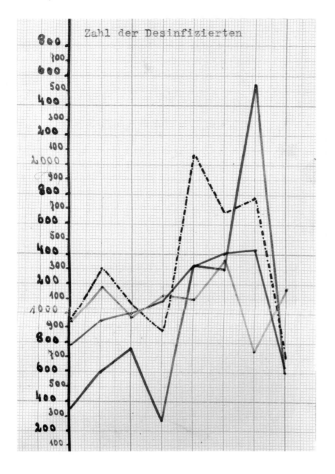

Zahl der Desinfizierten

A staff outing of nurses and orderlies from Grafeneck, a T-4 gassing center, ca. 1941.
Archiv des Landeswohlfahrtsverbandes Hessen, Kassel

Toward the end of the war, Operation T-4 officials compiled data on the number of patients "disinfected" at the six gassing facilities, and on the projected savings on food as a result of the program. The lines of the graph represent the number of deaths over an eight-month period, from January through August 1941, at Sonnenstein (blue), Bernburg (red), Hartheim (green), and Hadamar (black). *NARA, College Park, Md.*

for instance, saved Germany 13,492,440 kilograms of meat and sausage—a macabre utilitarianism designed to rationalize the eugenic and racial ideology that created the killing centers.

Hitler's stop order applied only to the gassing of the disabled; the T-4 killing centers could still be put to other use. In 1940, German concentration camps were growing in number and size, but they did not yet possess the facilities to kill large numbers of inmates at one time. Methods used to kill individual inmates during the prewar years—forced labor, harsh living conditions, beatings, and executions— were too slow to reduce the growing camp population.[21] The SS, therefore, turned to Hitler's KdF to determine how to utilize T-4's killing capabilities. Early in 1941, Reich Leader SS Himmler conferred with KdF chief Philipp Bouhler on "whether and how the personnel and the facilities of T-4 can be utilized for the concentration camps."[22] Soon after, in the spring of 1941, a new killing operation commenced, aimed at inmates in the German concentration camps.

The killing of selected inmates in the gas chambers of the T-4 killing centers was designated "Special Treatment 14f13." The selection of the victims was based on a collaboration between the SS camp physicians and T-4 physicians. Teams of T-4 physicians visited the camps, where they selected the victims from lists already prepared by the SS. Thus, the Bernburg and Sonnenstein killing centers continued to operate until 1943, when the growing need for concentration camp labor ended operation 14f13. Only the gas chamber at Hartheim, outside Linz, in Austria, remained operational. Located near the Mauthausen concentration camp, it had a special relationship with that camp and was used to gas Mauthausen inmates

Dr. Friedrich Mennecke, shown with his wife, Eva, was an expert physician for T-4 and Operation 14f13, which expanded the "euthanasia" program to include concentration camp inmates who were sick, infirm, and unable to work. *Bundesarchiv Berlin*

T-4 workers after hours at Hartheim, ca. 1940–42. *NARA, College Park, Md.*

until December 1944. Prisoners from the Dachau camp, near Munich, were also transported to Hartheim, where they were gassed.[23]

At Nuremberg, Brack swore under oath that no disabled Jewish patient died in the euthanasia killing centers. He lied. Brandt also lied at Nuremberg, claiming that he knew nothing about the fate of disabled Jews. Physicians involved in the killing of disabled Jews also lied when asked about their Jewish patients. All these lies were part of an elaborate scheme to falsify the record. And the liars succeeded, at Nuremberg and thereafter, in deceiving prosecutors, judges, and historians.[24]

The argument advanced by the T-4 perpetrators was that euthanasia was a form of deliverance, and that Jews did not deserve this benefit. It was, of course, true that positive eugenic measures never applied to Jews. But euthanasia was, in fact, a negative eugenic measure, and this always applied to Jews. We have evidence, therefore, that Jews were not exempted from the sterilization law. This also applied to the T-4 killings. Jews appeared on the lists of the earliest transports to the T-4 killing centers: The first name on the transport list from Eglfing-Haar to Grafeneck, of January 18, 1940, was Ludwig "Israel" Alexander.[25] But the regular killing process, including individual medical evaluations, was too slow and too uncertain for the T-4 managers when applied to Jews; they decided to transfer and kill Jews as a group, not on the basis of evaluated questionnaires but simply because they were Jews.[26]

The decision—to murder, systematically, disabled Jewish patients still in German hospitals—was apparently made in the spring of 1940. At that time, the Gestapo as well as T-4 started to collect statistics on institutionalized Jewish patients. In late March or early April, local offices of the Gestapo began to demand that Jewish

```
Der Oberbürgermeister                    Berlin C 2, den 18. Februar 1941.
der Reichshauptstadt Berlin              Breite Str. 23-24
 - Hauptgesundheitsamt -                 Fernruf: 52 59 81, App. 101
 -  HGA I W

                                         Heil-u.Pflegeanstalt Wuhlgarten,
           Auf Ihr Schreiben vom 1.2.41 an die    teile ich Ihnen
mit, daß Agnes Sara  S e n f f ,      wie auch zahlreiche andere
jüdische Insassen unserer Heil- und Pflegeanstalten, auf Anordnung
des Reichsverteidigungskommissars nach dem Generalgouvernement
Warschau verlegt worden ist.
           Die für Ihr Schreiben zuständige Dienststelle ist die
Gemeinnützige Kranken-Transport G.m.b.H., Berlin W 9, Potsdamer
Platz 1. Ich habe Ihr Schreiben dorthin abgegeben.
Herrn                                    In Vertretung :
    Hans  S c h ä f e r
Berlin - Charlottenburg
      Alt Lietzow 34
```

Agnes Senff, a Jewish patient killed in the "euthanasia" program, seen (right) in 1927, when she was well. *Wolfgang Haney, Berlin*

Letter documenting the transfer of Agnes Senff, a Jewish patient killed in the "euthanasia" program. The Nazis began murdering Jewish patients in mental hospitals in the spring of 1940, regardless of an individual's capacity to work. Nazi officials claimed that Jewish patients were being sent to a hospital in Chelm, in occupied Poland, an utter fabrication. Many of the patients were murdered at the Brandenburg killing facility outside Berlin. *Wolfgang Haney, Berlin*

communities provide them monthly reports on the number of Jewish patients; soon after, they also requested that all monthly changes be reported. On April 15, 1940, Herbert Linden, of the Reich Ministry of the Interior, asked all local authorities to report the number of Jewish disabled patients. His letter to state and provincial agencies administering state hospitals and nursing homes required them to submit, within three weeks, lists of Jewish patients 'suffering from mental illness or feeblemindedness."[27] The purpose of Linden's circular soon became apparent. Jewish patients in various hospitals and homes were transferred to a small number of institutions serving as assembly centers. From there, they were collected by T-4's buses and transported to the killing centers.

The disabled Jewish patients assigned to these Jewish transports had been chosen not on the basis of their questionnaires but solely on the basis of lists compiled by institutions in response to the Reich Ministry of the Interior circular. Unlike all other murdered disabled patients, the killing centers did not send out death certificates or letters of condolence. The disabled Jews were simply to disappear. But this changed as paperwork began to accumulate. Soon, relatives, welfare offices, insurance companies, and the courts inquired about the patients who had disappeared. At first, the institutions stonewalled, replying only that on orders of the ministry, the patient had been transferred to another institution via a Jewish transport, adding, "The name of that institution is not known." Thereupon, T-4 invented the Cholm-Chelm deception.[28]

Eventually, relatives and public agencies received death notices, as had the relatives of murdered German patients. But these notices did not come from killing

Nr. 343 - - - -

Chelm, Post Lublin ———, den 30.Januar - - 1941

D ie Agnes Sara Senff geborene Mosoner - - - - -

verheiratet - - - - - - - , mosaisch - - - - - - - ,

wohnhaft Chelm ————

ist am 30. Januar 1941 - - - - um 3 - - - Uhr 15 - - Minuten

in der Wohnung ———————— verstorben.

D ie Verstorbene war geboren am 19. Juli 1857 - - - - - -

in Berlin - - - - - - - - - - - - - - - - -

(Standesamt - - - - - - - - - - - - Nr - - - - - -)

Vater: -

Mutter: - - - - - - - - - - - - - - - - - - -

Die Verstorbene war — nicht — verheiratet - - - - - - - -

- -

- -

Eingetragen auf mündliche — schriftliche — Anzeige des Leiters der

Irrenanstalt Chelm ————

D Anzeigende ————

Vorgelesen, genehmigt und untergeschrieben

Der Standesbeamte
In Vertretung
ges. Alt

Todesursache: Altersschwäche Herzschlag

Eheschließung de Verstorbenen am in
(Standesamt Nr.

Nr. 343 - - - -

Chelm, Post Lublin ———, den 30.Januar - - 1941

D ie Agnes Sara Senff geborene Mosoner - - - - -

verheiratet - - - - - - , mosaisch - - - - - - - ,

Letter notifying the family that Agnes Senff, a Jewish mental patient, had died from a heart attack at the asylum at Chelm. The cause and location of death was a fabrication; Agnes was actually killed in the "euthanasia" program. *Wolfgang Haney, Berlin*

centers inside Germany, they arrived from the German-administered General Government in occupied Poland, on stationery with the heading, "Mental Asylum Chelm, Post Office Lublin." Chelm death notices were sent not only to relatives but also to various public agencies, especially those with financial responsibility for the patients. With true Germanic thoroughness, death notices were entered by local registry offices on the permanent birth records of the murdered Jewish patients.[29]

The entire Chelm enterprise, designed to enrich T-4's coffers, was completely amateurish. The letterhead was simple and did not have the normal appearance of a German institutional letterhead. In any event, it was not clear why a Polish institution near Lublin would use a German letterhead. Furthermore, the confusion over the name, sometimes spelled "Chelm," sometimes "Cholm," indicated that as far as forgery was concerned, the T-4 people were dilettantes. Still, no one, including German government agencies, seemed to notice these discrepancies. The same was true about the way payment was collected. The Chelm institution, near Lublin, asked that monies due be paid into "Post Office Account Berlin No. 17050," without explaining why a Polish institution would have an account in Berlin.[30]

The fraudulent letters were actually written in Berlin by T-4 officials, and a courier took the correspondence to Lublin for mailing so that the Lublin post-office cancellation would appear on the letters.[31] One exchange of correspondence can serve as an example. On November 7, 1940, Chelm notified Flora Tauber, in Vienna, that her son had died the previous day: "We must inform you that your son, Alfred Israel Tauber, who had been here for some time, has died here. We are enclosing two certified copies of the death certificate." On December 2, the mother wrote to

Diagnosed with schizophrenia, Julie "Sara" J., a stenographer from Berlin, was admitted to the Wittenau Clinic on October 17, 1941. On December 17, 1942, Julie was one of the last 20 Jewish patients transferred from Wittenau to the Jewish Hospital. She escaped the "euthanasia" program, but was later deported to the Auschwitz-Birkenau killing center. *Landesarchiv Berlin (A Rep. 003-04-04 Nr. 4)*

German troops advance through a village in Soviet Belorussia, in the opening days of the invasion of the Soviet Union, June 22–25, 1941. *Belorussky gosudarstvennyy arkhiv, Dzerzhinsk*

Jews from Lubny, Ukraine, rounded up for execution. On October 16, 1941, the SS murdered more than 1,300 people in a mass shooting at Lubny. *Heissisches Hauptstaatsarchiv, Wiesbaden (Abt. 495)*

the Lublin post-office box number listed on the Chelm stationery about her son's burial. The Chelm II police replied on April 7, 1941, that the urn containing her son's ashes had already been buried in the institution's cemetery "on orders from higher offices." Flora Tauber persisted. On April 16, she wrote once again, this time about her son's grave, requesting a memorial plaque. The Chelm II police answered that they could not accommodate her wishes. Since the institution cared for the grave at no cost to her, she was advised to wait until the end of the war when there might be a possibility of erecting such a plaque.[32]

The Chelm enterprise demonstrates how secret government activities can get out of hand. T-4 had orders to kill the Jewish patients, but its decision to manufacture the Chelm notices to make money was probably not specifically sanctioned from above. Considering the phobia about secrecy and the fear that Hitler's Chancellery would be exposed, the clumsy forgery format presented serious dangers to such a clandestine project. The decision to proceed with the scheme shows not only how greed operated but also that T-4 felt immune from normal bureaucratic constraints.

After the war, the Chelm-Cholm deception long continued to obscure the fate of disabled Jews. But the evidence is clear and incontrovertible that all disabled Jews were murdered in T-4 killing centers on German soil. The murder of disabled Jews transported from the assembly center at Berlin-Buch to the T-4 killing center at Brandenburg can serve as an example.

An eyewitness account comes from Herbert Kalisch, the T-4 electrician, who was interrogated in 1960 and 1961 by German prosecutors. On one occasion, he accompanied a transport of patients, and he testified that "as far as I remember, it was still in June 1940."

We drove in six large buses of the Reich railroads to the mental hospital Buch near Berlin, and there collected about 100 women with children and about 100 men, all members of the Jewish race.... The transport went to the city of Brandenburg on the Havel, to the old prison in the center of the city, which, being empty, had been remodeled into a crematorium. After arrival at the prison, the persons were put in cells, separated by gender. Still on the same day, immediately after arrival, about 20 persons at a time were taken from the cells. The persons were undressed completely, as they were told that they would be taken to another building for bathing and delousing. First they took women and children for gassing. To pacify these patients, physicians gave them a cursory examination. Thereafter, they were placed in a room with wooden benches, which looked, more or less, like a shower room. But before they entered the room, they were marked with consecutive numbers. The doors were locked as soon as the prescribed number of persons had entered the "shower room." At the ceiling were showerheads through which gas entered the room. The gas was ventilated after 15 to 20 minutes, as soon as one had discovered by looking through the peephole that all people inside were no longer alive. As the earlier examination had noted which persons had gold teeth, these persons could now be discovered by their marked number. The gold teeth were pulled from the dead people. Thereupon SS men stationed at the prison carried the dead people from the "shower room" and took them to the crematorium. On that very day, the entire transport was eliminated in this fashion.[33]

At a later interrogation, Kalisch enlarged on his testimony: "The transport that was gassed in the gas chamber of the former prison in Brandenburg on the Havel, in

The Jewish community of Mizocz, in occupied Poland, was herded into a ravine and executed in 1942. *Einsatzgruppen* squads of SS and police rounded up and killed more than one million Jews in such open-air shootings. *Instytut Pamieci Narodowej, Warsaw*

Still photographs from filmed testing of
new killing procedures at Mogilev,
Belorussia, in German-occupied USSR,
September 1941. German field policemen
from *Einsatzgruppe B* conducted the test.
NARA, College Park, Md.

Psychiatric patients were brought to the site...

ordered to undress, and sent into a small building...

about June 1940, contained only Jews, who I would estimate were men and women between the ages of 18 and 55."[34]

Kalisch's eyewitness testimony is not the only evidence we possess that Jewish patients were gassed in Brandenburg. The 1940 pocket diary of Irmfried Eberl survived the war. As physician-in-charge at Brandenburg, Eberl noted the arrival of transports for gassing, often listing the number of victims and usually indicating the composition by using the capital letter *M* for men *(Männer)*, *F* for women *(Frauen)*, and *J* for Jews *(Juden)*. The diary contains a relatively large number of *J* entries, and some match exactly the schedule of transfers known to us.[35]

The murder of disabled Jewish patients—which began about a year before the mass murder of Jews commenced in the occupied Soviet Union—formed an important link between euthanasia and the "Final Solution." The 1940 decision, made at the highest level, to kill disabled Jews as a group, regardless of their condition, pointed the way to the 1941 decision to kill all Jews.

On June 22, 1941, the German *Wehrmacht* invaded the Soviet Union, and the Nazi regime embarked on its second, and far more ambitious, killing operation. Mobile operational units of the SS, the so-called *Einsatzgruppen*, crossed the Soviet border immediately after the battle troops. In the occupied territory of the Soviet Union, these units shot large numbers of civilians in mass executions.[36] Their primary task was the murder of all Jews on Soviet soil.[37] The Germans labeled the murder of Soviet Jews, and the subsequent murder of all Jews within their jurisdiction, as the "Final Solution of the European Jewish Question." More than one million men, women, and children were killed in open-air shootings.[38] But they also murdered the

whose windows had been bricked up to leave only two small openings for hoses...

attached to the exhaust of a car. After five minutes, nothing appeared to have happened...

so another hose was fitted to a second vehicle. In another few minutes, the people were unconscious. Both vehicles were left running for another ten minutes.

Gypsies.[39] In addition, they also murdered the disabled, showing the link to the euthanasia program.[40] The quartermaster of the German army, General Eduard Wagner, thus recorded in September 1941: "Russians consider the feebleminded holy. Nevertheless, killing is necessary."[41]

It seems eminently reasonable to assume that the decision to kill the Jews followed the same pattern as the one to kill the disabled. As in the case of the policy against the disabled, the agencies charged with implementing Jewish policy continuously searched for new approaches, competing with each other for the most radical solution. Some have argued that this competition produced a decision that did not require the Führer's participation.[42] But the evidence for such a scenario is not convincing. Instead, as in the case of T-4, the argument is far more compelling that Hitler set the agenda, permitted his agents to prepare the ground, but reserved for himself the final decision. The date of the decision, which has consumed a great deal of debate, is less important.

Most likely, Hitler gave a verbal order—or authorization—to kill the Jews and appointed Heinrich Himmler as his agent.[43] Unlike T-4, however, he did not provide a written authorization. The reasons for this are not difficult to fathom. As too many people had read Hitler's earlier euthanasia authorization, such widespread knowledge could have implicated him in the killings; obviously, he refused to sign another such document. In addition, Himmler, his loyal paladin, could hardly insist that his Führer put his verbal order on paper. Still, Reinhard Heydrich, whose Central Office for Reich Security (RSHA) had to implement the order Hitler gave to Himmler, needed some written commission to compel

SS chief Heinrich Himmler *(left)* and Reinhard Heydrich, chief of the Reich Main Security Office, March 1938. Heydrich coordinated Nazi plans for the "Final Solution" and directed *Einsatzgruppen* activities in Eastern Europe.
AP/Wide World, New York

the cooperation of other government agencies. Hermann Göring, therefore, supplied a retroactive sanction in his letter of July 31, 1941.[44] Just as Hitler did not write but only signed the euthanasia authorization letter to Brandt and Bouhler prepared by the Chancellery of the Führer, Göring did not initiate but only signed the authorization prepared and submitted by Heydrich.[45]

The murder of the disabled preceded the murder of Jews and Gypsies, and it is reasonable to conclude that T-4's killing operation served as a model for the "Final Solution." The success of the euthanasia policy convinced the Nazi leadership that mass murder was technically feasible, that ordinary men and women were willing to kill large numbers of innocent human beings, and that the bureaucracy would cooperate in such an unprecedented enterprise. But the regime had also realized that mass murder on German soil posed problems, because public opinion seemed uneasy about such radical violation of the law. The mass murder of Jews and Gypsies was, therefore, moved to the East, into Poland and the occupied territories of the Soviet Union.

Jews deported from Lodz in 1942 arrive at the Chelmno killing center. Beginning in December 1941, some 150,000 Jews were gassed at Chelmno with deadly carbon monoxide exhaust fumes piped into sealed transport vans. *Zydowski Instytut Historyczny, Warsaw*

Formerly in charge of the Brandenburg and Bernburg "euthanasia" centers, SS physician Irmfried Eberl became first commandant of the Treblinka extermination camp, in occupied Poland, in July 1942. Here, Eberl is seen in the company of other "medical" personnel at the camp. *Ghetto Fighters' House, Kibbutz Lohamei HaGetaot*

FROM "EUTHANASIA" TO THE "FINAL SOLUTION"

Mass murder by execution, as, at first, practiced in the East, proved far too public; the perpetrators had to search for a better method. Himmler's men eventually realized, just as the T-4 killers had discovered earlier, that it was more efficient, and also less public, to bring the victims to a central killing place. It was only logical that these places would be modeled on the T-4 centers. To what degree the perpetrators of the "Final Solution" copied the T-4 system is revealed by the use of the term *Brack's devices*, referring to the T-4 administrator, when discussing the use of gas chambers.[46]

The first killing center of the "Final Solution" began functioning in December 1941 at Chelmno (Kulmhof, in German) in the Wartheland, a Polish territory annexed to Germany. Although it was a stationary killing center, it used the gas vans that circulated exhaust fumes into the van to kill the victims. To make use of previous T-4 experience, Herbert Lange, who had used vans to kill the disabled in the Wartheland and East Prussia, was chosen to head the Chelmno killing center. Some 150,000 Jews were gassed at Chelmno.[47]

At the same time, Himmler commissioned Odilo Globocnik, the SS and Police Leader in Lublin, to kill the Jews of Poland, an undertaking later named Operation Reinhard in honor of the assassinated Heydrich. To accomplish his mission, Globocnik established three killing centers in the General Government—Belzec, Sobibor, and Treblinka—which started to operate, one after the other, in the spring and summer of 1942. Unlike Chelmno, the camps of Operation Reinhard used stationary gas chambers, in which a diesel motor propelled gas fumes into the chambers.[48]

Killing Centers in Occupied Poland, 1942

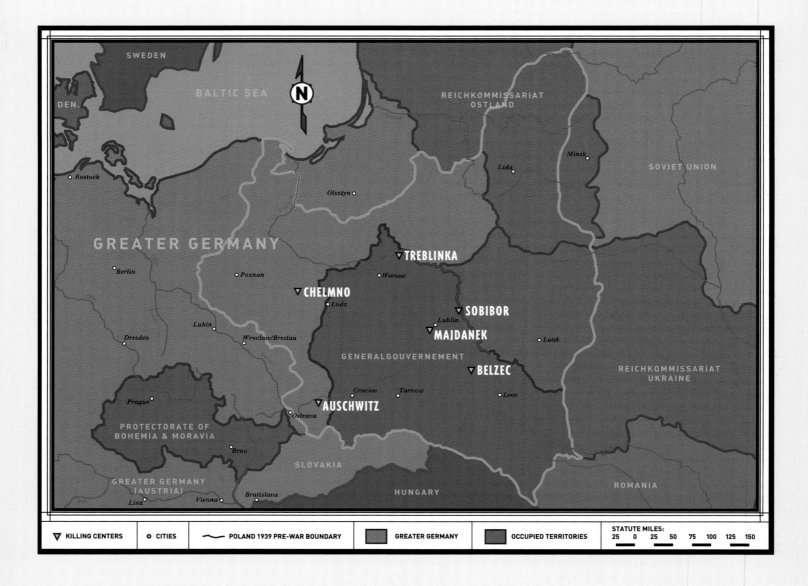

SWEDEN

DEN.

BALTIC SEA

N

REICHKOMMISSARIAT
OSTLAND

SOVIET UNION

•Rostock

Lida•

Minsk•

Olsztyn•

GREATER GERMANY

▽ TREBLINKA

Berlin•

Poznan•

•Warsaw

▽ CHELMNO

•Lodz

▽ SOBIBOR

Lublin•

Lubin•

▽ MAJDANEK

Dresden•

Wroclaw/Breslau•

Lutsk•

GENERALGOUVERNEMENT

REICHKOMMISSARIAT
UKRAINE

▽ BELZEC

Cracow•

Tarnow•

Prague•

Lvov•

▽ AUSCHWITZ

Ostrava•

PROTECTORATE OF
BOHEMIA & MORAVIA

Brno•

SLOVAKIA

GREATER GERMANY
(AUSTRIA)

Bratislava•

HUNGARY

ROMANIA

Linz•

Vienna•

▽ KILLING CENTERS | ○ CITIES | POLAND 1939 PRE-WAR BOUNDARY | GREATER GERMANY | OCCUPIED TERRITORIES | STATUTE MILES:
25 0 25 50 75 100 125 150

Hungarian Jews shortly after their arrival at Auschwitz, May 1944. *Yad Vashem, Jerusalem*

To accomplish this task, Globocnik turned to the Chancellery of the Führer to gain the support of T-4 for his enterprise. In September 1941, Bouhler and Brack visited Globocnik in Lublin, where they probably discussed their future collaboration.[49] During the 1941–42 winter, a number of T-4 men visited Lublin, and there can be no doubt that their sojourns were connected with the construction of killing centers. The T-4 chemist Helmut Kallmeyer visited Lublin in January or February 1942. Christian Wirth, a Stuttgart police officer who had served as troubleshooter for the T-4 killing centers, was also in Lublin in late fall or early winter 1941.[50] Erwin Lambert, the master mason of T-4, visited the General Government three times to construct gas chambers in Treblinka and Sobibor; he also directed construction work in several forced-labor camps nearby.[51]

Expert advice on the design and construction of killing centers was not the only contribution of the Chancellery. Because Globocnik needed staff, he subcontracted to T-4 for personnel to operate the killing centers of Operation Reinhard. In the second half of April, Globocnik conferred with Bouhler and Brack in Berlin, and they probably settled all remaining questions about the Chancellery's role. Eventually, T-4 men comprised almost the entire German personnel of the extermination camps of Operation Reinhard. The first group left in April; further staff members were posted east in June 1942. Altogether, at least 90 T-4 men were assigned to Belzec, Sobibor, and Treblinka. Irmfried Eberl, physician-in-charge at Brandenburg and, later, Bernburg, briefly served as the first commandant of Treblinka, and Christian Wirth served as inspector of all three killing centers of Operation Reinhard.[52]

The Auschwitz-Birkenau crematorium ovens were located in the same building as the gas chambers in order to speed up the extermination process. *Tsentral'nyi Muzei Vooruzhennykh Sil, Moscow*

A gas chamber at Auschwitz. The SS murdered about 1.1 million people at the Auschwitz camp complex. Nearly one million of the victims were Jews. *DÖW, Vienna*

The killing centers that the T-4 men ran in the Lublin region were modeled on those they had left in the Reich. But the much larger enterprise created conditions far worse than what had existed in Germany. Of course, brutalization and corruption of staff members had also been a by-product of the euthanasia killing enterprise inside Germany, but at home some restraints upon the killers still existed. Such restraints no longer applied in the East, especially as the sheer number of victims overwhelmed the machine of destruction. An estimated 900,000 Jews were gassed at Treblinka, 600,000 at Belzec, and 250,000 at Sobibor.[53] Sadism, torture, and corruption reached previously unimaginable proportions. An American judge, years later, described one of these camps as a "human abattoir."[54] Even Bouhler worried that "the absolute degradation and brutalization of the people involved" would make the T-4 staff assigned to Lublin no longer fit for the job of euthanasia inside the borders of the Reich.[55]

Because the killing task was so massive, Himmler also selected some of his concentration camps to serve as killing centers. He chose the newly established camp at Auschwitz, in Upper Silesia, and the so-called POW camp at Majdanek, a suburb of Lublin, to perform the killing function. Operating under the authority of the Inspectorate of the Concentration Camps, Auschwitz and Majdanek remained concentration camps while also running a killing center as part of their operation. At Auschwitz, the killing center was located at Birkenau, also known as Auschwitz II. The agent used to kill the victims differed slightly at Auschwitz, where the SS replaced carbon monoxide with hydrogen cyanide, known under the trade name Zyklon B, which was already in use as a pesticide in all concentration camps to fumigate barracks.

In Birkenau, the SS staff improved upon the extermination technique first used in the euthanasia killings. They introduced Zyklon B, which acted faster, and constructed a killing plant that combined gas chambers and stationary crematoriums in one building. They also identified and selected those prisoners still able to work so that they could exploit their labor before killing them. At Auschwitz-Birkenau, and also at Majdanek, the SS did not need the help of T-4 specialists. The T-4 technique was a basically simple German invention, one that any organization could learn to use. The concentration camps possessed both the organization and the manpower, as well as a commitment to savage brutality, to execute the killing task. About 1.1 million human beings were gassed in Auschwitz; as many as one million, probably, were Jews.[56]

In the postwar world, Auschwitz has come to symbolize genocide in the twentieth century. But Auschwitz was only the last, most perfect Nazi killing center. The entire killing enterprise started in January 1940 with the murder of the most helpless human beings, institutionalized disabled patients. It expanded in 1941 to include Jews and Gypsies. And by 1945, it had cost the lives of at least six million men, women, and children.

On the selection ramp at Auschwitz, an SS physician examines a Jew who recently arrived in a transport from Hungary. If judged healthy, the man could be selected for slave labor, a temporary reprieve from death. Spring 1944. *Yad Vashem, Jerusalem*

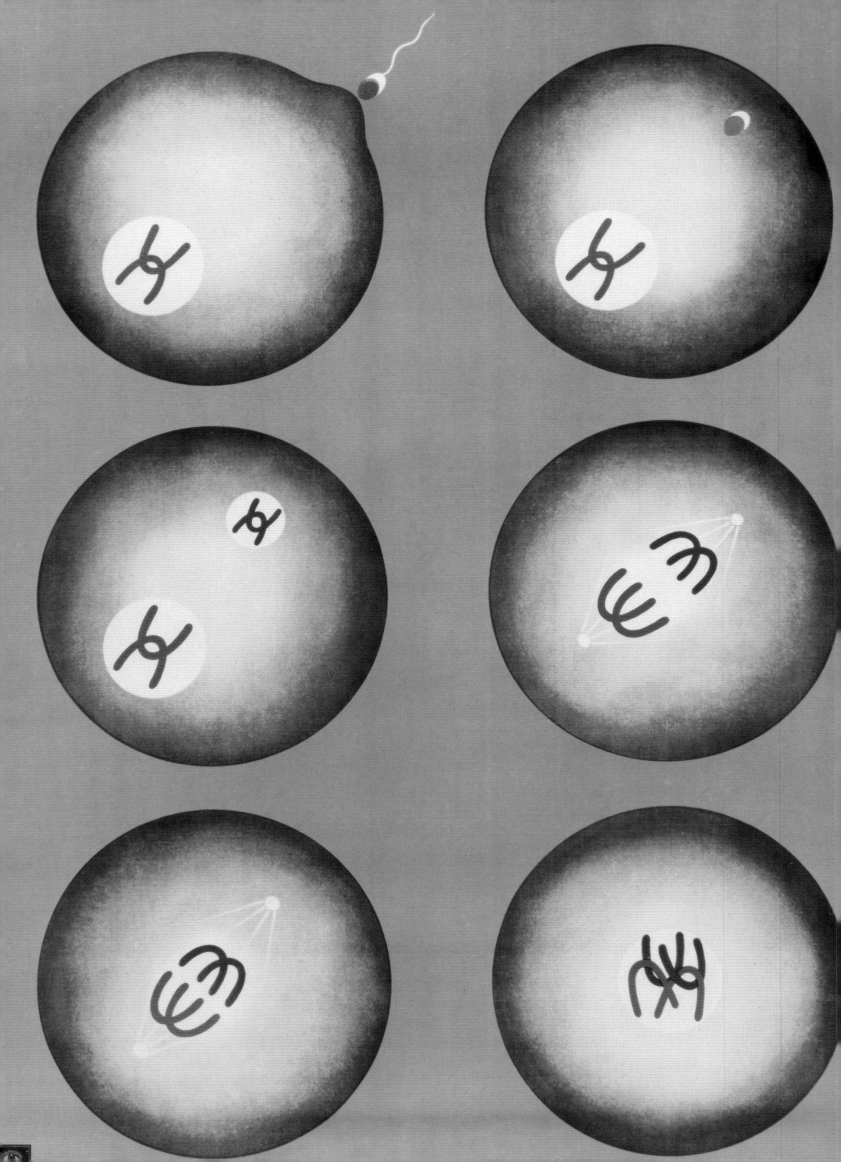

REFLECTIONS OF A GERMAN SCIENTIST

BY BENNO MÜLLER-HILL

The involvement of science, or, specifically, genetics, in the abhorrent crimes of Nazi Germany is one of the most disturbing events for scientists, and the public alike, to contemplate. Science is about knowledge and truth. So, we must ask ourselves, how could German scientists support antisemitism and the racial measures of the Nazis? Can science save face by claiming that what was practiced in Nazi Germany was not real science, that it was only pseudoscience? This depends on one's definition of *science*. I prefer, simply, to define *science* as what the majority of scientists working in the field call science at the time it is being done. Referees decide what can be published and what is to be funded—therefore, what is published in scientific journals and funded by grant agencies must be considered science. Under this definition, scientists—specifically, German human or medical geneticists (most of them did not yet call themselves human or medical geneticists)—were, during the 1930s and 1940s, deeply involved in the crimes of the Nazi government.

Those who were involved did not write detailed accounts after the collapse of the Third Reich, and, for several decades after 1945, historians of science did not concern themselves with this aspect of German history. Why was there virtually no interest among scientists and historians of science in describing and under-

Educational materials that promoted Nazi racial hygiene conflated benign scientific graphics, such as this, entitled "Fertilization," with overtly propagandistic material. *Deutsches Hygiene-Museum, Dresden*

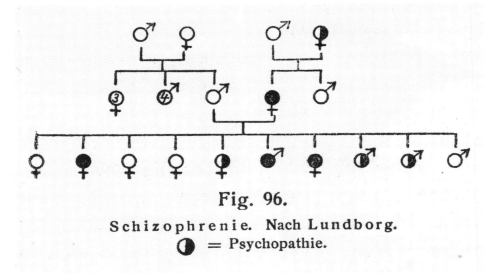

Family tree showing the manifestation of schizophrenic symptoms across three generations, from *Foundations of Human Genetics and Racial Hygiene*. USHMM Collection

Fig. 96.

S c h i z o p h r e n i e.   N a c h   L u n d b o r g.

◑ = Psychopathie.

standing this past? How could it have been that most of the scientists who had supported Nazi racial policies continued, after 1945, to work and publish the results of their research as though nothing had happened? These are unsettling questions. Today, human genetics is, once again, at the focal point of our interest, so it is imperative that this most unpleasant history be remembered if we are to prevent it being reincarnated in a modernized form.

GENETICS UNTIL 1923

Genetics as a science began in the year 1900 with the rediscovery of the work of Gregor Mendel. What, in 1866, Mendel's laws of inheritance had demonstrated to be true for peas—that transmission frequency and patterns of hereditary characteristics could be predicted—was, subsequently, also shown to be true for physical properties of many other species, such as corn, mice, certain flies *(Drosophila melanogaster)*, and, most important, humans. Naturally, the most difficult challenges were posed by the intellectual capabilities and behavioral differences of humans. Were these characteristics biologically inherited? Since humans could not be subjected to crossbreeding in the laboratory, one had instead to analyze families or twins. Identical twins should be more similar, or "concordant," than nonidentical twins if the trait analyzed is biologically inherited. Internationally, at the time, many scientists quickly concluded that intelligence and psychiatric diseases, like schizophrenia or manic depression, were genetically inherited in a Mendelian manner; moreover, they came to the conclusion that individuals of low

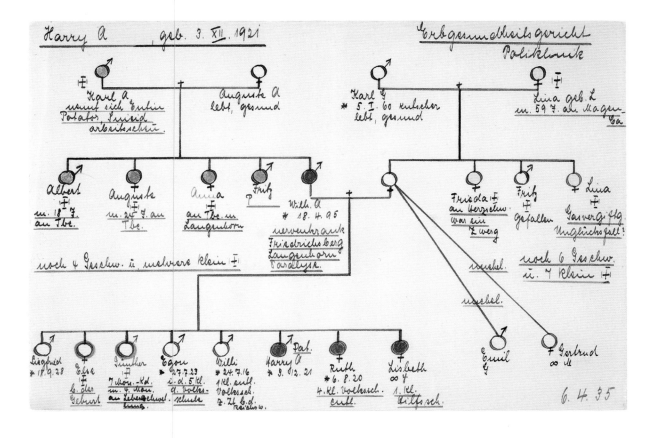

Heredity health card with family genealogy, prepared by staff at the Alsterdorf institution in Hamburg, ca. 1935. *Evangelische Stiftung Alsterdorf, Hamburg*

intelligence tended to breed faster—that is, have more children—than highly intelligent individuals. Being responsible scientists, they predicted accordingly that a terrible breakdown of European and American culture would result unless ways could be found to halt this process. Two possible solutions were proposed. One intended to solve the problem in a "positive" manner by encouraging the more intelligent persons to have more children, while the other solution took a "negative" approach, aiming to prohibit the less intelligent from having any children. The latter solution could only be effected successfully by confining or sterilizing these individuals. Those who endorsed these ideas in the United States and in Great Britain called themselves eugenicists. In Germany, Austria, and Switzerland, many eugenicists referred to themselves as racial hygienists. At first glance, there is little difference between German eugenics and racial hygiene, but closer examination of the scientists involved reveals the fact that racial hygienists often tended to be antisemitic; among the eugenicists, on the other hand, some were actually Jewish.

"Race" was a concept very much in use during this period, discussed and applied in scientific studies; it even influenced the issuance of laws in some countries. Blacks, who were labeled inferior by eugenicists, were said to have low intelligence for genetic reasons. In the United States, marriages between blacks and whites were outlawed in more than 30 states, and sexual relations between blacks and whites were punishable by law.[1] Race mixing was, in general, regarded as a process creating bad results. Despite the lack of any hard scientific evidence, almost all geneticists opposed racial mixing.

German Physicians' Journal, July 1, 1933. Universities, research institutes, and museums had been engaged in eugenics research and campaigns in the Weimar period became mouthpieces for Nazi racism. *National Library of Medicine, NIH, Bethesda, Md.*

GENETICS AND THE NAZIS, 1923–1933

The political demagogue Adolf Hitler was always an antisemite. But how did he come into contact with racial hygiene? On November 9, 1923, Hitler attempted a *putsch* in Munich. It failed. He was captured, tried, convicted for treason, and subsequently spent most of 1924 in a Bavarian jail. Imprisoned under rather liberal conditions, Hitler was able to write *Mein Kampf* during his jail term.[2] Among his friends in Munich was Julius Lehmann, a publisher of medical journals and literature as well as radically nationalist antisemitic books and pamphlets. In 1921, Lehmann had published the first German textbook on human genetics, *Foundations of Human Genetics and Racial Hygiene*.[3] The book was a great success, and when a second edition of the so-called Baur-Fischer-Lenz appeared in 1923, Lehmann sent a copy to his friend Hitler in his jail cell at Landsberg. Chapter 11 of the first volume of *Mein Kampf*, entitled "People and Race" *("Volk und Rasse"),* was inspired by the Baur-Fischer-Lenz. This was stated explicitly by one of the authors, Fritz Lenz, in an article he published, in 1931, on "The Attitude of National Socialism toward Racial Hygiene."[4] Lenz wrote that Hitler

The Kaiser Wilhelm Institute for Anthropology, Human Heredity, and Eugenics, Berlin, 1936. *Archiv zur Geschichte der Max-Planck-Gesellschaft, Berlin*

understood astonishingly well what genetics and racial hygiene were all about. In fact, he regarded him to be the only politician in Europe who really understood the significance of human genetics and racial hygiene. Lenz must have been thinking of the International Congress of Eugenics, in Rome, in 1929, where the American eugenicist Charles B. Davenport, from Cold Spring Harbor, New York, gave a memorandum, written by German anthropologist and eugenicist Eugen Fischer, to Mussolini, proposing eugenic measures for Italy.[5] "Maximum speed is necessary. The danger is enormous," was the bottom line of the memorandum. Mussolini, however, was not interested.

During these years, the only political-party leader truly interested in racial hygiene was Hitler. Most, if not all, German politicians were against involuntary sterilization of the unfit, but, according to the race hygienists, involuntary sterilization was precisely the best way to halt the impending disaster. Yet, for some German racial hygienists, the violent antisemitism of the Nazis was unpleasant. In the third edition of volume two of the Baur-Fischer-Lenz, appearing in 1931, Lenz wrote:

One has to regret the one-sided antisemitism of National Socialism. It seems that—unfortunately—the masses need such "anti" sentiments to become active.... That National Socialism tries honestly to improve the race cannot be doubted.... The question of genetic quality is a hundred times more important than the question of capitalism or socialism, and the fight between black-white-red and black-red-gold [respectively, the colors of the flags of the German Empire and Weimar Republic].[6]

Reluctantly, Lenz and his colleagues were willing to pay the price of antisemitism.

REFLECTIONS OF A GERMAN SCIENTIST

The Purge of Jews
German scientists such as Eugen Fischer collaborated with the Nazi regime in the removal of Jews from academic positions.

Dr. Julius Moses (1868–1942) served in Germany's national parliament, the Reichstag, from 1920 to 1932. A Social Democrat, he helped draft numerous health-care laws, including legislation aimed at protecting children and Germany's "crippled" population. Moses died, in the Theresienstadt ghetto, in September 1942. *Bildarchiv Preussischer Kulturbesitz, Berlin*

Dr. Felix Plaut (1877–1940), a pathologist who devoted much of his research to venereal disease, helped develop the first blood test for diagnosing syphilis. In 1935, he was dismissed from his position as a department head of the Kaiser Wilhelm Institute for Psychiatry, in Munich, by Ernst Rüdin, its director. Plaut committed suicide in 1940, during his exile in London. *Max-Planck-Institut für Psychiatrie, Munich*

THE SUCCESSFUL DEAL BETWEEN NAZIS AND GERMAN GENETICISTS

German scientists, here represented by Fischer and Lenz, hoped to get support for their views through legislation and through funding for race hygiene research. They also wanted, however, to remain independent scientists. The Nazis were willing to give them this; in return, they asked the scientists to accept and validate their violent antisemitism—and this is exactly what Fischer and Lenz did when the Nazis came to power. Instead of being critical of the antisemitic measures, they defended them as scientific necessities. Yet, neither did they say that Jews were inferior, referring to them simply as "different." Although the Nazi politicians were not particularly happy about this, they accepted it; consequently, the scientists got what they wanted—a law allowing involuntary sterilization of a defined group of people. Additionally, several geneticists, among them Fischer, aided the regime's illegal compulsory sterilization of several hundred mixed-race children in the Rhineland region. Moreover, the regime also planned to sterilize most "Gypsies," but, again, a law that would have allowed this never materialized.[7] Last, they discussed the sterilization of all German "quarter Jews," that is, those Germans who had just one Jewish grandfather or grandmother. With the onset of war, however, this project became unrealistic.

After 1933, Fischer steadily and frequently supported antisemitism. In 1933, he had already proposed a law, similar to the Nuremberg law, making marriage between Jews and Germans illegal. There are numerous examples of Fischer's anti-Jewish sentiment, but most revealing perhaps is a sentence he uttered in 1941–42. In what might have been his worst antisemitic statement, he claimed that "the morality and the actions of the Bolshevik Jews indicate such an incredible mentality that

Dr. Richard Goldschmidt (1878–1958) was a geneticist, the author of popular biology textbooks, and the codirector of the Kaiser Wilhelm Institute for Biology. During the 1920s, he promoted eugenic policies, including the sterilization of people with "undesirable" hereditary traits. In 1936, he emigrated to the United States and taught at the University of California at Berkeley. *Archiv zur Geschichte der Max-Planck-Gesellschaft, Berlin*

Dr. Georg Klemperer (1865–1946) was professor of medicine at the University of Berlin and director of internal medicine at Berlin's Moabit Hospital. His textbook *Basis of Clinical Diagnosis* was a standard medical training text. Klemperer emigrated to the United States in 1935. *Bundesarchiv Koblenz*

Dr. Magnus Hirschfeld (1868–1935), a physician, cofounded the Scientific-Humanitarian Committee, in 1897, to advocate for the civil rights of Germany's homosexuals. From 1919 to 1933, he directed the Institute for Sexual Science, in Berlin. Hirschfeld died, in exile, in France. *Ullstein Bild, Berlin*

one can only speak of inferiority and beings of a different species." This was the first time that he used the word *inferior* to describe Jews. By classifying them as a "different species," he essentially suggested that Jews could be killed like animals.[8]

One aspect of antisemitism should not be overlooked—the ousting of Jews from the field of medicine. Once in power, the Nazi regime moved quickly to remove Jewish influence, citing its overrepresentation in the medical profession. In Berlin, almost half of the medical professors were Jewish. By dismissing the Jewish professors, which is precisely what Fischer did while he was rector at Berlin University from 1933 to 1934, massive job opportunities for non-Jewish German academics were created. Many, who shamelessly accepted these newly vacant positions, justified their thievery by claiming to be "saving the field" from Jews.

The plant geneticist Erwin Baur also supported the Nazi regime; he hoped, in fact, to become minister of agriculture in Hitler's government. When the post went instead to the Nazi ideologue and national farmers' leader Walther Darré, Baur clashed with the new ministry. Moreover, in his own institute, Baur was attacked by young SS postdoctoral fellows and students, who considered him to be hopelessly old fashioned. The stress and strain of these developments precipitated a fatal heart attack in late 1933.

SCIENCE OR PSEUDOSCIENCE?

The power structure of Nazi Germany was not homogeneous. At one end were the technocrats who liked and supported science, and who increased the amount of research funding of the German Research Council roughly tenfold between 1932 and

The medicalization of antisemitism is reflected in this March 1941 German-made poster for occupied Poland: "Jews are lice. They cause typhus." Nazi officials advocated the establishment of sealed ghettos in Warsaw and other Polish cities, partly because they believed that Jews were spreading diseases. In fact, such ghettos actually worsened the public health crisis by creating overcrowded and unsanitary conditions. *Archiwum Panstwowe w Lublinie*

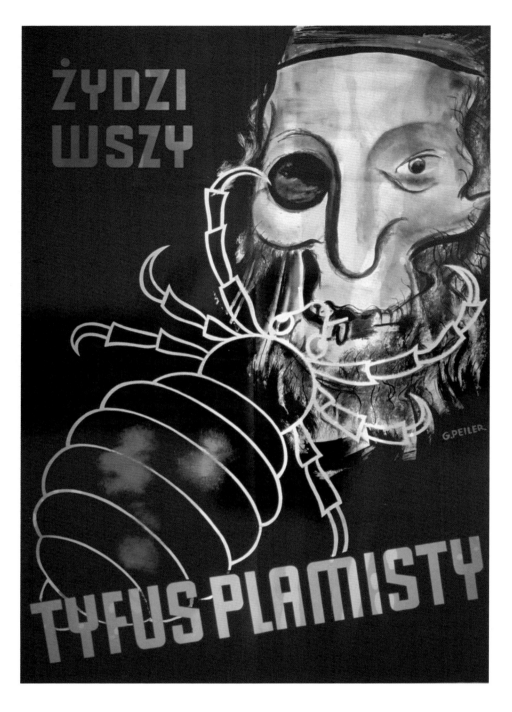

1939. They arranged for all medical schools to create professorships of racial hygiene and for medical genetics to become a standard part of the examination for the medical degree. On the other end were maniacs, like the virulently antisemitic Julius Streicher, head of the Nazi Party in Franconia and publisher of *The Attacker (Der Stürmer)*, a crude propaganda journal. To someone like Streicher, science—in particular, human genetics—was all nonsense. He claimed that just one instance of sexual intercourse between a German woman and a Jew damaged all of the woman's future offspring—that she could never again give birth to Aryan children, even if marrying an Aryan. Those who offered scientific evidence contradicting such theories—who thought they were serving and protecting science—found there were risks involved. Some experienced firsthand the intimidation tactics of a man like Streicher, who, on one occasion, threatened to "kill with [his] dog-whip" Professor Lothar Loeffler (a former assistant of Eugen Fischer) for giving an expert opinion proving Streicher wrong in a "Jewish" paternity case.

Hitler and other Nazi zealots linked a paranoid fear of a Jewish conspiracy to control the world to the threat of Soviet Communism (Bolshevism). The dual menace is portrayed as a biological threat in this image from the April 15, 1943, issue of the Nazi journal *Der Stürmer.* The six-pointed Star of David represents Jewish "microbes," and the hammer and sickle are Bolshevik "germs." *Institut für Zeitgeschichte, Munich*

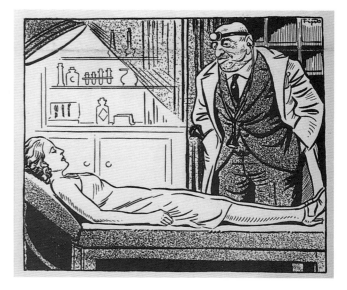

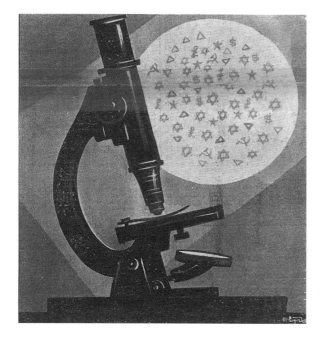

Der Stürmer (The Attacker), published by the virulently antisemitic Julius Streicher, depicts Jewish doctors as sexual predators. February 1935. *Staatsbibliothek zu Berlin*

So far, I have described Baur, Fischer, and Lenz as if they were real scientists who produced real science and not pseudoscience. Let us examine this issue closely. Fischer began his career as an anatomist, becoming professor of anatomy at the University of Freiburg, and only later developing an interest in human genetics. In 1927, he was made director of the newly founded Kaiser Wilhelm Institute for Anthropology, Human Heredity, and Eugenics, in Berlin. The building was partially funded by the Rockefeller Foundation. In that same year, Fischer served as president of the International Congress of Genetics, in Berlin. So, one can safely say that what he did was regarded as real science by his international colleagues and not as pseudoscience. The same was true for Erwin Baur. The American Nobel Prize–winner Hermann J. Muller praised Baur's part of the Baur-Fischer-Lenz as the best available text on human genetics.[9] Fritz Lenz, on the other hand, was more interested in eugenics than in genetics. Yet, he, too, was respected by his international colleagues in human genetics and was never accused of practicing pseudoscience.

During the 1920s and 1930s, twin research was a new and powerful method in human genetics. When Eugen Fischer became director of the Kaiser Wilhelm Institute for Anthropology, in Berlin, he wanted to initiate such research and hired as human genetics section chief Otmar von Verschuer, who had some experience in this type of research. The Rockefeller Foundation became interested and supported the project financially between 1932 and 1935. Verschuer studied hundreds of twins, and published his findings in a book about twin studies and tuberculosis susceptibility.[10] He was invited to speak about his twin research at the Royal Society, in London, in July 1939, and, in August 1939, at the International Congress of Biochemistry.[11] His work was obviously regarded as valid science by his peers.

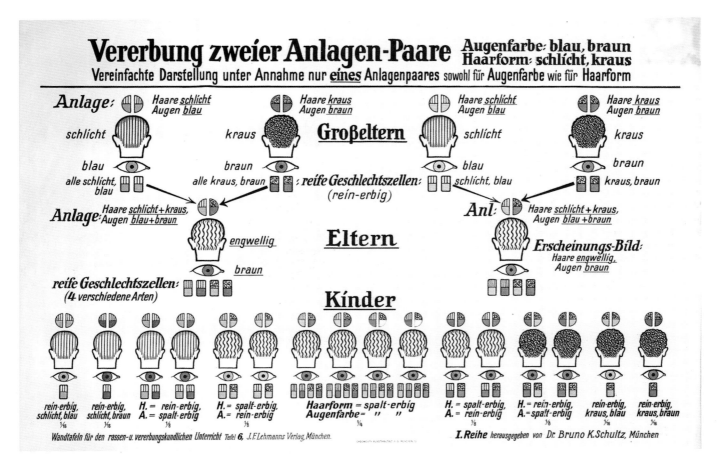

A chart that typifies the Nazi use of the laws of heredity discovered by the nineteenth-century Austrian botanist Gregor Mendel. The Nazis asserted—and many scientists during the Third Reich attempted to prove—that Mendelian principles of dominant and recessive traits in human inheritance predicted inferior offspring from "racially mixed" parents. *USHMM Collection, Gift of Werner Kraus*

In 1943, Verschuer initiated a research project in Auschwitz with camp doctor Josef Mengele, his former student and postdoctoral assistant.[12] They wanted to analyze the susceptibility of twins of various ethnic backgrounds to tuberculosis; for this, they used a test with so-called defense enzymes, discovered in 1909 by Emil Abderhalden.[13] Verschuer did not realize that defense enzymes did not exist, that they were an illusion promoted by Abderhalden. The entire project, therefore, was baseless. Today, it would be called pseudoscience, yet at the time it was regarded as valid science. In Berlin, Verschuer received technical help from Günther Hillmann, a graduate student of Nobel Prize—winner Adolf Butenandt. It is unclear whether Hillmann and Butenandt knew about the experiments in Auschwitz, or simply closed their eyes to what was happening.[14]

Equally respected internationally was the psychiatrist and geneticist Ernst Rüdin. A founding member of the German Society for Racial Hygiene, Rüdin, in 1931, became director of the Kaiser Wilhelm Institute for Psychiatry, in Munich, and was one of the scientists campaigning for a compulsory sterilization law. In the spring of 1933, his institute received a large monetary gift from James Loeb, an American Jewish benefactor, which funded the institute until 1940. Nevertheless, after the Nazis came to power, Rüdin fired his Jewish collaborator, Franz Kallmann. Forced to emigrate to the United States in 1936, Kallmann continued his work on the genetics of schizophrenia. Shortly before he left Germany, he proposed, at a conference in Berlin, that all individuals carrying the heterozygous gene for schizophrenia be forcibly sterilized.[15] Lenz spoke out publicly against him, arguing that Kallmann's proposal applied to roughly 10 to 20 percent of the total population.

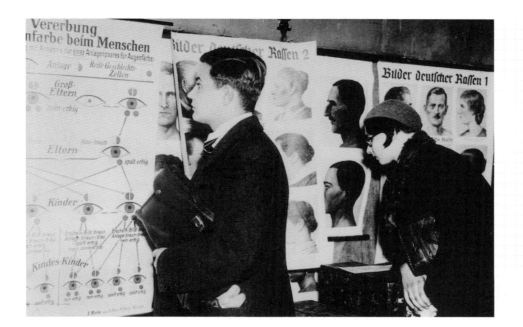

Geneticist Otmar von Verschuer in his laboratory for twin research at the Kaiser Wilhelm Institute, 1928. *Ullstein Bild, Berlin*

Visitors to a racial hygiene exhibition, Berlin, 1934. By displaying teaching posters on basic genetics, such as this one on the heredity of eye color in humans, with juxtaposed charts of the "superior," pure "Nordic race" and "inferior" races, Jews, and other "racial mixtures," Nazified eugenics hoped to establish a scientific basis for Nazi racism. *SV-Bilderdienst, Munich*

Fortunately, this plan was impossible to put into practice, since a test was not available. Kallmann's proposal, however, also indicated that geneticists were well aware that it would take many centuries until the number of homozygous gene carriers could be lowered. This fact is also mentioned in Baur-Fischer-Lenz, and in Hitler's *Mein Kampf*. German eugenicists thought that sterilizing homozygous individuals was only the beginning of a heroic task requiring many, many generations.

RACE HYGIENE, AN AMALGAM OF SCIENCE AND IDEOLOGY

This is not the entire story. What about the eugenic arguments of geneticists for the segregation of Jews? What about arguments that it was advisable to sterilize most Gypsies, since they were no longer the true descendants of the racially pure Gypsies but were instead the descendants of racially mixed criminal types? What about the arguments of psychiatrists that schizophrenics were inferior—that they were just empty shells it was permissible to kill?[16] Here, science was clearly mixed with ideology, and this particular mix was extremely destructive. Could it still be called true science? What about the proposals for a solution to the "Jewish Problem" —for a total and final solution? Words create their own reality, and words lead to actions. If psychiatrists referred to their patients as empty shells long enough, they could not argue against those who said that they should be discarded. It was this contagious mixture of science with ideology that was so very destructive. If this language was then used by scientists who respected science, it was far worse— because then it became utterly destructive. Mengele merely practiced what his

Researchers at the Kaiser Wilhelm
Institute for Psychiatry, Munich,
ca. 1930–35. *Max-Planck-Institut für
Psychiatrie, Munich*

teacher taught. Lenz, on the other hand, was a bit more moderate, yet he, too, was one
of the German race hygienists.

Should one call eugenics or race hygiene pseudoscience? The eugenicists did not
speak falsehoods when proposing their social programs. They lied when they claimed
that it was pure science and no ideology, because they accepted ideology. Fischer
described the situation, as he saw it, in an article he published in March 1943:

*It is a rare and special good fortune for a theoretical science to flourish at a time when
the prevailing ideology welcomes it, and its findings can immediately serve the policy
of the state. The study of human heredity was already sufficiently mature to provide
this, when years ago National Socialism was recasting not only the state but also
our ways of thinking and feeling. Not that National Socialism needed a "scientific"
foundation as proof that it was right, ideologies are formed through practical experience
and struggle rather than through laborious scientific theorizing. However the results of the
study of human heredity became absolutely indispensable as a basis for the important
laws and regulations created by the new state.*[17]

It should be clarified that the most popular German books about race were
not written by scientists but by authors lacking a genetic education, such as the racial
psychologist Ludwig Clauss and the Nordic propagandist Hans F. K. Günther, among
others. Clauss attempted to conjure up a vision of the "Nordic soul," while Günther,
a philologist turned anthropologist, sold more than 270,000 copies of his book
Brief Racial Study of the German People, which defined the "racially ideal" type.[18]

The contribution of the true scientists lay in providing the solid foundation that served to launch all of these books.

GERMAN HUMAN GENETICISTS AFTER 1945

After 1945, the German human geneticists and their international colleagues were all silent. None looked back at the Nazi past, and none wrote articles or books about it. The most outspoken comment came in 1955 from the grand old man Eugen Fischer:

It is certainly not the fault of eugenics, if godless and criminal misuse occurred in National Socialism without any knowledge of the genetic facts, and through the destruction of all human dignity. We deeply regret that as a reaction, true eugenic research was heavily hit, most heavily of course in Germany. Eugenics should not be accused in its international existence. One does not accuse Christian belief when one thinks that the crimes of the Inquisition, the witch trials, and the bloody wars of religion signify human confusion and crimes.[19]

It took another five years before Karl Saller's book on anthropology in the Nazi period appeared. After his critical account, *The Racial Theory of National Socialism in Science and Propaganda*, was published, in 1961, Saller was shunned by most of his German colleagues.[20] Total silence remained in effect until the beginning of the 1980s. Today, when most of the perpetrators are dead, the history of eugenics under the Nazis can finally be written.

Karl Brandt, Hitler's attending physician, was one of 23 defendants in the so-called Doctors Trial, conducted by U.S. military occupation authorities, at Nuremberg, in 1946 and 1947. Brandt was found guilty and sentenced to death by hanging. Many other physicians were never tried for crimes committed in the name of medicine and medical science. *USHMM Collection, Courtesy of John W. Mosenthal*

Eugen Fischer *(left)* is honored during a postwar "Eugen Fischer Day." In attendance were such scientists as Konrad Lorenz *(center)*, who later received the Nobel Prize for Medicine, and Otmar von Verschuer *(far right)*, genetics professor at the University of Münster. Ca. 1950s. *Archiv zur Geschichte der Max-Planck-Gesellschaft, Berlin*

HUMAN GENETICS TODAY

Genetics has grown over the last half century. Genes, which were once only ideas, have become a reality. They can now be isolated and their DNA sequence can be determined. If we speak of a genetic disease, then a specific mutant gene must be isolated. The analysis of the genetics of behavioral traits and psychiatric diseases has shown that, in general, no one single Mendelian gene is responsible. This has made the isolation of such genes difficult. So far, no mutant genes have been isolated for psychiatric diseases like schizophrenia and manic depression or for intelligence. As long as the genes are not isolated, ethnic groups cannot be compared, but this may actually happen in the near future. Therefore, it is most important that the social consequences of today's genetics are discussed among scientists and with the public in order to make misuse impossible. It must be made absolutely clear that science should never become the reason to justify injustices to a genetically defined group of humans.

What is the bottom line? Was Nazi racial science real science or pseudoscience? There is no doubt that science served crime, but was it pseudoscience? There is no simple, clear answer. Racial science under the Nazis was an amalgam of both honest, human genetics and pseudoscience. Like most science, racial science was well funded in Germany, so it was not money that was lacking—what was lacking was international review and discussion. Antisemitism, and the silencing of alternate viewpoints, made international collaboration difficult—even impossible. When the war ended, most of the German racial scientists continued their careers wearing the new mantle of human geneticists. There was no attempt to clarify what had happened,

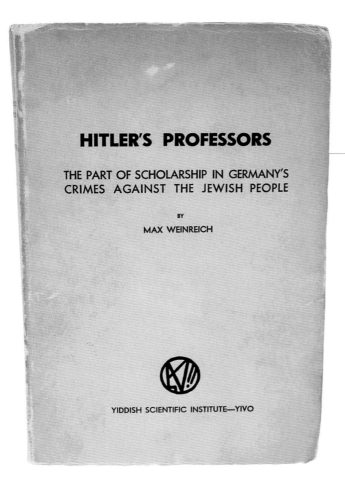

HITLER'S PROFESSORS

THE PART OF SCHOLARSHIP IN GERMANY'S
CRIMES AGAINST THE JEWISH PEOPLE

BY
MAX WEINREICH

YIDDISH SCIENTIFIC INSTITUTE—YIVO

Max Weinreich was one of the first
scholars to indict German academics for
their collaboration with the Nazi regime.
USHMM Collection

*"There were in the memory of mankind
Genghis Khans and Eugen Fischers, but
never before had a Genghis Khan joined
hands with an Eugen Fischer."*

— Max Weinreich, *Hitler's Professors* (1946)

and there were too few attempts to bring the guilty to justice. Decades passed before German scientists became reintegrated into the international community of scientists. Today, however, after the death of this generation, a new phase in human genetics is beginning.

REFLECTIONS OF A GERMAN SCIENTIST

CHRONOLOGY

1859
Charles Darwin's *On the Origin of Species by Means of Natural Selection* is published.

1869
British scientist Francis Galton's *Hereditary Genius* is published.

1883
Francis Galton coins the word *eugenics*. The German equivalent, *Rassenhygiene* (racial hygiene), is first used, in 1895, by Alfred Ploetz, a physician who studied under Swiss psychiatrist August Forel.

1900
Austrian monk Gregor Mendel's 1866 work demonstrating laws of heredity is rediscovered by botanists in Holland, Germany, and Austria.

1905
Alfred Ploetz establishes the German Society for Racial Hygiene.

1911
In the book *Heredity in Relation to Eugenics,* the American zoologist Charles B. Davenport defines *eugenics* as "the science of the improvement of the human race by better breeding." Davenport heads the Eugenics Record Office (ERO), at Cold Spring Harbor, New York.

1912
First International Eugenics Congress meets in London.

1913
German anthropologist Eugen Fischer publishes his study of the "Rehoboth Bastards," the racially mixed *(Mischlinge)* children in colonial German South-West Africa.

1914–18
World War I

1919
Germany becomes a republic under the Weimar Constitution.

1920
Authorization of the Destruction of Life Unworthy of Life (Die Freigabe der Vernichtung lebensunwerten Lebens), by jurist Alfred Binding and psychiatrist Karl Hoche, is published.

1921
Foundations of Human Genetics and Racial Hygiene (Grundriss der menschlichen Erblichkeitslehre und Rassenhygiene), by botanist Erwin Baur, anthropologist Eugen Fischer, and geneticist Fritz Lenz, is published.

1922
Philologist Hans F. K. Günther's *Racial Study of the German People (Rassenkunde des deutschen Volkes)* is published.

The State Institute for Racial Biology, the world's first, is created in Uppsala, Sweden, under the direction of Herman Lundborg, a physician and psychiatrist.

1923
The first endowed chair for racial hygiene in Germany, at the University of Munich, is filled by Fritz Lenz.

November
Adolf Hitler's beer-hall *putsch* fails, and the Nazi Party leader is imprisoned. While in prison, he reads, reportedly, *Foundations of Human Genetics and Racial Hygiene*, published and sent to him by a friend and admirer.

1927
The U.S. Supreme Court, in *Buck v. Bell,* upholds Virginia's state law sanctioning sterilization for the institutionalized hereditarily "unfit."

Spring
The German Society for Racial Hygiene produces Germany's first eugenics film, *The Curse of Heredity (Der Fluch der Vererbung).*

The Kaiser Wilhelm Institute for Anthropology, Human Heredity, and Eugenics, headed by Eugen Fischer, opens in Berlin.

1929

The National Socialist Physicians' League is formed in Germany.

Denmark introduces the first national sterilization law, which is applied largely to mentally retarded persons within institutions.

1932

A draft of a voluntary sterilization bill emerges from the Prussian Health Council.

1933

January 30
Adolf Hitler is appointed chancellor of Germany.

March 23
An Enabling Act is passed by the German Reichstag (parliament) and used by Hitler to establish his Nazi dictatorship.

April 1
An official, nationwide, one-day boycott of Jewish-owned businesses is called by the Nazi Party leadership.

April 7
The Law for the Restoration of the Professional Civil Service is introduced. It excludes most Jewish and "politically unreliable" civil servants and employees from working for the state. This includes university teaching and research posts.

April 22
Jewish physicians are banned from participating in the state medical insurance program.

July 14
The Law for the Prevention of Genetically Diseased Offspring is promulgated by the Hitler cabinet. This national, compulsory sterilization law takes effect on January 1, 1934, and is applied to persons judged hereditarily diseased who are living in or outside institutions.

November 24
The Law against Dangerous Habitual Criminals is published. Courts are authorized to commit "antisocial" individuals to state hospitals, impose protective custody on habitual criminals, and mandate castration for sexual offenders.

1934

October 1
The first course for SS doctors is given at the Kaiser Wilhelm Institute for Anthropology by Professor Eugen Fischer.

1935

January 1
A national law on sterilization goes into effect in Sweden under its Social Democratic government.

June 16–17
A committee of American scientists inspects the Eugenics Record Office (ERO), in Cold Spring Harbor, New York, at the behest of its funder, the Carnegie Institution of Washington. These experts sharply criticize the ERO's dated science and its mingling of science and political advocacy. The ERO loses funding in 1937 and is shut down at the end of 1939.

June 26
The Nazi sterilization law is amended to allow for abortion on "eugenic" grounds.

June 28
German officials revise Paragraph 175 of the German criminal code to broaden the grounds for punishing homosexual behavior.

September 2
Hitler promulgates the so-called Nuremberg racial laws at the Nazi Party rally, in Nuremberg. The Law for the Protection of German Blood and German Honor prohibits marriage and sexual relations between German Jews and "persons of German or related blood." A second law, the Reich Citizenship Law, confers "Reich citizenship" on German "Aryans" and only "state citizenship" or "subject" status for Jews. Under this law, decrees define who is a Jew and who is a *Mischling* (of mixed Jewish and "Aryan" parentage).

October 18
The Marital Health Law prohibits marriage if either partner has a mental condition, hereditary disease, severe contagious disease, tuberculosis, or any venereal disease.

December
SS chief Heinrich Himmler establishes the organization Fount of Life *(Lebensborn)* as part of his effort to combat abortion.

1936
February 6
The Reich Ministry of the Interior decrees that records for all patients in mental hospitals and institutions must include hereditary biological data.

February 20
The Nazi Racial Policy Office releases the film *Hereditarily Ill (Erbkrank).*

October 10
SS chief Heinrich Himmler creates the Reich Central Office for Combating Homosexuality and Abortion.

November
The Research Institute for Racial Hygiene and Population Biology of the Reich Health Office initiates a research program on "Gypsies," under the direction of Dr. Robert Ritter.

1937
April 15
Jews in German universities are prohibited from taking doctoral exams.

April–June
The so-called Rhineland bastards, children fathered by non-European French colonial soldiers, are forcibly sterilized.

1938
March 13
In the *Anschluss*, German troops cross the border into Austria, and Austria is incorporated into the German Reich.

September 28
The medical licenses of all Jewish doctors are revoked; Jewish doctors are limited to treating only other Jews.

November 9–10
In Nazi-led nationwide pogroms, called *Kristallnacht* (The Night of Broken Glass), synagogues and Jewish homes and businesses are looted and burned. Nearly 30,000 German and Austrian Jewish men are deported to concentration camps.

1939
August 18
The Reich Ministry of the Interior orders the reporting of all infants and children up to the age of three with serious mental or physical disabilities.

September 1
German forces invade Poland; World War II begins.

September 21
The Reich Ministry of the Interior orders the reporting of all institutions caring for "mental patients, epileptics, and the feebleminded."

September 29–November 1
Special SS mobile killing squads *(Einsatzgruppen)* murder 2,342 hospitalized psychiatric patients in Kocborowo, near Bydgoszcz, Poland.

October
To make room for ethnic German settlers, the SS begins expelling Poles and Jews from their homes in the Danzig Corridor and Warthegau, the area of occupied Poland annexed to the Reich. By the end of 1940, an estimated 325,000 people have been deported eastward into the General Government, the German-occupied territory of central and eastern Poland.

October–December
The SS shoots or gasses, in hermetically sealed vans, 4,400 "incurable" patients in Polish mental hospitals at Koscian (near Posen) and Chelm-Lubelski.

October
Hitler issues a secret memo authorizing doctors "to grant a mercy death to patients judged incurably sick." This memo is backdated to September 1 to associate the "euthanasia" program with the war effort.

December–January
Patients from the Tiegenhof hospital, in Prussia, are murdered in gassing vans.

1940
January
The systematic poisoning of patients by gas is officially inaugurated at the Brandenburg "euthanasia" facility.

April 30
The Lodz ghetto is ordered sealed.

October
Dr. Julius Hallervorden removes the brains from the corpses of 40 children killed at the Brandenburg-Görden pediatric "euthanasia" ward.

October
The Warsaw ghetto is established.

1941
January
The gassing of patients begins at the Hadamar "euthanasia" facility.

Spring
In Operation 14f13, SS chief Heinrich Himmler orders physicians involved in "euthanasia" to select for murder any ailing or exhausted concentration camp prisoners unfit for work. Tens of thousands of prisoners chosen in this manner are gassed at the Sonnenstein, Bernburg, and Hartheim "euthanasia" facilities during the next four years.

June 22
Operation Barbarossa, the German invasion of the Soviet Union, begins. Soon after, SS *Einsatzgruppen* killings begin in Soviet territory.

August 3
Bishop Clemens August von Galen denounces "euthanasia" killings, in a sermon in Münster.

August 24
The first phase of the "euthanasia" program ends after Hitler issues a stop order. Some 70,000 patients from 100 German hospitals have been killed by gassing at six facilities in Germany and Austria.

September
Soviet prisoners of war are used in experiments to test Zyklon B gassing at Auschwitz.

September 29–30
Members of *Einsatzgruppe C* murder more than 33,000 Jews at Babi Yar, near Kiev, Ukraine.

December
Gassing of Jews in sealed vans begins at Chelmno, in occupied Poland.

1942
January 20
Fifteen Nazi and senior government officials meet at Wannsee, in Berlin, to plan the fulfillment of the "Final Solution," the extermination of Europe's Jews.

March
The gassing of Jews begins at the Belzec killing center. Christian Wirth, formerly employed in the "euthanasia" program, and many other superfluous staff from this halted program help carry out the mass murder.

Spring
Anthropologists associated with the Institute for German Work in the East, in Cracow, conduct a study of Jewish families in Tarnow, in occupied Poland.

May
The gassing of Jews begins in the Sobibor killing center. Franz Stangl, previously stationed at the Hartheim "euthanasia" facility, serves briefly as commandant at Sobibor.

July
The Treblinka extermination camp, near Warsaw, begins operation. "Euthanasia" physician Irmfried Eberl is its first commandant.

July 19
Under instructions from Hitler, Himmler orders the deportation, to extermination camps or closed labor camps, of all Jews remaining in occupied Poland's General Government.

Summer
Adult "euthanasia" begins again on a broad scale at a number of institutions throughout Germany and Austria. Lethal overdoses of medication and starvation, rather than gassing, are the new modes of killing.

October 1
Otmar von Verschuer becomes the director of the Kaiser Wilhelm Institute for Anthropology, Human Heredity, and Eugenics.

December 16
Himmler issues an order for the deportation of "all Roma Gypsies, all part Gypsies, and all non-German Gypsies of Balkan origin" to the Auschwitz concentration camp.

December
Dr. Carl Clauberg arrives at Auschwitz, where he begins experiments on prisoners to develop a method of mass sterilization.

1943

March 9
A new law imposes the death penalty on anyone who "impairs the vitality of the German people by carrying out abortions."

May 30
SS doctor Josef Mengele arrives at Auschwitz.

August 18
Otmar von Verschuer, director of the Kaiser Wilhelm Institute for Anthropology, cooperates with Mengele on a research project using the diverse racial groups in the Auschwitz concentration camp.

1944

May 15–July 9
More than 430,000 Hungarian Jews are deported to Auschwitz, where most are gassed.

June 6
Allied military forces invade Western Europe on D-Day.

1945

January 27
Soviet troops enter Auschwitz.

March–April!
"Euthanasia" continues in institutions not yet liberated by the Allies.

April 30
Hitler commits suicide in his bunker in Berlin.

May 7
Germany surrenders and the war in Europe ends.

1946–47

December 9, 1946–August 20, 1947
Twenty-three German physicians and administrators are prosecuted for war crimes and crimes against humanity. Sixteen doctors are found guilty, and seven are sentenced to death. Many scientists, including Eugen Fischer, Otmar von Verschuer, and Julius Hallervorden, escape punishment and continue their careers.

ENDNOTES

INTRODUCTION

1 Francis Galton, "Hereditary Talent and Character," *Macmillan's Magazine* 12, no. 68 (1865), 165.

2 L. C. Dunn, *A Short History of Genetics: The Development of Some of the Main Lines of Thought, 1864–1939* (Ames: Iowa State University Press, 1991), 89–94.

3 Paul Weindling, *Health, Race and German Politics between National Unification and Nazism, 1870–1945* (Cambridge: Cambridge University Press, 1989), 63–89.

4 Martin S. Pernick, *The Black Stork: Eugenics and the Death of "Defective" Babies in American Medicine and Motion Pictures since 1915* (New York: Oxford University Press, 1996), fig. 6; *Eugenik, Erblehre, Erbpflege* 1, no. 11 (1931): 237–42.

5 Weindling, *Health, Race and German Politics*, 82; Richard F. Wetzell, *Inventing the Criminal: A History of German Criminology, 1880–1945* (Chapel Hill: University of North Carolina Press, 2000), chaps. 1–2.

6 Weindling, *Health, Race and German Politics*, chaps. 5–6.

7 Philip R. Reilly, *The Surgical Solution: A History of Involuntary Sterilization in the United States* (Baltimore: Johns Hopkins University Press, 1991), 34.

8 Wendy Kline, *Building a Better Race: Gender, Sexuality, and Eugenics from the Turn of the Century to the Baby Boom* (Berkeley: University of California Press, 2001); Angus McLaren, *Our Own Master Race: Eugenics in Canada, 1885–1945* (Toronto: McClelland & Stewart, 1990).

9 Felix Tietze, "Sterilisierung zu eugenischen Zwecken," *Volksaufartung, Erbkunde, Eheberatung*, 8/9 (1929): 169–212.

10 Erwin Baur, Eugen Fischer, and Fritz Lenz, *Human Heredity*, Eden and Cedar Paul, trans., 3d ed. (London: Allen & Unwin, 1931), 604–8.

11 Adolf Hitler, *Mein Kampf*, Ralph Manheim, trans. (Boston: Houghton Mifflin, 1971), 403–4.

12 Michael Burleigh and Wolfgang Wippermann, *The Racial State: Germany 1933–1945* (Cambridge: Cambridge University Press, 1991), 69.

13 Fritz Lenz, "Eugenics in Germany," *The Journal of Heredity* 16, no. 5 (May 1924): 229.

14 Benno Müller-Hill, *Murderous Science: The Elimination by Scientific Selection of Jews, Gypsies, and Others in Germany, 1933–1945*, George R. Fraser, trans. (Plainview, N.Y.: Cold Spring Harbor Laboratory Press, 1998), 13. For a general discussion of how German scientists lent legitimacy to Nazi policies, see also Robert Proctor, *Racial Hygiene: Medicine under the Nazis* (Cambridge, Mass.: Harvard University Press, 1988).

15 Benno Müller-Hill, *Tödliche Wissenschaft: Die Aussonderung von Juden, Zigeunern und Geisteskranken, 1933–1945* (Reinbeck bei Hamburg: Rowohlt, 1984); Ernst Klee, *"Euthanasie" im NS-Staat: Die "Vernichtung lebensunwerten Lebens"* (Frankfurt am Main: S. Fischer, 1983).

16 Amt der Oberösterreichischen Landesregierung–Landeskulturdirektion, *Wert des Lebens: Gedenken, lernen, begreifen* (Linz: Trauner Verlag, 2003).

17 Volkhard Knigge and Jürgen Seifert, *Vom Antlitz zur Maske: Wien, Weimar, Buchenwald 1939* (Weimar: Nationale Mahn- und Gedenkstätte Buchenwald, 1999). The Natural History Museum's continuing search for Jewish survivors studied by Vienna anthropologists is important in reconstructing the history of the Nazi-era research.

18 Carola Sachse and Benoit Massin, *Biowissenschaftliche Forschung an Kaiser-Wilhelm-Instituten und die Verbrechen des NS-Regimes. Informationen über den gegenwärtigen Wissensstand*, Preprint from the Research Program, "History of the Kaiser Wilhelm Society in the National Socialist Era" (Berlin: Max Planck Society, 2000).

19 Gerhard Baader, Johannes Cramer, and Bettina Winter, *"Verlegt nach Hadamar." Die Geschichte einer NS-"Euthanasie"-Anstalt* (Kassel: Landeswohlfahrtsverband Hessen, 1991); Christian Pross and Götz Aly, *Der Wert des Menschen: Medizin in Deutschland, 1918–1945* (Berlin: Edition Hentrich, 1989), published in an abridged English version as *The Value of the Human Being* (Berlin: Edition Hentrich, 1991); Arbeitsgruppe zur Erforschung der Geschichte der Karl-Bonhoeffer-Nervenklinik, *Totgeschwiegen, 1933–1945: Zur Geschichte der Wittenauer Heilstätten Seit 1957 Karl-Bonhoeffer-Nervenklinik* (Berlin: Edition Hentrich, 1989).

20 Dokumentationsarchiv des österreichischen Widerstandes, *Der Krieg gegen die "Euthanasie": Zur Geschichte der NS-Medizin in Wien,* http://www.gedenkstaettesteinhof.at/; Sammlung Prinzhorn/Wunderhorn, *Todesursache: Euthanasie. Verdeckte Morde in der NS-Zeit* (Heidelberg: Verlag Das Wunderhorn, 2002); Stiftung Deutsches Hygiene-Museum, *Der [im]perfekte Mensch: Vom Recht auf Unvollkommenheit* (Ostfildern-Ruit: Hatje Cantz Verlag, 2000).

GERMAN EUGENICS, 1890–1933

1 Paul Weindling, *Health, Race and German Politics between National Unification and Nazism, 1870–1945* (Cambridge: Cambridge University Press, 1989), 486–87; Jeremy Noakes and Geoffrey Pridham, eds., *Nazism: A History in Documents and Eyewitness Accounts, 1919–1945*, vol. 2 (New York: Schocken Books, 1988), 1001–2; Christian Pross and Götz Aly, *The Value of the Human Being: Medicine in Germany, 1918–1945*, trans. Marc Iwand (Berlin: Ärztekammer Berlin, 1991), 12.

2 Sheila Faith Weiss, "The Race Hygiene Movement in Germany," *Osiris*, 2d ser., 3 (1987): 196–97; Peter Weingart, Jürgen Kroll, and Kurt Bayertz, *Rasse, Blut und Gene. Geschichte der Eugenik und Rassenhygiene in Deutschland* (Frankfurt am Main: Suhrkamp, 1988), 114–24.

3 Sheila Faith Weiss, *Race Hygiene and National Efficiency: The Eugenics of Wilhelm Schallmayer* (Berkeley and Los Angeles: University of California Press, 1987), 27–37.

4 Wilhelm Schallmayer, *Vererbung und Auslese im Lebenslauf der Völker: Eine staatswissenschaftliche Studie auf Grund der neueren Biologie* (Jena: Gustav Fischer, 1903), x.

5 Alfred Ploetz, *Die Tüchtigkeit unsrer Rasse und der Schutz der Schwachen. Ein Versuch über Rassenhygiene und ihr Verhältnis zu den humanen Idealen, besonders zum Socialismus* (Berlin: Fischer, 1895), 5.

6 Weindling, *Health, Race and German Politics*, 141–42.

7 Weiss, "Race Hygiene Movement," 207.

8 Hans-Walter Schmuhl, "Rassenhygiene in Deutschland—Eugenik in der Sowjetunion: Ein Vergleich," in *Im Dschungel der Macht. Intellektuelle Professionen unter Stalin und Hitler*, Dietrich Beyrau, ed. (Göttingen: Vandenhoeck and Ruprecht, 2000), 362.

9 Weiss, "Race Hygiene Movement," 209; Schmuhl, "Rassenhygiene in Deutschland," 365; Weindling, *Health, Race and German Politics*, 144–47.

10 Ibid., 211–13.

11 Weiss, *Race Hygiene and National Efficiency*, 50–59.

12 Weindling, *Health, Race and German Politics*, chap. 6.

13 Ibid., 404.

14 Sheila Faith Weiss, "Race and Class in Fritz Lenz's Eugenics," *Medizinhistorisches Journal* 27 (1992): 17n41; Niels C. Lösch, *Rasse als Konstrukt. Leben und Werk Eugen Fischers* (Frankfurt am Main: Peter Lang, 1997), 119.

15 Baur to American geneticist and eugenicist A. F. Blakeslee, 1921, in Bentley Glass, "A Hidden Chapter of German Eugenics between the Two World Wars," *Proceedings of the American Philosophical Society* 125 (1981): 364.

16 Weindling, *Health, Race and German Politics*, 406–9.

17 Ibid.

18 Donald J. Dietrich, "Catholic Eugenics in Germany, 1920–1945: Hermann Muckermann, S. J. and Joseph Mayer," *Journal of Church and State* 34 (1992): 575–99; Michael Schwartz, "Konfessionelle Milieus und Weimarer Eugenik," *Historische Zeitschrift* 265 (1995): 403–48; Schwartz, *Sozialistische Eugenik: Eugenische Sozialtechnologien in Debatten und Politik der deutschen Sozialdemokratie 1890–1933* (Bonn: Dietz, 1995).

19 Sheila Faith Weiss, "Pedagogy, Professionalism, and Politics: Biology Instruction during the Third Reich," in *Science, Technology and National Socialism*, Monika Rennenberg and Mark Walker, eds. (New York: Cambridge University Press, 1994), 184–96, 377–85.

20 Weiss, "Race Hygiene Movement," 215.

21 Heiner Fangerau, *Etablierung Eines Rassenhygienischen Standartwerkes 1921–1941. Der Baur-Fischer-Lenz im Spiegel der Zeitgenössischen Rezensionsliteratur. Marburger Schriften zur Medizingeschichte* 43 (Frankfurt am Main: Peter Lang, 2001).

22 Erwin Baur, Eugen Fischer, Fritz Lenz, *Grundriss der menschlichen Erblichkeitslehre und Rassenhygiene*, 2 vols. (Munich: J. F. Lehmann, 1921). Here, I have quoted from the 1931 English translation of the 3d German edition of the book, vol. 1 (1927), *Human Heredity*, Eden and Cedar Paul, trans. (London: Allen & Unwin; New York: Macmillan Company, 1931), 668, 671.

23 Weiss, "Race and Class in Fritz Lenz's Eugenics," 12–16.

24 Maria Günther, *Die Institutionalisierung der Rassenhygiene an den deutschen Hochschulen vor 1933* (medical diss., Mainz, privately printed, 1982), 61.

25 Volker Roelcke, "Psychiatrische Wissenschaft im Kontext nationalsozialistischer Politik und 'Euthanasie.' Zur Rolle von Ernst Rüdin und der Deutschen Forschungsanstalt für Psychiatrie/Kaiser-Wilhelm-Institut," in *Geschichte der Kaiser-Wilhelm-Gesellschaft im Nationalsozialismus. Bestandsaufnahme und Perspektiven der Forschung*, vol. 1, Doris Kaufmann, ed. (Göttingen: Wallstein, 2000), 116.

26 Weindling, *Health, Race and German Politics*, 384.

27 Weiss, "Humangenetik und Politik als gegenseitige Ressourcen": Das Kaiser-Wilhelm-Institut für Anthropologie, menschliche Erblehre und Eugenik, 1927–45. Preprint from the Research Program, "History of the Kaiser Wilhelm Society in the National Socialist Era" (Berlin: Max Planck Society, forthcoming 2004).

28 Weindling, *Health, Race and German Politics*, 309–10, 437, 554.

29 Weiss, "Race Hygiene Movement," 222.

30 Sabine Schleiermacher, *Sozialethik im Spannungsfeld von Sozial- und Rassenhygiene. Der Mediziner Hans Harmsen im Centralausschuss für die Innere Mission. Abhandlungen zur Geschichte der Medizin und der Naturwissenschaft* 85 (Berlin: Matthiesen, 1998). Quotation taken from Schleiermacher, "The Eugenics Politics of Protestant Welfare Organizations in Germany During the Weimar Republic" (lecture, American Historical Society Meetings, Atlanta, Ga., 1996).

31 Weiss, "Race Hygiene Movement," 225.

32 Jonathan Harwood, *Styles of Scientific Thought: The German Genetics Community, 1900–1933* (Chicago: University of Chicago Press, 1993); Susanne Heim, *"Die reine Luft der wissenschaftlichen Forschung": Zum Selbstverständnis der Wissenschaftler der Kaiser-Wilhelm-Gesllschaft.* Preprint from Research Program, "History of the Kaiser Wilhelm Society in the National Socialist Era" (Berlin: Max Planck Society, 2002); see also *Autarkie und Ostexpansion: Pflanzenzucht und Agrarforschung im Nationalsozialismus,* Susanne Heim, ed. (Göttingen: Wallstein, 2002).

33 Hans-Peter Kröner, *Von der Rassenhygiene zur Humangenetik. Das Kaiser-Wilhelm-Institut für Anthropologie, menschliche Erblehre und Eugenik nach dem Kriege* (Stuttgart: Gustav Fischer, 1998), 18.

34 Weiss, "Race and Class in Fritz Lenz's Eugenics," 17n42.

35 *Archiv der Max-Planck-Gesellschaft* (AMPG) I Rep 3 n.8 *Tätigkeitsbericht* Jg. 1931/32.

INTERNATIONAL EUGENICS

1 Francis Galton, *Inquiries into the Human Faculty* (London: Macmillan, 1883), 24–25. The most recent biography of Galton is Nicholas Wright Gillham, *A Life of Sir Francis Galton: From African Exploration to the Birth of Eugenics* (New York: Oxford University Press, 2001).

2 Entry into the various national eugenics movements can be obtained in Mark B. Adams, ed., *The Well-Born Science: Eugenics in Germany, France, Brazil, and Russia* (New York: Oxford University Press, 1990); Nancy L. Stepan, *The Hour of Eugenics: Race, Gender, and Nation in Latin America* (Ithaca, N.Y.: Cornell University Press, 1991); Diane B. Paul, *Controlling Human Heredity, 1865 to the Present* (Amherst, N.Y.: Humanity Books, 1995).

3 Daniel J. Kevles, *In the Name of Eugenics: Genetics and the Uses of Human Heredity* (Cambridge, Mass.: Harvard University Press, 1995), chap. 2

4 Ibid.

5 Garland Allen, "The Eugenics Record Office at Cold Spring Harbor, 1910–1940: An Essay in Institutional History," *Osiris*, 2d. ser., 2 (1986): 225–64.

6 Charles B. Davenport, *Heredity in Relation to Eugenics* (New York: Henry Holt, 1911).

7 Kevles, *Name of Eugenics*, 62.

8 Edward J. Larson, *Sex, Race, and Science: Eugenics in the Deep South* (Baltimore: Johns Hopkins University Press, 1995), 2.

9 Mark B. Adams, "The Soviet Nature-Nurture Debate," in Loren R. Graham, ed., *Science and the Soviet Social Order* (Cambridge, Mass.: Harvard University Press, 1990), 101.

10 Ibid., 102, 106.

11 Gunnar Broberg and Nils Roll-Hansen, eds., *Eugenics and the Welfare State: Sterilization Policy in Denmark, Sweden, Norway, and Finland* (East Lansing: Michigan State University Press, 1996), 78, 197.

12 Kevles, *Name of Eugenics*, 74.

13 Davenport, *Heredity in Relation to Eugenics,* 216, 218–19, 221–22.

14 Kevles, *Name of Eugenics*, 63.

15 Stefan Kühl, *The Nazi Connection: Eugenics, American Racism, and German National Socialism* (New York: Oxford University Press, 1994), chap. 2; Edwin Black, *War against the Weak: Eugenics and America's Campaign to Create a Master Race* (New York: Four Walls Eight Windows, 2003), 240.

16 Ibid., 62–63.

17 Kevles, *Name of Eugenics*, 96–97, 102–3.

18 Larson, *Sex, Race, and Science*, 81.

19 Philip R. Reilly, *The Surgical Solution: A History of Involuntary Sterilization in the United States* (Baltimore: Johns Hopkins University Press, 1991); Angus McLaren, *Our Own Master Race: Eugenics in Canada, 1885–1945* (Toronto: McClelland & Stewart, 1990); Daniel J. Kevles, "Eugenics in North America," in Robert A. Peel, ed., *Essays in the History of Eugenics* (London: Galton Institute, 1998), 208–26.

20 Larson, *Sex, Race, and Science*, 2; Marouf A. Hasian, Jr., *The Rhetoric of Eugenics in Anglo-American Thought* (Athens and London: University of Georgia Press, 1996).

21 *Buck v. Bell*, 274 U.S. 201–7 (1927); Kevles, *Name of Eugenics*, 110–12.

22 Kevles, "Eugenics in North America."

23 Ibid., 136–47.

24 Broberg and Roll-Hansen, *Eugenics and the Welfare State*, 104–5.

25 Kühl, *The Nazi Connection*, chap. 2.

26 On German eugenics, see Robert Proctor, *Racial Hygiene: Medicine under the Nazis* (Cambridge, Mass.: Harvard University Press, 1988).

27 Kevles, *Name of Eugenics*, 118.

28 Julian S. Huxley and A. C. Haddon, *We Europeans: A Survey of "Racial" Problems* (London: Jonathan Cape, 1935), 18, 184, 68, 91, 96–97, 25–26, 267–68.

29 Larson, *Sex, Race, and Science*, 146.

30 Clarence Darrow, "The Eugenics Cult," *American Mercury* 30 (1926): 135.

31 Kevles, *Name of Eugenics*, 268.

NAZI STERILIZATION AND REPRODUCTIVE POLICIES

1   Wilhelm Frick, *Bevölkerungs- und Rassenpolitik. Ansprache auf der ersten Sitzung des Sachverständigenbeirats für Bevölkerungs- und Rassenpolitik am 28. Juni 1933* (Berlin: Reichsausschuss für Volksgesundheitsdienst, 1933).

2   Arthur Gütt, Ernst Rüdin, and Falk Ruttke, *Gesetz zur Verhütung erbkranken Nachwuchses vom 14. Juli 1933 mit Auszug aus dem Gesetz gegen gefährliche Gewohnheitsverbrecher und über Massnahmen der Sicherung und Besserung vom 24. November 1933* (Munich: J. F. Lehmann, 1934), 5, 60; 1936.

3   Gisela Bock, *Zwangssterilisation im Nationalsozialismus: Studien zur Rassenpolitik und Frauenpolitik* (Opladen: Westdeutscher Verlag, 1986), 230–42, 312; Henry Friedlander, *The Origins of Nazi Genocide: From Euthanasia to the Final Solution* (Chapel Hill: University of North Carolina Press, 1995), 27–30. The lower age limit for sterilization was ten. Men could be sterilized at any age above this, women over 50 were usually not. By far, most sterilizations were performed on persons between 18 and 45.

4   Stefan Kühl, *Die Internationale der Rassisten. Aufstieg und Niedergang der internationalen Bewegung für Eugenik und Rassenhygiene im 20. Jahrhundert* (Frankfurt am Main: Campus Verlag, 1997). For the period before 1933, Sheila Faith Weiss, *Race Hygiene and National Efficiency: The Eugenics of Wilhelm Schallmayer* (Berkeley and Los Angeles: University of California Press, 1987).

5   Erwin Baur, Eugen Fischer, and Fritz Lenz, *Grundriss der Menschlichen Erblichkeitslehre und Rassenhygiene*, 2 vols. (Munich: J. F. Lehmann, 1921, 1923, 1931, 1936, 1940); Erwin Baur et al., *Human Heredity*, Eden and Cedar Paul, trans. (London: Allen & Unwin; New York: Macmillan Company, 1931).

6   Hans-Walter Schmuhl, *Rassenhygiene, Nationalsozialismus, Euthanasie* (Göttingen: Vandenhoeck and Ruprecht, 1987), 100–102.

7   Matthias M. Weber, *Ernst Rüdin. Eine kritische Biographie* (Berlin: Springer Verlag, 1993), 129–30.

8   Quote from Bock, *Zwangssterilisation*, 51.

9   Weber, *Ernst Rüdin*, 175; Bock, *Zwangssterilisation*, 112.

10 Ernst Rüdin, "Aufgaben und Ziele der Deutschen Gesellschaft für Rassenhygiene," *Archiv für Rassen- und Gesellschaftsbiologie* 28 (1934): 228.

11 Bock, *Zwangssterilisation*, 86–87.

12 There were few such cases. Self-applications could not be withdrawn and were highly suspect; the courts usually rejected them.

13 For the manifold methods of compulsion, see Bock, *Zwangssterilisation*, chap. 5.

14 Hans Burkhart, *Der rassenhygienische Gedanke und seine Grundlagen* (Munich: Reinhardt, 1930), 93; Martin Staemmler, "Die Sterilisierung Minderwertiger vom Standpunkt des Nationalsozialismus," in *Eugenik–Erblehre–Erbpflege* 3 (1933): 97.

15 *Eugenic News* 18 (1933): 89–90.

16 Erich Ristow, *Erbgesundheitsrecht* (Stuttgart: Kohlhammer, 1935), 111; Gütt, Rüdin, Ruttke, *Gesetz zur Verhütung* (1936), 221; Bock, *Zwangssterilisation*, 111.

17 Ristow, *Erbgesundheitsrecht*, 27. For the "may-or-must" debate, see Bock, *Zwangssterilisation*, 202–5, 396–400.

18 Alfons Labisch and Florian Tennstedt, *Der Weg zum "Gesetz über die Vereinheitlichung des Gesundheitswesens," vom 3. Juli 1934* (Düsseldorf: Akademie für öffentliches Gesundheitswesen, 1985), 325.

19 Hans Luxenburger, *Psychiatrische Erblehre* (Munich: J. F. Lehmann, 1938), 109. See especially vol. 1 of series *Handbuch der Erbkrankheiten*, edited by Arthur Gütt: Alfred Dubitscher, *Der Schwachsinn* (Leipzig: Thieme, 1937); and vol. 2: Berthold Kihn and Hans Luxenburger, *Die Schizophrenie* (Leipzig: Thieme, 1940).

20 Gunnar Broberg and Nils Roll-Hansen, eds., *Eugenics and the Welfare State: Sterilization Policy in Denmark, Sweden, Norway, and Finland* (East Lansing: Michigan State University Press, 1996); Kühl, *Internationale der Rassisten*, especially chap. 3; Bock, *Zwangssterilisation*, 302–3.

21 Quoted in ibid., 243–44.

22 Ernst Rüdin, "Das deutsche Sterilisationsgesetz," in *Erblehre und Rassenhygiene im völkischen Staat*, Rüdin, ed. (Munich: J. F. Lehmann, 1934), 161.

23 Gütt, Rüdin, Ruttke, *Gesetz zur Verhütung* (1936), 121, 129.

24 *Eugenic News*, 89–90.

25 Bock, *Zwangssterilisation*, 352–53.

26 Diemut Majer, *"Fremdvölkische" im Dritten Reich* (Boppard: Boldt, 1981), 859.

27 Bock, *Zwangssterilisation*, 99, 160–61, 382–88, 436–38.

28 Ibid., 152, 156, for figures and sources.

29 Wallace R. Deuel, *People under Hitler* (New York: Harcourt, Brace and Company, 1942), 221; Bock, *Zwangssterilisation*, 95.

30 Burkhard Jellonnek and Rüdiger Lautmann, eds., *Nationalsozialistischer Terror gegen Homosexuelle* (Paderborn: Ferdinand Schöningh, 2002); Günter Grau, ed., *Hidden Holocaust? Gay and Lesbian Persecution in Germany 1933–45*, Patrick Camiller, trans. (London: Cassell, 1995).

31 Georg Lilienthal, *Der "Lebensborn e.V.": ein Instrument nationalsozialistischer Rassenpolitik* (Frankfurt am Main: Fischer Taschenbuch Verlag, 1993), 229.

THE "SCIENCE OF RACE"

1 Otto Aichel and Otmar von Verschuer, eds., *Festband Eugen Fischer zum 60. Geburtstage* (Stuttgart: Schweizerbart, 1934).

2 Eberhard Geyer, "Wissenschaft am Scheideweg," *Archiv für Rassen- und Gesellschaftsbiologie* 37 (1944): 1–6.

3 Michael Schwartz, "Sozialismus und Eugenik. Zur fälligen Revision eines Geschichtsbildes," *Internationale wissenschaftliche Korrespondenz zur Geschichte der deutschen Arbeiterbewegung* 25 (1989): 465–89; Schwartz, *Sozialistische Eugenik. Eugenische Sozialtechnologien in Debatten und Politik der deutschen Sozialdemokratie, 1890–1933* (Bonn: Dietz, 1995).

4 Peter Weingart, Jürgen Kroll, and Kurt Bayertz, *Rasse, Blut und Gene. Geschichte der Eugenik und Rassenhygiene in Deutschland* (Frankfurt: Suhrkamp, 1988), 243–44.

5 Charles G. Seligman, "Presidential Address. Anthropology and Psychology: A Study of Some Points of Contact," *Journal of the Royal Anthropological Institute of Great Britain and Ireland* 54 (1924): 13–46, 28–30; Elazar Barkan, *The Retreat of Scientific Racism: Changing Concepts of Race in Britain and the United States between the World Wars* (Cambridge: Cambridge University Press, 1992), 30–34.

6 Hans F. K. Günther, *Rassenkunde des deutschen Volkes* (Munich: J. F. Lehmann, 1922, 1933); Günther, *Rassenkunde Europas* (Munich: J. F. Lehmann, 1926); Günther, *Rassenkunde des jüdischen Volkes* (Munich: J. F. Lehmann, 1929).

7 Eugen Fischer and Hans F. K. Günther, *Deutsche Köpfe nordischer Rasse* (Munich: J. F. Lehmann, 1927).

8 Benoit Massin, "Anthropologie raciale et national-socialisme. Heurs et malheurs du paradigme de la 'race,'" in Josiane Olff-Nathan, ed., *La science sous le Troisième Reich* (Paris: Seuil, 1993), 197–262.

9 Benoit Massin, "Anthropologie und Humangenetik im Nationalsozialismus, oder: Wie schreiben deutsche Wissenschaftler ihre eigene Wissenschaftsgeschichte?," in Heidrun Kaupen-Haas, ed., *Wissenschaftlicher Rassismus* (Frankfurt am Main: Campus Verlag, 1999), 12–64; Robert Proctor, "From *Anthropologie* to *Rassenkunde* in the German Anthropological Tradition," in George W. Stocking, Jr., ed., *Bones, Bodies, Behavior: Essays on Biological Anthropology* (Madison: University of Wisconsin Press, 1988), 138–79.

10 Reiner Pommerin, *"Sterilisierung der Rheinlandbastarde": Das Schicksal einer farbigen deutschen Minderheit, 1918–1937* (Düsseldorf: Droste, 1979).

11 See Niels C. Lösch, *Rasse als Konstrukt: Leben und Werk Eugen Fischers* (Frankfurt: Peter Lang, 1997), 344–49.

12 Eugen Fischer, *Die Rehobother Bastards und das Bastardierungsproblem beim Menschen: anthropologische und ethnographische Studien am Rehobother Bastardvolk in Deutsch-Südwest-Afrika* (Jena: G. Fischer, 1913).

13 Wolfgang Abel, "Zähne und Kiefer in ihrer Wechselbeziehung bei Buschmännern, Hottentotten, Negern und ihren Bastarden," *Zeitschrift für Morphologie und Anthropologie* 31 (1933): 314–61.

14 Wolfgang Abel, "Bastarde am Rhein," *Neues Volk* 2 (1934): 4–7.

15 Heidrun Kaupen-Haas, "Die Bevölkerungsplaner im Sachverständigenbeirat für Bevölkerungs-und Rassenpolitik," in Kaupen-Haas, ed., *Der Griff nach der Bevölkerung. Aktualität und Kontinuität nazistischer Bevölkerungspolitik* (Nördlingen: Greno, 1986), 104–20.

16 See Peter Liebermann, "Psychiatrie und Kriminologie," in Wolfgang Blaschke et al., eds., *Nachhilfe zur Erinnerung. 600 Jahre Universität zu Köln* (Cologne: Pahl-Rugenstein, 1988), 6–68.

17 See Wolfgang Ayass, *"Asoziale" im Nationalsozialismus* (Stuttgart: Klett-Cotta, 1995).

18 Joachim S. Hohmann, *Robert Ritter und die Erben der Kriminalbiologie. "Zigeunerforschung" im Nationalsozialismus und in Westdeutschland im Zeichen des Rassismus* (Frankfurt: Peter Lang, 1991).

19 Wolfgang Ayass et al., *Feinderklärung und Prävention. Kriminalbiologie, Zigeunerforschung und Asozialenpolitik* (Berlin: Rotbuch Verlag, 1988).

20 Michael Zimmermann, *Rassenutopie und Genozid: Die nationalsozialistische "Lösung der Zigeunerfrage"* (Hamburg: Christians, 1996).

21 Benoit Massin, "From Virchow to Fischer: Physical Anthropology and 'Modern Race Theories' in Wilhelmine Germany (1890–1914)," in George W. Stocking, Jr., ed., *Volksgeist as Method and Ethic: Essays on Boasian Ethnography and the German Anthropological Tradition*, vol. 8, *History of Anthropology* (Madison: University of Wisconsin Press, 1996), 79–154; Massin, *Le savant, la race, et la politique. La conversion de la "sci-*

ence de l'Homme" allemande à la "science de la race" (1890–1914) (Ph.D. diss., EHESS, Paris, 2003).

22 "10 Jahre Verlobungs- und Heiratsbefehl in der Schutzstaffel," *Volk und Rasse* 1 (1942): 1–4.

23 Robert L. Koehl, *RKFDV: German Resettlement and Population Policy, 1939–1945: A History of the Reich Commission for the Strengthening of Germandom* (Cambridge: Harvard University Press, 1957); Isabel Heinemann, *"Rasse, Siedlung, deutsches Blut." Das Rasse- und Siedlungshauptamt der SS und die rassenpolitische Neuordnung Europas* (Göttingen: Wallstein Verlag, 2003).

24 Isabel Heinemann, "Another Type of Perpetrator: The SS Racial Experts and Forced Population Movements in the Occupied Regions," *Holocaust and Genocide Studies* 15 (2001): 387–411.

25 Carola Sachse and Benoit Massin, *Biowissenschaftliche Forschung an Kaiser-Wilhelm-Instituten und die Verbrechen des NS-Regimes. Informationen über den gegenwärtigen Wissensstand*, Preprint from the Research Program, "History of the Kaiser Wilhelm Society in the National Socialist Era" (Berlin: Max Planck Society, 2000).

26 Berlin Document Center File, Josef Mengele; Michael Burleigh, "Die Stunde der Experten," in Mechtild Rössler and Sabine Schleiermacher, eds., *Der "Generalplan Ost." Hauptlinien der nationalsozialistischen Planungs- und Vernichtungspolitik* (Berlin: Akademie Verlag, 1993).

27 Renate Rissom, *Fritz Lenz und die Rassenhygiene* (Husum: Matthiesen Verlag, 1983), 83.

28 Helmut Heiber, "Der Generalplan Ost," *Vierteljahreshefte für Zeitgeschichte* 6 (1958): 281–325, 312–13.

29 Annegret Kiefer, *Das Problem einer "Jüdischen Rasse." Eine Diskussion zwischen Wissenschaft und Ideologie, 1870–1930* (Frankfurt: Peter Lang, 1991); Massin, *Le savant, la race, et la politique.*

30 See Georg Lilienthal, "Die jüdischen 'Rassenmerkmale.' Zur Geschichte der Anthropologie der Juden," *Medizinhistorisches Journal* 28 (1993): 173–98. For example: Fritz Wagenseil, "Beiträge zur physischen Anthropologie der spaniolischen Juden und zur jüdischen Rassenfrage," *ZMA* 23 (1925): 33–150. The paper by Karl Saller, "Beitrag zur Anthropologie der Ostjuden," *ZMA* 32 (1933): 125–31, was published in 1933 but researched during the Weimar Republic.

31 Günther, *Rassenkunde des jüdischen Volkes.*

32 Otmar von Verschuer, *Erbpathologie, Ein Lehrbuch für Ärzte und Medizinstudierende* (Dresden: Steinkopf, 1937), 4; Verschuer, *Leitfaden der Rassenhygiene* (Leipzig: Thieme, 1941), 126–27, 2d ed. (1944), 138–39.

33 Verschuer to Fischer, November 5, 1937, University Archive Münster, Private Papers Verschuer.

34 Otmar von Verschuer, "Was kann der Historiker, der Genealoge und der Statistiker zur Erforschung des biologischen Problems der Judenfrage beitragen?," in *Forschungen zur Judenfrage*, vol. 2 (Hamburg: Hanseatische Verlagsanstalt, 1937), 216–22.

35 Eugen Fischer, "Rassenentstehung und älteste Rassengeschichte der Hebräer," *Forschungen zur Judenfrage*, vol. 3 (Hamburg: Hanseatische Verlagsanstalt, 1938), 121–36.

36 Dora M. Koenner, "Vorläufiger Bericht über rassenkundliche Aufnahmen an Juden," *Verhandlungen der Deutschen Gesellschaft für Rassenforschung* 10 (1940): 121–26; see also in the same volume, Eberhard Geyer, "Ansprache," 126.

37 Ronald Hirte, "Die anthropologische Untersuchung am Stadion," in Volkhard Knigge and Jürgen Seifert, eds., *Vom Antlitz zur Maske. Wien–Weimar–Buchenwald 1939* (Weimar: Stiftung Gedenkstätten Buchenwald und Mittelbau-Dora, Stiftung Weimarer Klassik, 1999), 26–28.

38 Ronald Hirte, "Anthropologie und Menschenverachtung. Bilder einer Ausstellung, Wien 1939," in Knigge and Seifert, *Vom Antlitz zur Maske*, 20–25.

39 Götz Aly, "Das Posener Tagebuch des Anatomen Hermann Voss," in *Biedermann und Schreibtischtäter. Materialen zur deutschen Täter-Biographie, Beiträge zur NS Gesundheits- und Sozialpolitik* (Berlin: Rotbuch Verlag, 1987), 15–66.

40 Felicitas Heimann-Jelinek, "Zur Geschichte einer Austellung. Masken. Versuch über die Schoa," in Fritz Bauer Institut, ed., *"Beseitigung des jüdischen Einflusses." Antisemitische Forschung, Eliten und Karrieren im Nationalsozialismus* (Frankfurt am Main: Campus Verlag, 1999), 131–45; Maria Teschler-Nicola and Margit Berner, "Die Anthropologische Abteilung des Naturhistorischen Museums in der NS-Zeit: Berichte und Dokumente von Forschungs- und Sammlungsaktivitäten 1938–1945," in *Senatsprojekt der Universität Wien. Untersuchungen zur Anatomischen Wissenschaft in Wien 1938–1945* (Vienna: Akademischer Senat der Universität Wien, 1988), 333–58. Classified as a "minor National Socialist," Wastl was suspended from his post at the museum in 1945 and retired in 1948. Until his death in 1968, he worked as a freelance genetics expert, issuing lineage documents for the courts.

41 Michael Burleigh, *Germany Turns Eastwards: A Study of Ostforschung in the Third Reich* (Cambridge: Cambridge University Press, 1988), 253–90; Gretchen E. Schafft and Gerhard Zeidler, *Register to the Materials of the Institut für Deutsche Ostarbeit*, National Anthropological Archives, 1998. I thank Gretchen E. Schafft for her draft chapter on "Scientific Racism in Service of the Reich: German Anthropologists in the Nazi Era," which includes a section on the IdO.

42 Götz Aly and Susanne Heim, *Vordenker der Vernichtung. Auschwitz und die deutschen Pläne für eine neue europäische Ordnung* (Frankfurt: Fischer Taschenbuch Verlag, 1993), 198–202; Götz Aly, *Macht – Geist – Wahn. Kontinuitäten deutschen Denkens* (Berlin: Argon, 1997), 93–98.

43 Archives of the Max Planck Society (AMPG), I, Rep. 1a / 2409, KWI for Anthropology, October 11, 1940.

44 Eugen Fischer and Gerhard Kittel, *Das antike Weltjudentum, Forschungen zur Judenfrage*, 7 (Hamburg: Hanseatische Verlagsanstalt, 1943).

45 David Martin Luebke and Sybil Milton, "Locating the Victim: An Overview of Census-Taking, Tabulation Technology, and Persecution in Nazi Germany," *Annals of the History of Computing* 16/30 (1994): 25–39.

46 Georg Lilienthal, "Anthropology and National Socialism," in Israel Gutman, ed., *Encyclopedia of the Holocaust,* vol. 1 (New York: Macmillan, 1990), 48–52; Lilienthal, "Anthropologie und Nationalsozialismus: Das erb- und rassenkundliche Abstammungsgutachten," *Jahrbuch des Instituts für Geschichte der Medizin der Robert Bosch Stiftung* 6 (1989): 71–91.

47 Hans-Peter Kröner, "Von der Vaterschaftsbestimmung zum Rassegutachten," *Berichte zur Wissenschafts-geschichte* 22 (1999): 257–64.

48 Beate Meyer, *"Jüdische Mischlinge": Rassenpolitik und Verfolgungserfahrung, 1933–1945* (Hamburg: Dölling and Galitz), 1999.

49 Edouard Conte and Cornelia Essner, *La Quête de la race. Une anthropologie du nazisme* (Paris: Hachette, 1995), 363–65.

50 Bundesarchiv Koblenz, R73 / 1542. DFG / Verschuer.

51 Universitätsarchiv Münster, Private Papers Verschuer. See all quotations in Benno Müller-Hill, "Das Blut von Auschwitz und das Schweigen der Gelehrten," in *Geschichte der Kaiser-Wilhelm-Gesellschaft im Nationalsozialismus*, vol. 1 (Göttingen: Wallstein, 2000), 210–11.

52 Niederschrift über die Sitzung des Kuratoriums des KWI für Anthropologie am 9 Januar 1941, Anlage: Erbbiologische Centralsammlung, AMPG/ Abt. I / Rep.1A / 2404 / 4 and 2400 / Bl. 192 and 194; Erich Nehse, "Beiträge zur Morphologie, Variabilität und Vererbung der menschlichen Kopfbehaarung," *Zeitschrift für Morphologie und Anthropologie* 36 (1937): 151–82; Rita Hauschild, "Rassenunterschiede zwischen negriden und europiden Primordialcranien des 3. Fetalmonats. Ein Beitrag zur Entstehung der Schädelform," *Zeitschrift für Morphologie und Anthropologie* 36 (1937): 215–79.

53 Hans Hesse, *Augen aus Auschwitz. Ein Lehrstück über nationalsozialistischen Rassenwahn und medizinische Forschungen. Der Fall Dr. Karin Magnussen* (Hessen: Klartext, 2001); Ernst Klee, *Deutsche Medizin im Dritten Reich. Karrieren vor und nach 1945* (Frankfurt: S. Fischer, 2001), 348–81.

NAZI "EUTHANASIA" PROGRAMS

1 Karl Binding and Alfred Hoche, *Die Freigabe der Vernichtung lebensunwerten Lebens. Ihr Mass und ihre Form* (Leipzig: Meiner, 1920).

2 Ewald Meltzer, *Das Problem der Abkürzung "lebensunwerten" Lebens* (Halle: Marhold Verlag, 1925), 88–90, 98–99.

3 Dr. Kuhne, "Offene Fürsorge," *Allgemeine Zeitschrift für Psychiatrie* (1929): 359; Valentin Faltlhauser, "Erfahrungen des Erlanger Fürsorgearztes," *Allgemeine Zeitschrift für Psychiatrie* (1925): 121.

4 Bernhard Richarz, *Heilen, Pflegen, Töten. Zur Alltagsgeschichte einer Heil- und Pflegeanstalt bis zum Ende des Nationalsozialismus* (Göttingen: Verlag für Medizinische Psychologie, 1987), 78.

5 Michael Freeden, "Eugenics and Progressive Thought: A Study of Ideological Affinity," *The Historical Journal* 22 (1979): 667.

6 Horst Dickel, *"Die sind doch alle unheilbar." Zwangssterilisation und Tötung der "Minderwertigen" im Rheingau, 1934–1945* (Wiesbaden: Hessisches Institut für Bildungsplanung und Schulentwicklung, 1988), 68–69.

7 Josef Ackermann, *Heinrich Himmler als Ideologe* (Göttingen: Musterschmidt, 1970), 183; Ernst Klee, *Euthanasie im NS-Staat. Die "Vernichtung lebensunwerten Lebens"* (Frankfurt am Main: Fischer, 1983), 52; Johannes Tuchel, ed., *"Kein Recht auf Leben." Beiträge und Dokumente zur Entrechtung und Vernichtung "lebensunwerten Lebens im Nationalsozialismus"* (Berlin: Wissenschaftlicher Autoren-Verlag, 1984).

8 Bundesarchiv Koblenz, R18/5586: RMdI Runderlass, August 18, 1939.

9 Some children were also murdered by gassing after being caught up in the adult euthanasia program.

10 Michael Burleigh and Wolfgang Wippermann, *The Racial State: Germany, 1933–1945* (Cambridge: Cambridge University Press, 1991), 144.

11 Ibid., 144–50.

12 Michael Burleigh, *Death and Deliverance: "Euthanasia" in Germany, 1900–1945* (Cambridge: Cambridge University Press, 1994; repr. London: Pan Macmillan, 2002), 113–29.

13 Ibid., 135–40.

14 Christina Vanja and Martin Vogt, "Zu melden sind sämtliche Patienten," in Vanja, ed., *Euthanasie in Hadamar. Die nationalsozialistische Vernichtungspolitik in hessischen Anstalten* (Kassel: Landeswohl-fahrtsverband Hessen, 1991), 29.

15 Burleigh, *Death and Deliverance*, 150–52.

16 Ibid., 162–70.

17 Peter Löffler, ed., *Clemens August Graf von Galen: Akten, Briefe und Predigten 1933–1946*, vol. 2 (Mainz: Matthias Grünewald Verlag, 1988), 543.

18   Burleigh, *Death and Deliverance*, 174–80.

19   Burleigh and Wippermann, *The Racial State*, 153–61.

20   Ibid., 161–64; Burleigh, *Death and Deliverance*, 220–37; Gordon J. Horowitz, *In the Shadow of Death: Living Outside the Gates of Mauthausen* (New York: Maxwell Macmillan International, 1990).

21   "Aktion Reinhard," in Ernst Klee, *Euthanasie im NS–Staat*; Burleigh, *Death and Deliverance*, 220–37.

22   Ibid., 238–66.

23   Ernst Klee, *Was Sie taten–was sie wurden. Ärzte, Juristen und andere Beteiligte am Kranken- oder Judenmord* (Frankfurt am Main: Fischer Taschenbuch Verlag, 1988); Burleigh, *Death and Deliverance*, 269–90.

FROM "EUTHANASIA" TO THE "FINAL SOLUTION"

1   For a more detailed account of the history discussed in this essay, see Henry Friedlander, *The Origins of Nazi Genocide: From Euthanasia to the Final Solution* (Chapel Hill: University of North Carolina Press, 1995).

2   Gisela Bock, *Zwangssterilisation im Nationalsozialismus: Studien zur Rassenpolitik und Frauenpolitik* (Opladen: Westdeutscher Verlag, 1986), 103.

3   Arthur Gütt, Ernst Rüdin, and Falk Ruttke, *Gesetz zur Verhütung erbkranken Nachwuchses vom 14. Juli 1933 nebst Ausführungsverordnungen, bearbeitet und erläutert*, 1st ed. (Munich: J. F. Lehmann, 1934), 6.

4   Joseph Walk, ed., *Das Sonderrecht für die Juden im NS-Staat: Eine Sammlung der gesetzlichen Massnahmen und Richtlinien—Inhalt und Bedeutung* (Heidelberg: C. F. Müller Juristischer Verlag, 1981).

5   Arthur Gütt, Herbert Linden, and Franz Massfeller, *Blutschutz- und Ehegesundheitsgesetz: Gesetz zum Schutze des deutschen Blutes und der deutschen Ehre und Gesetz zum Schutze der Erbgesundheit des deutschen Volkes nebst Durchführungsverordnungen sowie einschlägigen Bestimmungen, dargestellt, medizinisch und juristisch erläutert*, 1st ed. (Munich: J. F. Lehmann, 1936), 21, 25çff.

6   Uwe Dietrich Adam, *Judenpolitik im Dritten Reich* (Düsseldorf: Droste Verlag, 1979), 125–31; Karl Schleunes, *The Twisted Road to Auschwitz* (Urbana: University of Illinois Press, 1970), 121–25.

7   Cited in Gütt, Linden, and Massfeller, *Blutschutz- und Ehegesundheitsgesetz*, 21.

8   Ibid., 16.

9   See Sybil Milton, "Vorstufe zur Vernichtung: Die Zigeunerlager nach 1933," *Vierteljahrshefte für Zeitgeschichte* 43 (1995): 115–30.

10   See Franz Calvelli-Adorno, "Die rassische Verfolgung der Zigeuner vor dem 1. März 1943," *Rechtssprechung zum Widergutmachungsrecht* 12 (December 1961): 529–37.

11   Walk, *Sonderrecht für die Juden*, 146n81.

12   Leo Alexander, "Medical Science under Dictatorship," *New England Journal of Medicine* 241, no. 2 (1949): 40.

13   National Archives and Records Administration (NARA), RG 238: interrogation Karl Brandt, October 1, 1945, p.m., 7–8.

14   Dokumentationsarchiv des österreichischen Widerstandes (DÖW), file E18370/3: Kriminalpolizei Linz, interrogation Vinzenz Nohel, September 4, 1945; DÖW, file E18370/1: Staatsanwaltschaft (StA) Frankfurt, Js 18/61, Generalstaatsanwalt (GStA), interrogation Georg Renno, February 1, 1965, 3–4, 7, 17, and Landgericht (LG) Frankfurt, Untersuchungsrichter, Verfahren Js 18/61 (GStA), interrogation Fritz Tauscher, Hamburg, June 2, 1964; Hessisches Hauptstaatsarchiv, Wiesbaden, (HHStA), 461/32061/7: LG Frankfurt, Verfahren Adolf Wahlmann, Hans-Bodo Gorgass, Irmgard Huber, 4a KLs 7/47 (4a Js 3/46), Protokoll der öffentlichen Sitzung der 4. Strafkammer, February 24, 1947, 16–18 (testimony Hans-Bodo Gorgass).

15   Friedlander, *Origins of Nazi Genocide*, 86–110.

16   Ibid.

17   Ibid.

18   Ibid.

19   Ibid.

20   NARA, RG 338, Microfilm Publication T-1021, roll 18, "Hartheim Statistics," 1. Although the microfilm has always been available, the original was lost for some time. This writer, together with archivist Richard Boylan, rediscovered it at the Suitland depot of NARA. It is now at Archive II, and was for a time on display at the USHMM.

21   Richard Breitman, *The Architect of Genocide: Himmler and the Final Solution* (New York: Alfred A. Knopf, 1991), 87–88.

22   GStA Frankfurt, Anklage Georg Renno, Hans-Joachim Becker und Friedrich Robert Lorent, Js 18/61 (GStA), Js 7/63 (GStA), Js 5/65 (GStA), November 7, 1967, 48; LG Frankfurt, Urteil Hans-Joachim Becker und Friedrich Robert Lorent, Ks 1/69 (GStA), May 27, 1970, 49.

23   See Henry Friedlander, "The Nazi Concentration Camps," in *Human Responses to the Holocaust*, Michael Ryan, ed. (New York: Edwin Mellon Press, 1981), 47–48; Walter Grode, *Die "Sonderbehandlung 14f13" in den Konzentrationslagern des Dritten Reiches: Ein Beitrag zur Dynamik faschistischer Vernichtungspolitik* (Frankfurt: Peter Lang, 1987), 82.

24   Friedlander, *Origins of Nazi Genocide*, 187–245.

25   Beginning in January 1939, the Nazis forced German-Jewish men to adopt the middle name "Israel."

26 Ibid., 263–83; see also Gerhard Schmidt, *Selektion in der Heilanstalt, 1939–1945* (Frankfurt: Edition Suhrkamp, 1983), 73.

27 For copies of the circular, see Hauptstaatsarchiv (HStA) Stuttgart, Bestand J355: Reich Ministry of the Interior (sig. Linden) to Württemberg Ministry of the Interior, April 15, 1940, and Staatsanwaltschaft (StA) Hamburg, Verfahren Lensch und Struve, 147 Js 58/67, Gesundheitsbehörde, Bd. 1: Reich Ministry of the Interior (sig. Linden) to Reichsstatthalter in Hamburg, April 15, 1940.

28 Nuremberg Doc. NO–1143 contains numerous such letters from Eglfing-Haar to welfare offices, insurance companies, and state attorneys (copies in Boston University Library, Leo Alexander Collection, box 57).

29 Friedlander, *Origins of Nazi Genocide*, 263–83.

30 Ibid, 280–83; Schmidt, *Selektion in der Heilanstalt*, 75.

31 Friedlander, *Origins of Nazi Genocide*, 263–83.

32 DÖW, file 4608.

33 StA Stuttgart, Verfahren Albert Widmann, Ks 19/62 (19 Js 328/60), interrogation Herbert Kalisch, Mannheim, January 25, 1960.

34 Ibid., March 4, 1960.

35 GStA Frankfurt, Irmfried Eberl Taschenkalender 1940. On the front is stamped: "Dr. med. Irmfried Eberl, Berlin-Schöneberg, Innsbrucker Str. 34/1. Aufg./II, Fernruf 716279."

36 Helmut Krausnick and Hans-Heinrich Wilhelm, *Die Truppe des Weltanschauungskrieges: Die Einsatzgruppen der Sicherheitspolizei und des SD, 1938–1942* (Stuttgart: Deutsche Verlagsanstalt, 1981), 173–205; Krausnick, "Judenverfolgung," in Hans Buchheim et al., *Anatomie des SS-Staates,* vol. 2 (Munich: Deutscher Taschenbuch Verlag, 1967), 235–366.

37 See Alfred Streim, "The Tasks of the SS Einsatzgruppen," *Simon Wiesenthal Center Annual* 4 (1987): 309–28; "Correspondence (Krausnick and Streim)," *Wiesenthal Center Annual* 6 (1989): 311–47.

38 Raul Hilberg, *The Destruction of the European Jews* (New York: Holmes and Meier, 1985), 1219.

39 On Gypsies, see Ronald Headland, *Messages of Murder: A Study of the Reports of the Einsatzgruppen of the Security Police and the Security Service, 1941–1943* (Rutherford, N.J.: Fairleigh Dickinson University Press, 1992), 53–54, 63–64, 71, 114, 142, 157, 169; Adelheid L. Rüter-Ehlermann and C. F. Rüter, eds., *Justiz und NS-Verbrechen (JuNSV)* (Amsterdam: University Press Amsterdam, 1968–89), vol. 20, no. 588: LG Essen, 29 Ks 1/64, March 29, 1965; ZStL, Sammlung UdSSR, Bd. 245Ac, 318 (from 1945 Soviet report).

40 On the disabled, see U.S. Military Tribunal, Transcript of the Proceedings in Case 1, 2545–47; Nuremberg Doc. L-180: Einsatzgruppe A Gesamtbericht bis zum 15. October 1941 (Stahlecker report), 37.

41 Nuremberg Doc. NO-1758.

42 Hans Mommsen, "Die Realisierung des Utopischen: Die 'Endlösung der Judenfrage' im Dritten Reich," *Geschichte und Gesellschaft* 9 (1983): 381–420; Götz Aly, *"Endlösung": Völkerverschiebung und der Mord an den europäischen Juden* (Frankfurt: Fischer, 1995).

43 See Gerald Fleming, *Hitler and the Final Solution* (Berkeley: University of California Press, 1984).

44 Nuremberg Docs. PS–710, NG–2586: Hermann Göring to Reinhard Heydrich, July 31, 1941.

45 Hilberg, *Destruction of the European Jews,* 401.

46 See Nuremberg Doc. NO-365: Alfred Wetzel to Heinrich Lohse, October 25, 1941. See also ibid. NO-997: Reichsminister für die besetzten Ostgebiete to Lohse, draft, October 1941.

47 *JuNSV,* vol. 21, no. 594: LG Bonn, 8 Ks 3/62, March 30, 1963 (Chelmno trial); Adalbert Rückerl, *NS-Verbrechen vor Gericht* (Heidelberg: C. F. Müller Juristischer Verlag, 1982), 243–94; Hilberg, *European Jews,* 1219.

48 Adalbert Rückerl, *NS-Vernichtungslager im Spiegel deutscher Strafprozesse* (Munich: Deutscher Taschenbuch Verlag, 1977), 87–242.

49 U.S. Military Tribunal, Transcript of the Proceedings in Case 1, 7514 (testimony Viktor Brack).

50 LG Hagen, Urteil Werner Dubois, 11 Ks 1/64, December 20, 1966, 35–36; see also Christopher Browning, *Fateful Months: Essays on the Emergence of the Final Solution* (New York: Holmes and Meier, 1985), 30–31.

51 LG Hagen, Urteil Dubois, 11 Ks 1/64, December 20, 1966, 268–73.

52 Rückerl, *NS-Vernichtungslager,* 117–18; Friedlander, *Origins of Nazi Genocide,* 284–302.

53 Ibid., 287.

54 *Fedorenko v. United States,* 449 U.S. 490, 493 (1981).

55 U.S. Military Tribunal, Transcript of the Proceedings in Case 1, 7516 (testimony Viktor Brack).

56 Franciszek Piper, *Die Zahl der Opfer von Auschwitz,* Jochen August, trans. (Oswiecim: Verlag Staatliches Museum, 1993); Hilberg, *Destruction of the European Jews,* 3d ed. (New Haven: Yale University Press, 2003), 1320.

REFLECTIONS OF A GERMAN SCIENTIST

1 Geza von Hoffmann, *Die Rassenhygiene in den Vereinigten Staaten von Nordamerika* (Munich: J. F. Lehmann, 1913).

2 Adolf Hitler, *Mein Kampf* (Munich: Franz Eher Verlag, vol. 1, 1925; vol. 2, 1927).

3   Erwin Baur, Eugen Fischer, and Fritz Lenz, *Grundriss der Menschlichen Erblichkeitslehre und Rassenhygiene*, 2 vols. (Munich: J. F. Lehmann), *Menschliche Erblichkeitslehre*, 1921, 1923, 1927, 1936. *Menschliche Auslese und Rassenhygiene (Eugenik)*, 1921, 1923, 1931.

4   Fritz Lenz, "Die Stellung des Nationalsozialismus zur Rassenhygiene," *Archiv für Rassenhygiene und Gesellschaftsbiologie* 29 (1931): 300.

5   Friedrich Burgdörfer, "Eugenische Tagung in Rom," *Allgemeines Statistisches Archiv* 20 (1930): 442–44.

6   Lenz, *Menschliche Auslese und Rassenhygiene (Eugenik)* (1931), 317.

7   Himmler ordered "*Zigeunermischlinge*" (racially mixed, or "hybrid," Gypsies) to Auschwitz on December 16, 1942; this was carried out in 1943. Exempt from this order were Roma and Sinti who could show consistent employment and fixed residence (but most could not); those serving in the German army or who had been decorated; and those working in the armaments industry whose employer could demonstrate that they were essential for the war effort. In this so-called Auschwitz decree, it was specifically stated that Sinti/Roma above the age of 12 who remained in Germany should be immediately and compulsorily sterilized. The *Reichszentrale zur Bekämpfung des Zigeunerunwesens* (Central Office for the Combating of the Gypsy Pest) pushed for the immediate execution of this action, urging physicians to register completed procedures with the public health office and the Reich Criminal Police. Karola Fings and Frank Sparing, "*z. Zt. Zigeunerlager*": *Die Verfolgung der Düsseldorfer Sinti und Roma im Nationalsozialismus* (Cologne: Kölner Volksblatt-Verlag, 1992), 77.

8   Karl Saller, *Die Rassenlehre des Nationalsozialismus in Wissenschaft und Propaganda* (Darmstadt: Progress-Verlag, 1961); Benno Müller-Hill, *Murderous Science: The Elimination by Scientific Selection of Jews, Gypsies, and Others in Germany, 1933–1945*, George R. Fraser, trans. (Plainview, N.Y.: Cold Spring Harbor Laboratory Press, 1998).

9   Hermann J. Muller, review of *The Scientific Basis of Evolution*, by Thomas Hunt Morgan, *Birth Control Review* 17 (1933): 19–21; repr. in *Studies in Genetics: Selected Papers of H. J. Muller* (Bloomington: Indiana University Press, 1962), 541–44.

10 Otmar von Verschuer and Karl Diehl, *Zwillingstuberkulose. Zwillingsforschung und erbliche Tuberkulosedisposition* (Jena: Gustav Fischer Verlag, 1933).

11 Otmar von Verschuer, "Twin Research from the Time of Francis Galton to the Present Day," *Proceedings of the Royal Society* (B) 128 (1940): 62–81.

12 Benno Müller-Hill, "The Blood from Auschwitz and the Silence of the Scholars," *History and Philosophy of the Life Sciences* 21 (1999): 331–65.

13 Ute Deichmann and Benno Müller-Hill, "The Fraud of Abderhalden's Enzymes," *Nature* 393 (1998): 109–11.

14 Benno Müller-Hill, "Selective Perception: The Letters of Adolf Butenandt, Nobel Prize Winner and President of the Max Planck Society," *Comprehensive Biochemistry* 42 (2003): 548–79.

15 Franz Kallmann, "Die Fruchtbarkeit der Schizophrenen," in *Bevölkerungsfragen. Bericht des Internationalen Kongresses für Bevölkerungsfragen*, Berlin, August 26, 1935, Hans Harmsen and Franz Lohse, eds. (Munich: J. F. Lehmann, 1936).

16 Müller-Hill, *Murderous Science*, 42–43, 100–03.

17 Eugen Fischer, "Erbe als Schicksal," *Deutsche Allgemeine Zeitung*, 28 March 1943.

18 Ludwig Clauss, *Die Nordische Seele* (Munich: J. F. Lehmann, 1932); Clauss, *Rasse und Seele* (Munich: J. F. Lehmann, 1926); Clauss, *Rasse und Charakter* (Munich: J. F. Lehmann, 1938); Hans F. K. Günther, *Kleine Rassenkunde des Deutschen Volkes* (Munich: J. F. Lehmann, 1929); Günther, *Rassenkunde des jüdischen Volkes* (Munich: J. F. Lehmann, 1929); Günther, *Kleine Rassenkunde Europas* (Munich: J. F. Lehmann, 1925).

19 Eugen Fischer, "Die Wissenschaft vom Menschen," in *Gestalter unserer Zeit, Vol. 4, Erforscher des Lebens* (Oldenburg: Gerhard Stalling Verlag, 1955), 272–87.

20 Karl Saller, *Die Rassenlehre des Nationalsozialismus in Wissenschaft und Propaganda* (Darmstadt: Progress-Verlag, 1961); Müller-Hill, *Murderous Science*, 92.

FURTHER READING

Adams, Mark B., ed. *The Well-Born Science: Eugenics in Germany, France, Brazil, and Russia.* New York: Oxford University Press, 1990.

Allen, Garland. "The Eugenics Record Office at Cold Spring Harbor, 1910–1940: An Essay in Institutional History," *Osiris*, 2d ser., 2 (1986): 225–64.

Aly, Götz, et al. *Cleansing the Fatherland: Nazi Medicine and Racial Hygiene.* Baltimore: Johns Hopkins University Press, 1994.

Aly, Götz, and Susanne Heim. *Architects of Annihilation.* Translated by A. G. Blunden. Princeton: Princeton University Press, 2002.

Bock, Gisela. "Racism and Sexism in Nazi Germany: Motherhood, Compulsory Sterilization, and the State." In *When Biology Became Destiny: Women in Weimar and Nazi Germany*, edited by Renate Bridenthal, Atina Grossmann, and Marion Kaplan, 271–96. New York: Monthly Review Press, 1984.

Brand-Claussen, Bettina, Inge Jádi, and Caroline Douglas. *Beyond Reason: Art and Psychosis, Works from the Prinzhorn Collection.* London: Hayward Gallery; Berkeley: University of California Press, 1996.

Broberg, Gunnar, and Nils Roll-Hansen, eds. *Eugenics and the Welfare State: Sterilization Policy in Denmark, Sweden, Norway, and Finland.* East Lansing: Michigan State University Press, 1996.

Browning, Christopher. *The Path to Genocide.* New York: Cambridge University Press, 1992.

Burleigh, Michael. *Death and Deliverance: "Euthanasia" in Germany, 1900–1945.* Cambridge: Cambridge University Press, 1994.

———. *Germany Turns Eastwards: A Study of* Ostforschung *in the Third Reich.* Cambridge: Cambridge University Press, 1988.

———, and Wolfgang Wippermann. *The Racial State: Germany, 1933–1945.* Cambridge: Cambridge University Press, 1991.

Caplan, Arthur, ed. *When Medicine Went Mad: Bioethics and the Holocaust.* Totowa, N.J.: Humana Press, 1992.

Dikötter, Frank. *Imperfect Conceptions: Medical Knowledge, Birth Defects, and Eugenics in China.* New York: Columbia University Press, 1998.

Dunn, Leslie C. *A Short History of Genetics: The Development of Some of the Main Lines of Thought: 1864–1939.* (Ames: Iowa State University Press, 1991).

Ehmann, Annegret. "From Colonial Racism to Nazi Population Policy: The Role of the So-called Mischlinge." In *The Holocaust and History: The Known, the Unknown, the Disputed, and the Reexamined,* edited by Michael Berenbaum and Abraham J. Peck, 115–33. Bloomington and Indianapolis: Indiana University Press, 1998.

Friedlander, Henry. *The Origins of Nazi Genocide: From Euthanasia to the Final Solution.* Chapel Hill: University of North Carolina Press, 1995.

Friedländer, Saul. *Nazi Germany and the Jews.* Vol. 1, *The Years of Persecution.* New York: HarperCollins Publishers, 1997.

Gillham, Nicholas Wright. *A Life of Sir Francis Galton: From African Exploration to the Birth of Eugenics.* New York: Oxford University Press, 2001.

Gould, Stephen Jay. *The Mismeasure of Man.* New York: Norton, 1996.

Graham, Loren R. "Science and Values: The Eugenics Movement in Germany and Russia in the 1920s." *American Historical Review* 82 (1977): 1133–64.

Grossmann, Atina. *Reforming Sex: The German Movement for Birth Control and Abortion Reform, 1920–1950*. New York: Oxford University Press, 1995.

Heberer, Patricia. "Targeting the 'Unfit' and Radical Public Health Strategies in Nazi Germany." In *Deaf People in Hitler's Europe*, edited by Donna Ryan and Stan Schuchman, 49–70. Washington, D.C.: Gallaudet University Press, 2002.

Kater, Michael. *Doctors under Hitler*. Chapel Hill: University of North Carolina Press, 1989.

Kevles, Daniel J. *In the Name of Eugenics: Genetics and the Uses of Human Heredity*. Cambridge, Mass.: Harvard University Press, 1995.

Kline, Wendy. *Building a Better Race: Gender, Sexuality, and Eugenics from the Turn of the Century to the Baby Boom*. Berkeley: University of California Press, 2001.

Koehl, Robert L. *RKFDV: German Resettlement and Population Policy, 1939–1945: A History of the Reich Commission for the Strengthening of Germandom*. Cambridge, Mass.: Harvard University Press, 1957.

Koonz, Claudia. *Mothers in the Fatherland: Women, the Family, and Nazi Politics*. New York: St. Martin's Press, 1987.

Kühl, Stefan. *The Nazi Connection: Eugenics, American Racism, and German National Socialism*. New York: Oxford University Press, 1994.

Larson, Edward J. *Sex, Race, and Science: Eugenics in the Deep South*. Baltimore: Johns Hopkins University Press, 1995.

Lifton, Robert J. *The Nazi Doctors: Medical Killing and the Psychology of Genocide*. New York: Basic Books, 1986.

Lombardo, Paul. "Medicine, Eugenics, and the Supreme Court: From Coercive Sterilization to Reproductive Freedom." *Journal of Contemporary Health Law and Policy* 13 (1996): 1–25.

Massin, Benoit. "From Virchow to Fischer: Physical Anthropology and 'Modern Race Theories' in Wilhelmine Germany (1890–1914)." In *Volksgeist as Method and Ethic: Essays on Boasian Ethnography and the German Anthropological Tradition*, edited by George W. Stocking, Jr., 79–154. Madison: University of Wisconsin Press, 1996.

McLaren, Angus. *Our Own Master Race: Eugenics in Canada, 1885–1945*. Toronto: McClelland & Stewart, 1990.

Michalczyk, John, ed. *Medicine, Ethics, and the Third Reich*. Kansas City: Sheed and Ward, 1994.

Mosse, George L. *Toward the Final Solution: A History of European Racism*. New York: Howard Fertig, 1978.

Müller-Hill, Benno. *Murderous Science: The Elimination by Scientific Selection of Jews, Gypsies, and Others in Germany, 1933–1945*. Translated by George R. Fraser. Plainview, N.Y.: Cold Spring Harbor Laboratory Press, 1998.

Noakes, Jeremy. "Nazism and Eugenics: The Background to the Nazi Sterilization Law of 14 July 1933." In *Ideas into Politics*, edited by Roger J. Bullen et al., 75–94. London: Croom Helm, 1984.

Patai, Raphael, and Jennifer Patai. *The Myth of the Jewish Race*. 2d ed. Detroit: Wayne State University Press, 1989.

Paul, Diane B. *Controlling Human Heredity, 1865 to the Present*. Amherst, N.Y.: Humanity Books, 1995.

Pernick, Martin S. *The Black Stork: Eugenics and the Death of "Defective" Babies in American Medicine and Motion Pictures since 1915*. New York: Oxford University Press, 1996.

———. "Eugenics and Public Health in American History." *American Journal of Public Health* 87, no.11 (November 1997): 1767–72.

Pine, Lisa. *Nazi Family Policy, 1933–1945*. Oxford: Berg, 1997.

Proctor, Robert. "From *Anthropologie* to *Rassenkunde* in the German Anthropological Tradition." In *Bones, Bodies, Behavior: Essays on Biological Anthropology*, edited by George W. Stocking, Jr., 138–79. Madison: University of Wisconsin Press, 1988.

———. *Racial Hygiene: Medicine under the Nazis*. Cambridge, Mass.: Harvard University Press, 1988.

Pross, Christian, and Götz Aly. *The Value of the Human Being: Medicine in Germany, 1918–1945*. Berlin: Ärtzekammer Berlin, 1991.

Rafter, Nicole Hahn, ed. *White Trash: The Eugenic Family Studies, 1877–1919*. Boston: Northeastern University Press, 1988.

Reilly, Philip R. *The Surgical Solution: A History of Involuntary Sterilization in the United States*. Baltimore: Johns Hopkins University Press, 1991.

Renneberg, Monika, and Mark Walker, eds. *Science, Technology, and National Socialism*. Cambridge: Cambridge University Press, 1994.

Schneider, William. *Quality and Quantity: The Quest for Biological Regeneration in Twentieth-Century France*. Cambridge: Cambridge University Press, 1990.

Seidelman, William E. "Power, Responsibility, and Abuse in Medicine: Lessons from Germany." In *New Perspectives on the Holocaust: A Guide for Teachers and Scholars*, edited by Rochelle L. Millen, 319–42. New York: New York University Press, 1996.

Selden, Steven. *Inheriting Shame: The Story of Eugenics and Racism in America*. New York: Teachers College Press, 1999.

Stepan, Nancy L. *The Hour of Eugenics: Race, Gender, and Nation in Latin America*. Ithaca, N.Y.: Cornell University Press, 1991.

Stephenson, Jill. *Women in Nazi Germany*. New York: Longman, 2001.

Weindling, Paul. "Eugenics and the Welfare State during the Weimar Republic." In *State, Social Policy, and Social Change in Germany, 1880–1994*, edited by W. R. Lee and Eve Rosenhaft, 134–63. New York: Berg, 1997.

———. *Health, Race and German Politics between National Unification and Nazism, 1870–1945*. Cambridge: Cambridge University Press, 1989.

Weingart, Peter. "German Eugenics between Science and Politics." *Osiris*, 2d ser., 5 (1989): 60–282.

Weinreich, Max. *Hitler's Professors: The Part of Scholarship in Germany's Crimes against the Jewish People*. New York: Yiddish Scientific Institute-YIVO, 1946.

Weiss, Sheila Faith. *Race Hygiene and National Efficiency: The Eugenics of Wilhelm Schallmayer*. Berkeley: University of California Press, 1987.

Wetzell, Richard F. *Inventing the Criminal: A History of German Criminology, 1880–1945*. Chapel Hill: University of North Carolina Press, 2000.

Weyers, Wolfgang. *Death of Medicine in Nazi Germany: Dermatology and Dermatopathology under the Swastika*. Lanham, Md.: Madison Books, 1998.

VIDEOGRAPHY

Healing by Killing. Directed by Nitzan Aviram. New Israel Foundation for Cinema and Television, 1996.

Homo Sapiens 1900. Directed and written by Peter Cohen. First Run/Icarus Films, 1998.

In the Shadow of the Reich: Nazi Medicine. Directed by John Michalczyk. First Run Features, 1997.

Selling Murder: The Killing Films of the Third Reich. Directed by Joanna Mack. Written by Michael Burleigh. Domino Films, 1991.

INDEX

Page numbers in *italics* refer to captions